THE
DIRTY
SQUAD

THE
DIRTY
SQUAD

The Inside Story of
the Obscene Publications
Branch

Michael Hames

LITTLE, BROWN AND COMPANY

A *Little, Brown* Book

First published in Great Britain in 2000
by Little, Brown & Company

A CIP catalogue record for this book
is available from the British Library.

ISBN: 0 316 85321 6

*The names of some individuals in this book
have been changed.*

Typeset by M Rules
Printed and bound in Great Britain
by Clays Ltd, St Ives plc

Little, Brown & Company (UK)
Brettenham House
Lancaster Place
London WC2E 7EN

To my wife, Caroline

Contents

PART THREE

Acknowledgements

I have received the full and generous support of all of my former colleagues in the writing of this book, in particular Detective Chief Inspector Bob McLachlan, Lennie Yeoell and the present and former staff of the Dirty Squad, now renamed the Paedophile Unit of the Organised Crime Group at New Scotland Yard.

Special thanks to my agent, Roger Houghton of Lucas Alexander Whitley; my editor and great friend, Hugh Miller; and Andrew Gordon of Little, Brown, all of whom made this book readable. Among many others who encouraged and inspired me, I'd like to thank Ann Winterton MP; Richard Monk OBE, QPM; Roger Beam; Mick McGovern; and Robert and Marion Fleming. My thanks also to Spike Milligan Productions for permission to use copyright material.

Lastly, my family and, in particular, my wife Caroline, who has supported me by believing in this project and putting up with the inevitable long periods of isolation.

Prologue

I had run all the way from Chelsea Police Station to Hans Crescent. I stood for a minute to catch my breath, hardly able to tell where I was, for the place had been devastated. It looked more like a battleground than a West London street. The air stank of oil and burning rubber. Black smoke hung in a pall, clinging to the walls and shattered awnings of Harrods and the wrecked shops and offices on the other side of the road. Splintered glass and smashed brick littered the pavement and blocked the roadway. I stared at twisted bodies scattered along the street, their arms and legs sticking up at crazy angles. Slowly it dawned on me they were shop dummies, sucked out through Harrods' windows when the car bomb exploded.

There were real bodies too, in doorways and on the road, none of them moving. Torn and mangled remains of cars were scattered across piles of broken masonry. The Austin 1300 that had carried the bomb was no more than a smoking clump of fused black metal. When I looked up I saw a car bonnet hanging over a parapet.

My boss, Peter Ryan, was there already. I helped him to put the outer and inner cordons in place. As we worked I saw what seemed to be the scorched body of a police officer lying under a burning car. Further along the road a policewoman lay motionless. As far as I could tell she hadn't been marked by the blast, but I knew she was dead. I tilted my head to see her face and felt a jab of shock as I recognised her. Jane Arbuthnot. I had been joking with her a few days before, not far from this spot.

There was no time to dwell on anything, but I knew this was one of the days in my life that would never leave me. I went about my duty in a detached overdrive, working methodically like everybody else, learning the scale of the catastrophe in gradual stages. Jane Arbuthnot was dead and so was Sergeant Noel Lane, the officer under the burning car; a dog handler, John Gordon, had lost a leg and several fingers, and some days later he would lose the other leg; John's dog, Queenie, was so badly injured she had to be shot at the scene by an officer of the Diplomatic Protection Group; Inspector Steve Dodd and Sergeants Chris Stanger and Andy Melham were critically injured. Roughly a hundred members of the public had been hit by the blast and three of them were also dead.

I looked up the road towards Knightsbridge. It was a cold, darkening Saturday afternoon with bright Christmas lights in the shop windows. Crowds of shoppers stood behind the cordon, motionless for the most part, and silent, all sense of safety gone.

Earlier that day, 17 December 1983, Peter Ryan had been

standing in for me at Chelsea Police Station. The drill was that Peter, a chief superintendent, and myself, then a superintendent, took it in turn to be Senior Duty Officer at the station. Terrorist intelligence that winter had said the IRA were going to strike somewhere in London before Christmas, and the attack would probably be in the West End. That meant that while precautionary measures were in force, Chelsea Division had to be supervised at all times by either the officer in charge or his assistant. On 17 December it was my turn on the rota, but Peter swapped a day with me so I could attend a black-tie function in central London.

While I was at home in Harrow getting ready, a call came through asking me to ring B District Control. It was urgent. I called them and the district chief superintendent, Mike Jones, told me to get to Chelsea as fast as I could.

'A bomb's gone off at Harrods,' he said.

I asked him how big it was.

'Deaths and casualties as far as we can tell. There are police among the casualties.'

I was driven at breakneck speed in a private car from Harrow to Chelsea and got there in twenty minutes. I changed from dinner jacket into uniform and took a quick briefing. An hour earlier, at 1:20 P.M., a bomb had exploded in Hans Crescent, at the side of Harrods, shortly after the police had been tipped off that a device had been planted in the vicinity of the store. Since there was no clear indication where the bomb was, it was decided not to evacuate the store, because that could result in shoppers being shepherded into the area of an explosion. The bomb went off outside the store while officers were still looking for it.

There was no chance of me driving to the scene because

the roads had been closed off. I left the station on foot and ran through the back streets up to Hans Crescent.

It was vital to get people out of the vicinity of the explosion and it was just as important, from an investigative point of view, to preserve the scene. Police officers were arriving now from all over London to help. As we cleared the area and made it secure we all knew there could be another bomb nearby, ticking down to zero. It is a standard ploy of the IRA to have a second device set to detonate after the first explosion.

By stages the Anti-Terrorist Branch took charge of the on-scene investigation. The army arrived too, and with the help of their detection equipment they were finally able to tell us there were no other bombs in the area.

By late afternoon we had done all we could at the scene. I rounded up the officers from Chelsea who had been called out, many of them stained with the blood of people they had tended. We went back to the station in a van. I herded them all into my office, gave them paper cups and got out the whisky. I was still pouring when Deputy Assistant Commissioner John Cracknell walked in. He looked at us all in silence for a moment, then nodded.

'Carry on,' he said.

On the evening television news the Commissioner, Sir Kenneth Newman, confirmed there had been a telephone warning about the bomb, but it had been deliberately intended to mislead the police about other devices.

'At 12:44 P.M. today,' he said, 'the Central London Samaritans informed the Metropolitan Police that they had received a telephone message claiming to be from the IRA, and warning of bombs placed in and around Harrods store and in Oxford Street. The text of the message was, I quote, "This is the IRA. Car bomb outside Harrods. Two bombs in Harrods. One in Oxford Street, one in Littlewood's Oxford Street." Following receipt of that message police units were sent to investigate.'

Later the Prime Minister, Margaret Thatcher, spoke in a BBC TV interview about her own reaction to the bombing: 'I heard the news on the way from Chequers to London to attend a carol concert for a cancer fund for children. We were totally shocked by it. It is a crime against humanity, and at Christmas it's particularly cruel. We express the deepest sympathy for all of those who have lost their lives, and those who are injured, and we are thinking very deeply of them at this time. I know that many many friends will gather round to do everything they can to comfort them. I think whoever did it, it is just totally brutal and barbaric, but there are very evil people in our society and we have to do everything we can to catch them. Our police are very brave. On a Christmas Saturday so many people will take their children shopping. It would be a day out, it would be a pleasure, a delight. And then for it to end like that, in total tragedy, bringing grief to so many people – it's difficult to understand the minds of people who can do that.'

By early evening things had begun to settle at the station and I decided I could tackle the matter of our two dead officers. The Casualty Bureau at the Yard was co-ordinating the job of informing the families of civilians who had been killed or injured. I called the bureau and spoke to the senior officer. I told him I wanted to let the families of the dead officers know what had happened.

'You can't do that,' he told me briskly. 'Not without first being absolutely sure these officers are dead, and even when that much has been determined you can't talk to the relatives without the authority of the Assistant Commissioner, Personnel.'

'Look,' I said, hanging on to my temper, 'go and tell him right now, I've been to see the bodies and I can promise you they're dead. I want to let the families know. We need to do it now, because the publicity's enormous, rumours are flying, and the relatives have been phoning us. We can't put them off any longer.'

'You can't tell the families,' he insisted. 'Not without the appropriate authority from the Assistant Commissioner, Personnel.'

We ended up shouting at each other. I bawled at him and demanded clearance, but he stood his bureaucratic ground. He came back at me with the same argument, over and over. He wasn't going to shift. Finally I told him to fuck off and hung up.

I was determined to let the families know what had happened. I went to Deputy Assistant Commissioner Cracknell. I told him what I wanted to do, and how I was being obstructed.

'Okay, Mike,' he said. 'We'll do it on my authority.'

He said I should go and speak to Jane Arbuthnot's parents. He would get the Acting Commander at Croydon to take the bad news to Noel Lane's family.

I asked a WPC to come with me to the Arbuthnots' house in Fulham. On the way over I thought about Jane. She was twenty-two, an attractive, outgoing, feisty girl who loved her job. I could picture her, see her smiling. My throat began to swell and I felt a touch of pressure behind the eyes. I made myself think of Jane's family. I imagined how much tougher it would be for them. It was important that I represent some kind of stability in the turmoil of their grief. I sat up straight behind the wheel, concentrated on driving and kept my mind off Jane.

I pulled up opposite the Arbuthnot house. As we got out I heard Charlie, Jane's younger brother.

'It's true!' he shouted. 'It's true!'

When we reached the front door Jane's father opened it. He looked stricken.

'Janie's dead, isn't she?' he said.

'I'm afraid so.' I put my arms around him.

We went into the parlour where the family were waiting. Their pain and anger were palpable. Jake, Jane's father, was a retired lieutenant commander, Royal Navy. He understood, even in the grip of terrible loss, that nothing would be gained if he abandoned his composure; his wife Sue was as self-effacing and strong as he was. During the hour I spent with the family there were only a couple of moments when it seemed their restraint would collapse. When we left, I promised I would come back later, and I reassured the family that from then on, the Metropolitan Police would be their guardian.

By late evening the sad work was over and done, but that was only a start. I now had to take responsibility for the welfare of the injured police officers and their dependants, which meant I had to visit a lot of people. I had to comfort them, reassure them and help them materially in any way I could.

For a start I got the comedian Spike Milligan, an old friend, to come round the wards with me and pump up the patients' morale. I laid on comfortable hire cars with police drivers for the families of the injured officers. The drivers doubled as liaison officers and kept me posted on any problems within the family groups. I arranged the funeral of Jane Arbuthnot at St Luke's Church in Chelsea. At the service Sergeant Mike Thwaites delivered a fine eulogy that left no one in the church unmoved.

My pal Steve Dodd had been critically injured in the blast and now he was on life support in Central Middlesex Hospital. Shrapnel was lodged in his brain and in several other parts of his body. Every surgical and clinical effort had been made to sustain and stabilise him, but on the seventh day after the bombing he went into serious decline.

I spoke to the ITU consultant in charge of Steve's case on the morning of Christmas Eve. He told me that Steve's brain was losing control of his immune system and now, on top of the damage from the explosion, his body was being overrun by infection. The consultant said that in spite of everything his team had done, there was no chance that Steve could cope without mechanical support. His brain was hopelessly damaged and the removal of support therapy would certainly mean that he would die.

The machines were withdrawn later that day. I did what I could to prepare the family for the inevitable. As time wore on they began to accept what was happening. At six o'clock Steve passed away.

I scribbled out a press release on a memo pad:

Despite every effort and maximum supportive therapy, Mr Dodd's condition deteriorated rapidly and he developed circulatory failure. Regrettably, he died in the Intensive Therapy Unit of the hospital at 6:00 P.M.

I phoned the Assistant Commissioner to let him know what had happened. He in turn told the Commissioner, who told the Home Secretary and the Prime Minister, who had asked to be kept informed.

When I left the hospital nurses were singing carols to the patients. As the culmination of the worst Christmas I could remember, it was heartbreaking.

Back at Chelsea Police Station I learned, with enormous relief and gratitude, that Inspector Sue Williams had shopped for me and got presents for my children. She had even wrapped everything, so that all I had to do was fill in the tags. I thought of my daughters and began to feel bleak and alone. Self-pity had never been a component of my nature, but the circumstances of the past week had shifted my perspectives. Although my children no longer lived with me I could see them whenever I wanted; even so, being separated from them at that moment felt unbearable.

Later in the evening a call came through from 10 Downing Street. A secretary on the Prime Minister's staff wanted to know the home address of Steve Dodd's widow. I explained that we couldn't give out that information, because Mrs Dodd was being protected from the attentions of the press and poison-pen cranks. It was imperative, I added, that the fewest number of people should know the address.

The secretary said that the Prime Minister wanted to write to Mrs Dodd that very night. I thought about it and finally I said that was fine. If the letter could be brought to my office by messenger, I would see that a police officer delivered it to Mrs Dodd straight away.

That evening Margaret Thatcher, who was at Chequers, sat down and wrote a six-page letter in longhand, telling Mrs Dodd that Steve had died for his country, and in doing so he had left the entire population of Britain in her debt. She went on to express how she, as another wife and mother, could sympathise and commiserate with the widow of a good man at this darkest and most dreadful hour.

I went home very late, carrying the presents for my children which I would deliver the next day. My empty flat was cold; I was exhausted and my spirits were at rock bottom. I sat down and tried to think about Steve and Jane in happier times. But I could only recall them the way I had seen them last, remote and solemn in their death. I had never felt so low or so desolate in my life. I lay down on the bed and cried.

PART ONE

1
The Best of Times

Because my father was granted a 72-hour pass in July 1944, I was born in time for the grand finale of the Second World War. My birth was uncomplicated and took place on 7 February 1945 in a hospital opposite Colchester Royal Grammar School, where eleven years later I would be a pupil. When Mum left hospital she took me home to Mersea Island, ten miles south of Colchester, where she and Dad had rented a place where she could live in relative safety while he was off soldiering with the Royal Artillery.

On St Valentine's Day 1945, exactly one week after I was born, RAF and USAF planes carried out an extended bombing raid on Dresden. They dropped so much high explosive that they created a fire-storm which took three days to burn itself out and reduced the city to a smoking ruin. It was overkill, but it drained away the last dregs of Nazi resistance. By the end of April Hitler was dead and Germany had surrendered to the Allies. On 6 August an atomic bomb fell on the Japanese city of Hiroshima, and on the 9th Nagasaki was destroyed. Japan surrendered five days later, and for the first time in six years the world was at peace. Weary fighting men began to return to their families. My father was among the last of the British soldiers to be demobbed, but finally he came home to Mersea Island and said hello to his new son.

My recollections of the toddler days on the island are patchy, but they call up a sensation of warmth and harmony. Years later I realised that the timing of my birth could hardly have been better. In spite of being bomb-battered, decimated and sickened by war, the country I was born into had turned the corner and showed every sign of winning. I was a brand-new member of a people with more hope than they had known since before the depression of the 1930s.

By the time I was old enough to attend primary school another war was brewing, in Korea this time, but in Britain the peace had taken hold and there were glimmers of prosperity. My dad was back at work in Colchester as a clerk with the Inland Revenue, and if we were not exactly well-off we didn't appear to want for anything. There was an enclosing sense of security. The country was alive with enterprise, people had direction and there was every reason to be ambitious. I am sure those years gave me my optimistic nature, because my curiosity about life grew in pace with the postwar brightening of Britain.

Mersea Island was a good place to grow up. It is a peninsula roughly six miles long by three miles wide at its broadest part. At certain high tides the single road from Colchester, called the Strood, is submerged, and Mersea becomes a true island. There are remains of Roman villas there and in later years Mersea became the haunt of smugglers and the home ground of some notable old families. The island is featured in a novel, *Mehala*, by Sabine Baring-Gould, who wrote 'Onward Christian Soldiers' and who was, for a time, the vicar of East Mersea.

I recall most of all the sense of open space that I enjoyed as a child. Mersea had stood relatively still in the 1920s and '30s, gently aloof from change, so even by the 1940s it was not densely populated. Very few of the roads were properly metalled, and the ones where we lived were simple tracks of clay and packed earth. Our house was down by the sea, a big place where we occupied the top floor and another family lived underneath. A spacious garden surrounded us, with woods behind the house and an expanse of greensward in front, sloping down to the coast road. I used to bathe in the sea with other kids, or just play on the deserted beach, then walk home with bare feet, carrying my shoes and socks.

The best times on the beach, or so my memory tells me, were when I was there with my father, who was always good company. He was fun, an ageless companion who always slipped in a measure of instruction with the horseplay. On the beach he taught me – and later my brother Eric, eighteen months my junior – to play cricket. He taught us to play football, too, and although it didn't please my mother, he also taught us to box. Boxing, like so much else he knew and did well, was one of the things Dad had learned in the army. He boxed impressively, but his personality was not at all aggressive. He was a softly-spoken man with great natural kindness and an old-fashioned courtesy in his dealings with people. He was a father who commanded respect and he managed that by kindness, too. He was energetic, tireless and endlessly enthusiastic, and he gave me so much that honed my capability, in mostly painless ways, and helped shape my outlook on life.

He was Robert Benjamin Hames, born in 1897 in Lambeth.

He served in both world wars, joining up for the first time in 1914; by 1915 he was old enough to go to France, where he survived the Battle of the Somme and later saw action in Salonika and Egypt.

In July 1925, seven years after the Great War ended, he married his first wife, Elsie May Tiller, and in December of the following year they had a son, Kenneth Robert Hames. Elsie died in the seventeenth year of their marriage.

Dad joined up for the second time in 1939, at the age of forty-two, as a private soldier in the Royal Artillery. Within a few months he was promoted to Company Quartermaster, then in July 1940 he became Battalion Quartermaster Sergeant. At the end of the Second World War he was sent out to Belgium to help protect the firemen of the National Fire Service, who were putting out a spate of arson attacks on the homes of Belgians who had collaborated with the Germans.

On 17 May 1944, a little over a year before the war ended, Dad married my mother at Marylebone Register Office. Before the wedding she was Myrtle Grace Stace, a soldier's daughter from Worcester. She had gone into service as soon as she left school and eventually became a parlour maid in the household of a Mr and Mrs Simpson. The wife, Wallis Warfield Simpson, eventually divorced her husband and married the Duke of Windsor who, as King Edward VIII, abdicated in 1938 so that the marriage could take place. My mother actually served at table during a private dinner between the King and Mrs Simpson, and on that occasion Mum accidentally tipped some of the pudding on the King's trousers.

During the war she worked at Kodak's premises in Wealdstone, Harrow, which had been commandeered to make bombs for the war effort. It was during that time that she met Dad, in Stanmore, where she was living with her sister.

My mother, like my father, gave her children all the love they ever needed, and she expressed more pride than they could ever live up to. At times she could be strict, but necessarily so, because her two boys were a handful. She made a home that was the warm centre of our lives, where the smallest event could become a memory to treasure. When my sister Pat was born in 1952, I remember being allowed upstairs with Eric to see the new baby, and I still recall what a breathless, emotional event it was as we stood there and gazed, hushed and full of wonder, at the tiny sleeping head nestled in the crook of Mum's arm.

At primary school we were asked to do an essay on what we would like to be when we grew up. I said I wanted to be a comedian, and I am sure I meant it at the time. Our teacher, Mrs Chesney, thought that was terribly silly. So silly, in fact, that she began making fun of me. I must have been a sensitive soul even then, because I remember I got so upset at the way she went on that I threw a pen at her.

The variety of career paths open to a young man was expanding, although for a woman the clock had more or less stood still since before the war. It was true that more girls were going to university, and more than ever were getting jobs in industry and commerce, but wherever their ambition or aptitude took them, they found themselves in a two-tier system. The social paradigm was hard to shift: a woman's place was indoors, being a wife and home-maker, not troubling her head with things like trade, technology, politics and all the other stuff that was the proper province of men. In the workplace, women's gender automatically meant that in terms of advancement they would do less well than men with the same – or often fewer – qualifications. Women would certainly earn less than men, even when they did exactly the same jobs.

But I was a boy, and boys had never had it so good. Pals at school talked about following their fathers' trades: carpenters, butchers, fishermen; others had more glamorous ideas: pilots, heart surgeons, magazine photographers; the really practical ones talked about being chemists, accountants, lawyers. At eight or nine I didn't really want to be a comedian any more. If my relish lay in any direction it was probably towards adventure. That was what I wanted, a job with plenty of adventure – I had a fuzzy notion about being some kind of hired, swashbuckling righter-of-wrongs in the pay of an Eastern potentate. Or maybe a naval commando. Or a spy. Nothing was fixed. My future was still a sea of fluid possibilities.

But that was bound to change. There was, after all, the hand of influence, my father's hand, guiding me, involving me, giving me a sense of proportion that would eventually set an ambition stirring. Looking back I can detect the small beginnings of my ambition, camouflaged in the turbulence of boyhood.

As soon as he was back home from the war, Dad joined the Home Guard and the British Legion. Apart from the fact that this made him very busy in the evenings and at weekends, it meant that every year the whole family had to attend the county British Legion Rally.

If I hadn't been so travel-sick on the coach every time we went, I think I would have been more conscious of what a real insider I was at these big events. My mother was a member of the Women's Section of the British Legion, and her father was President of the British Legion at Burnham-on-Crouch. At every rally we joined up with Granddad, Grandma, and a host of other involved relatives. We must have looked to others there like a benign Mafia.

What I see, looking back on those days, is something poignantly old-fashioned. The patriotism of my family would seem strange nowadays, even cranky. But it was never eccentric, never flag-waving or arrogant. It was a modest, abiding, *practical* loyalty that the family possessed without ever really questioning it. I grew up in a household tacitly dedicated to King and Country, and tied into that allegiance was the notion of duty as a necessity, as a builder of character.

As if his job and his other pursuits weren't enough to occupy his time, my father joined the St John Ambulance Brigade. That was in 1955, when I was ten. In due course he began setting up the St John Ambulance Cadets on Mersea Island. He encouraged my brother and me to join and we did, along with a lot of our friends. In the end there were about thirty boys and girls in the Cadets, which was a lot for a small community like ours. Under Dad's gentle, firm leadership we all studied and trained until we began to win cups and competition prizes at county level. As time passed and my skills grew, I was more and more aware of how much weight my father placed on the duty of the individual to serve the community. To be inclined that way himself was a part of his disposition, a fundamental quality of the man. Since I loved my dad I loved his principles, and so I absorbed them without resistance.

As the year wore on I began taking an interest in what was happening in the world at large; inevitably, it was my father's own interest in current affairs that aroused my curiosity about the bigger picture. Between the spring of 1955 and April 1956 there was a lot to take in. Churchill resigned as Prime

Minister; football authorities from eight countries set up a contest to be called the European Cup; in London a 28-year-old woman called Ruth Ellis was found guilty of the murder of her lover and hanged at Holloway Prison; Albert Einstein died, so did Thomas Mann, Alfred Kinsey, and James Dean; commercial television began in London; British troops were sent to break up the fighting between Greeks and Turks in Cyprus; and traffic wardens appeared on the streets of Britain.

About that time my sense of fairness seemed to develop a very sensitive edge. I certainly knew injustice when I saw it, and I knew that injustice inflicted on the helpless was the worst kind of all. In school I was in the top set for the 11-plus, maths and English. One of the other lads in the set had trouble with his grasp of maths; I forget the details, but there was some little thing he could not manage to do. And because he couldn't do it, he was beaten. I can remember being absolutely furious. The boy had simply failed to master some trivial technique of calculation, and because he couldn't do it an adult deliberately caused him pain. I had never been so indignant in all my eleven years.

It was only when I passed my 11-plus that I realised my parents were short of money. Not long after the warmly-greeted news that I would be going to Colchester Royal Grammar School, there began a series of anxious little huddles between Mum and Dad, murmured discussions about how to divert funds and liquefy savings; a lad with my antennae couldn't miss stuff like that, no matter how discreet they thought they were being. The fact was, a boy going to grammar school needed a lot of kit. I had to have the uniform, a rugger outfit, cricket whites, lab coats, plus numerous other odds and ends which added up to serious money. It was sad to see how my parents had to marshal their slim resources and cut back, just so that I could go forward.

When I started travelling to school by bus, a half-hour journey, my chronic travel-sickness promptly vanished. I never probed the psychology of that, if there was any. Later, I got a weekend gardening job, working for a man called Colonel Lang, who lived on the front at Mersea. It was dirty work but it paid six shillings a week, which meant I was now able to be an independent saver. Eventually I bought myself a bike out of my earnings from the gardening job, and I went to and from school on that. It was a Dawes with drop handlebars and derailleur gears. It cost me £12 and it was the *business*.

I enjoyed grammar school. I had a seriously good time. I wasn't unpopular and nobody picked on me. The work was hard, it could even be called arduous, but it was that way because we were expected to excel academically. There was respite, we played a lot of games, and although I wasn't a great sportsman I thoroughly enjoyed throwing myself about.

Here and there, inevitably, there were dark patches. I hadn't been at Colchester Royal Grammar very long when I witnessed another instance of injustice that had a much harder impact on me than the incident at primary school. In my class there was a boy rather too tall for his age, nearly six feet. His parents made him wear short trousers, which made him look incredibly awkward. One day it was alleged that he tried to steal something from Woolworth's. A successful thief has to be inconspicuous, so it must have been the daftest thing the boy ever did. He was caught. Woolworth's didn't prosecute, but what happened to him at school was worse than anything the law could have done to him.

Morning assemblies at Colchester Royal Grammar were

heavily disciplined. There were six hundred boys, eight full prefects, maybe a dozen prefects-designate, and a head boy. Head boys, for some reason, always looked about thirty-five years old. I remember this one glared a lot and barked 'Shurrup!' at the least sound from the assembly, while the prefects went round smacking heads and clipping ears. The atmosphere was invariably tense, and the tension built as the headmaster, Jack Elam, made his way down the middle of the assembly hall, his gown flowing out behind him. He was trailed at a respectful distance by a prefect, who would read the lesson. Following the lesson the school orchestra accompanied us as we sang a hymn. Then we had the *Nunc Dimittis* and School Notices, after which the head would sweep off again.

Assembly on the day after they caught the boy was a grim affair. The head called for him and the rest of us watched in silence as the poor lad gangled his way up to the dais. He stood there looking wretched as he was told, loudly, that he would be expelled. And then, incredibly, the headmaster beat him. Right before my pained and astonished eyes he ordered the boy, in his pathetic short trousers, to bend over and take six strokes of the cane on his backside.

I could hardly believe it. The boy was being expelled, that was his punishment and it was a terrible one, so why inflict this violence on him? I felt as if I was the one who had been assaulted. He didn't cry but I nearly did. I gulped back tears of anger. If this was meant to be a warning to the rest of us, in my case it failed. It had no effect on my feelings about whether I would take a straight or crooked path in life. If it did anything, it contributed to my convictions on corporal punishment.

Somewhere around the second form I got it into my head

that I wanted to join the police force when I left school. It was the beginning of an ambition, I suppose, a simple wish that a policeman was what I would become.

The older I got the faster my schooldays passed. As I went through the fourth and fifth forms the wish to be a policeman hardened into serious hope, and then it became determination. It stayed with me all the way through my final exams.

I sat a total of eight O-levels and passed seven. I failed Latin, the only exam I have ever failed, although a lot of us in my set failed that one and it infuriated many, because in those days you had to have a Latin O-level to get into Oxford or Cambridge. Not that *that* mattered to me. There would have been a fine sense of completeness if I had passed Latin, but on the other hand I didn't need it to get into the police.

The school authorities were not impressed when they learned about my career plans. In those days, a police officer was regarded as an artisan. You didn't need a grammar-school education to become one of *those*. The headmaster told me as much: 'You're wasting your education, boy.'

The prevailing attitude towards a police career belonged to a set of prejudices that was disintegrating far too slowly. But I didn't care what people thought, I was stubborn about what I wanted to make of my life. The public service instinct was now a strand of my character, so by joining the police I could satisfy that *and* my serious little craving for adventure. I was exhilarated at the prospect. I'd read a lot of fiction, lots of it about the police, books like *The Big Five at Scotland Yard*; I thought how great it was going to be, how fantastic to play goodies and baddies for real. That was my naïve view of the life up ahead, and it was backed with severe determination.

I am sure, now, that if I had not joined the police I would have gone into the army. The impulse had nothing to do with a desire to hide behind a uniform, nothing to do with aggression or a desire for easy authority. It truly had everything to do with adventure. To me, adventure meant being in a job where I would experience the exciting, the phenomenal and the amazing all at once, preferably most of the time. I could think of nothing better to want.

2
Shaping Up

I decided that the Essex Constabulary just would not do. I wanted to be a Scotland Yard detective, nothing less. So I applied to the Metropolitan Police, filling in all my details on the form with scrupulous honesty and feeling a real jolt of excitement as I popped the envelope into the letterbox. Then I went home to wait for the response that would tell me when I could start the process that would turn me into a cadet. The wait seemed endless, but a letter finally arrived. It told me I had been turned down.

That was a blow, the worst I had ever had. The possibility of rejection had never occurred to me. I was devastated, and also seriously mystified. I couldn't imagine where I had gone wrong, and since it was Met policy not to tell applicants why they had failed, it seemed I would never find out. But Dad came to the rescue. He had an old friend, Major Peter Young, a well-connected man who worked in advertising in the City. Dad explained what had happened and Major Young said he

would see what he could do. He made enquiries in the appropriate place, and eventually he obtained an answer.

'Young Michael isn't heavy enough,' he told my father.
'Feed him up and flesh him out a bit, then get him to apply
again.'

I put on several pounds before I sent in my second application. Sure enough, this time they invited me to attend for
interview and a medical examination. Before I knew it, I was
accepted. I was going to be a policeman after all. I was
relieved and overjoyed at the same time. So were Mum and
Dad, even though they hated the idea of me leaving home.

'Promise you'll write,' Mum said.

I promised. I also pointed out that while I was a cadet I
would be home most weekends. That didn't seem to console
her. When it came time for me to leave we all felt a bit
gloomy, and Mum and Dad looking openly sad did nothing to
help me as I tried to look stoic and manly, striding up to the
bus with my bags. I had been homesick before I got out of the
house and as I struggled along the aisle and stowed my case
on the rack I could scarcely make myself turn round and
wave to my folks in case I blubbered and let myself down. I
managed a courageous wave and a tight little smile before I
took my seat, faced the front, and shut my eyes for a count of
twenty, seeing my mother's tearful face and Dad's big soulful
eyes long after they had been left behind.

Less than twenty-four hours later my homesickness had
vanished. I was caught up in the intricacies and exertions of
becoming a police cadet.

My parents wrote to me every week, and when I came back
at weekends I sometimes brought my washing, which pleased
Mum, because that made it obvious I still needed her. Dad, for
his part, simply emanated an amazing pride in me.

I was at Hendon for eight months. The overall purpose of that phase of training was to knock us into shape and instil some discipline. The accent of training was on developing the cadet as an individual; serious police work would come later. We were pushed around and bullied to a certain extent, but all the time we were reminded that the harshness was for our benefit, it was to shake out the flabby remnants of our softie schooldays.

There were regular examinations and I came top of my intake in academic studies; one or two of the lads called me a swot, but that didn't matter, because I was presented with a book on motor mechanics – my own choice.

Overall, my stay at Hendon was like being at a tough boarding school. We lived in rooms of three and I shared with Stuart Campbell, who later became a detective superintendent in the Anti-Terrorist Squad, and Alan Briggs, who finished up as a Class One driver in the Diplomatic Protection Group. We remained friends throughout our careers.

We played a lot of sport at the college and it was decidedly rough. We went on intensive walks, sometimes carrying handicaps like telegraph poles, and we weren't allowed to stop for catastrophes like splinters or blisters. After Hendon we moved on to Ashford in Kent for the second phase of training, which lasted eight months and was much, much harder. There were incredibly tough obstacle courses: I remember one cadet was crossing a wire bridge twenty feet above the ground, and he fell off it. He broke his arm, but the instructor made him get back up on the bridge and cross it properly before he could go to hospital.

There was no doubt the training worked. They made hard lads out of us. When I left Ashford I had the kind of stamina that told me I could run all day. I was afraid of nobody and I felt myself to be in peak condition. Some of the young people in the police nowadays admit they get frightened, yet we were fearless. We knew all the techniques, we could save our own necks while we disarmed and disabled. We could take a hammering and know beforehand that we would give as good as we got. The right mixture of science and calculated brutality prepared us to be simultaneously one man's doom and another's salvation. Much later, when I became headmaster at Hendon, I was aware that things had gone soft in the ensuing years. But at least we still had a cadet system. It has gone now. That was a very bad administrative move.

When I was at grammar school we didn't think about girls very much; it was all football and rugby and Latin prep. There wasn't the sexual pressure back then. You didn't *have* to go out with a girl.

Eventually you did go out with one, of course. I don't remember my first girlfriend's name, but she was very attractive and for a while I think I was besotted with her. I remember her father had a smallholding, and she used to get on the bus which took the long route from Mersea to Colchester, and I sometimes used to take that bus just to see if she got on it. I managed eventually to make her acquaintance and by gradual stages we became friends. Eventually I took her to the Odeon, which had double seats in the back row, where I was able to put my arm round the young lady and kiss her. I don't think I did more than that – I was too well brought up for the libidinous stuff. That probably explains why I only went out with her twice. She probably found me too backward.

I met my first serious girlfriend when I was eighteen. She was Jacky, the daughter of George, the newly arrived bank manager at Barclays, which was the only bank on Mersea Island. The first time I saw Jacky she was walking her dog on the beach. She looked good to me.

We started going out on her sixteenth birthday. Shortly afterwards I passed my driving test. Dad bought me my first car, a Ford Prefect, which I reckoned added a fair chunk to my magnetism and helped boost my rating with Jacky.

The relationship turned serious very quickly, and that worried Jacky's parents. I was a police cadet, a virtual nothing, while their daughter was a bright student at the County High School for Girls, where she had obtained nine O-levels and was doing three A-levels. They didn't want anyone disturbing her balance or shifting her focus, least of all *me*. It frightened them half to death when, at the age of seventeen, Jacky told them we wanted to get married.

They recovered quickly and countered with a civilised proposition. We should wait, they said, until Jacky had gone to university and obtained her degree. When she was twenty-one, they would be happy to smile on our union. Not that they could have done much else by then. I suppose they were hoping that by the time Jacky was twenty-one she would have enough emotional maturity to drop me and take up with someone more suitable.

Jacky went ahead and got her A-levels, then applied to do a degree course in psychology. She wrote to one place only, London University, because I was working in London. She was accepted at Bedford College, which stands in the inner circle of Regent's Park. At that time I was a constable at Albany Street on the other side of the park. I viewed it as a terrific omen and a superbly convenient arrangement.

We were inseparable. We made the effort to be with each other at every opportunity, both of us going home to the island every weekend we could. We went for long walks on the beach, we listened to the Beatles, we went swimming off the deserted shoreline at East Mersea. We were in love, nothing could have been surer, and naturally we assumed it would last for ever.

Jacky stayed in hall at Bedford College for the first year, but her second and third years were spent in a one-room flat at Victoria Road, Kilburn, where she paid a rent of £6.16.6d a week. It was there, as a young constable, that I began to experience the routines of married life alongside my growing capability as a law enforcer. In that tiny place Jacky used to cook for me and for some of the other lads I worked with. Like any diligent wife on a budget she would buy fresh vegetables in the market and shop carefully for the best bargains. Sometimes she would spring surprise treats on me. Domestic routines developed in the midst of our almost daily contact; we had been seeing each other for years, but now we were a firmly established couple. Those unexceptional days were among the most idyllic of my life.

A look back at daily life for a constable in the Met during the 1960s can evoke a sense of period, as well as showing us what a change there has been in the routine duties and procedures of everyday police work. I was a PC in 1964; that year Sonny and Cher were in the charts, and right now Cher is still there, doing better than ever, so in a sense it wasn't so long ago. But the changes in police work have been enormous, most significantly in the technology.

I came out of training school and went to Albany Street with Mike Dixon. We had been cadets together and were at the training school together. At Albany Street we were on the same shift. Our warrant numbers were adjoining; I was

153441 and he was 153440, because alphabetically D comes before H. Mike later went into Special Branch and finished up as a detective superintendent, now retired.

I was a nineteen-year-old probationer. At first I stayed in the old Paddington Green station, in the dormitory, where there were partitions on each side of the bed space which did not reach all the way to the ceiling. I was there only a short time, then I moved to the single men's quarters at Camden Town.

The shifts we worked were 6-till-2, 2-till-10, and 10-till-6; the shift pattern was six weeks on days, three weeks on nights. Three weeks on nights was a good idea, it gave you a chance to get adjusted, whereas now it's only one week of nights and by the time an officer begins to adjust to the change he is due to go back on days again.

We would line up in the parade shed at Albany Street, where the sergeant would take the parade and post us to our respective beats and patrols, which we were not supposed to leave. We would be given the times at which we could take refreshment, and these times varied on a day-to-day basis. So if I was on early turn, the sergeant might say, 'One-seven-six, you're two-beat, refreshments at 9 A.M.' We would also be told where we could take our refreshments. For example, if I was at the Camden Town end of the beat, I would take refreshment at the section house.

At parade the sergeant would also give out information about people who were wanted, and there would often be details of property that owners or tenants had asked the police to keep an eye on while they were away. All of this would be read out from the Parade Book. In those days the Car List was still in operation. When someone reported a car stolen the details went to the Central Vehicle Index (CVI) and every hour, on the hour, a teleprinter list came out from Scotland Yard detailing all of the vehicles that had been reported stolen, together with cancellations of details on earlier lists where the vehicles in question had been recovered. It was the job of the Second Reserve Officer, who sat in the room where all the phones were located, to put the numbers of these cars on a strip index, in alphabetical order, and then take them off the display when they were cancelled. The details of cars stolen or recovered locally were read out at parade, and so were the details of cars wanted in connection with crimes, where fingerprints would be required. What with one thing and another, we put a considerable amount of information in our notebooks each and every day.

At five minutes to six the sergeant would say, 'Appointments, please.' Along with everybody else I would respond by producing my truncheon, my whistle (to which was attached a key to open any of the Tardis-type police boxes), my pocket book, accident reports – both personal injury and damage only. The sergeant would look round to make sure that each constable present had all the necessary items, and if anybody didn't then he was in trouble. Sometimes a constable would forget his truncheon, and if he wasn't able to borrow one quickly, he would sometimes just stick up his hand as if he was holding a truncheon, and occasionally he got away with that.

A constable was expected to be smartly turned out. Shoes and uniform would be inspected; if someone had long hair he was told to get it cut before next parade.

Back in the 1960s police cars had radios but police officers did not. There were other radios available, but they were so heavy as to be useless. I used them sometimes on plain-clothes duty, but to be practical they had to be in a car, and they only covered a range of about half a mile. So the main means of long-range communication were car radio, telephone and teleprinter. The drawback to today's prevalent use of radios is that officers listen to them all the time, so part of their attention, as trained observers, is always absent from the immediate scene. I don't doubt that the lack of a radio made a constable less efficient than he is now, but on the other hand, when I spoke to anyone on my beat, I could give that person my whole attention, instead of keeping one ear tuned to my talking brooch.

One big advantage to having a radio, though, is that making arrests without one was downright arduous. Handcuffs were not issued, so it was a case of putting an arm or wrist lock on the detainee and walking with him or her to the nearest telephone and calling for transport. Alternatively the prisoner could be walked all the way to the station.

Once I was on my beat, I was expected to work it and not leave it without authority. I was also expected, once before and once after refreshments, to 'make a ring'. To explain: we had Beat Books, and if I was on a particular beat it would say in the Beat Book *You will make a ring from Number One box* (which for the record was situated at the corner of Camden High Street and Kentish Town Road) *at 8:30 A.M.* When I got to the box in question, I would pick up the phone which would connect me directly to Albany Street; the telephonist would record the time I rang in, and would tell me if there were any messages for me. If there was a variation – that is, if I made my ring late because I was chasing someone, or I had been attending the scene of a crime – I had to write the reason in a book kept in the phone box. If anybody wanted to reach me while I was on my beat, the blue light on top of the police box would be flashed by remote control from the police station and it would go on flashing until the telephone was picked up and the message or instructions had been passed on.

We all developed our own methods of policing our beats. I always thoroughly checked the commercial and industrial properties on my beat by actually trying the doors, especially on nights, and I adopted a practice of standing still, in the early hours of the morning, just watching people move, getting acquainted with the patterns of activity. I became familiar with the cars that were around all the time, so that I could soon spot a stranger and keep an eye on it. I remember one night I telephoned the station with three car checks, and two turned out to be stolen. Observers see much more by standing still than they ever will by walking. Nowadays officers patrol in cars, listening to their radios. They see nothing and they are always partially distracted, so they effectively exist on a plane quite removed from the reality beyond their windscreens.

I had my first experience of corruption while I was still a probationer. It involved a man called Vasos Avramides, nicknamed Pataros, who owned a club in Drummond Street that was patronised largely by prostitutes and petty criminals. One night, working a late shift, I saw Vasos driving along in his car with his girlfriend sitting beside him. I flagged him down. I knew he had been disqualified from driving, but I wasn't sure if the disqualification was still in force. In those days we had no radios and at that moment I was nowhere near a telephone, so I couldn't check the status of the disqualification. I gave Vasos a form and explained that it required him to produce his driving licence and insurance at Albany Street Police Station.

Near the end of the shift I went back to the station to hand in my reports. While I was there I looked in the Disqualified Drivers Register, a very thick book, and I saw that the disqualification of Vasos Avramides still had two months to run. So I had caught him breaking the law.

Around noon the next day there was a knock on my door at the section house. It was one of the Crime Squad officers. He stood there and chatted a while, working his way around to something. Finally he said, 'I hear you stopped Pataros last night.'

I said that was right.

He nodded slowly, frowning, then he named another of the officers at the station. 'He says Pataros is a good informant. He wonders whether you could forget it.'

I stared at him. 'Listen,' I said, getting annoyed, 'if this bloke wants to talk to me, let him come round here himself, instead of sending you.'

He went away. Half an hour later I opened the door to the other officer in person. He was a fat man, wheezing with the effort of climbing the stairs.

'Hello, mate,' he said. 'It seems I've upset you.'

'No, you haven't. Not yet.'

'Well . . .' He shrugged. 'The thing is, you stopped Vasos Avramides last night, which was fair enough. But he's a very good informant, and it would be useful if you just forgot all about it.'

I told him I couldn't do that.

He did a slow blink. 'It'll be worth your while.'

'What does that mean?'

'A hundred quid.'

Now I was getting indignant. I was getting scared, too. I asked him what he would get out of the deal.

He shrugged again. 'I'll be all right.'

'Sorry,' I said, 'I don't want to know about it.'

'Listen, son . . .'

'I'm not interested.'

When he had gone I went next door and talked to another officer. I told him what had happened, without naming the man involved. I admitted I was worried. For all I knew I could be framed for something, or a nasty physical reprisal could be taken against me. The other officer was sympathetic but he was a probationer like me, so he had no more idea what to do than I had.

That night, when I reported at the station to start my shift, I went to the inspector in charge and told him what had happened. Again, I didn't name the officer who tried to bribe me. It would be stupid to do that because it would force a showdown, which would mean that the uncorroborated word of a probationer would be pitched against the word of a seasoned senior officer. Which would torpedo my career.

The inspector listened to me and when I had finished he told me to carry on as usual. 'Don't worry,' he said, 'you've got nothing to fear. I'll back you up on this one.'

The following day I was called in to see the superintendent. He said he had heard about my problem. 'What I want you to do is go and serve summonses personally on Vasos Avramides,' he said. 'Take somebody with you, one of your colleagues. We'll get this to court as quickly as possible and dispose of the matter.'

I took Tony Mulvaney with me down to the Greek's club. I knocked at the side door and Pataros answered it himself. He took a second to register who I was, then suddenly he was all over me, grinning, patting my arm, gushing goodwill.

'Mr Hames! Good to see you! Come in, come in!'

I stayed where I was, brandishing the paperwork. 'I've got these summonses for you.'

He waved the papers aside. 'I plead guilty, I plead guilty. But I will say I had to take my girlfriend to hospital.'

'Listen,' I said, 'I don't want to talk to you about it.'

'Why not?' He stared at me wide-eyed, overdoing the bafflement. 'You don't want money, what do you want? Jewellery for your girlfriend? Maybe something else – what?'

'Just cop these,' I said, shoving the summonses at him. 'I'll see you in court.'

The case went before the Clerkenwell Magistrates. Vasos Avramides was fined £50 for driving while disqualified and £10 for driving without insurance. He was also disqualified for a further six months. The legal route cost him less than the proposed bribe.

That experience turned me off any ideas I had about joining the Crime Squad at Albany Street. I still wanted to be a detective, but I was far from comfortable with certain things going on there.

In 1967, at a time when I was attached to West Ham Magistrates' Court as a cadet in the third phase of training, an old station sergeant asked me if I had ever seen a dead body. I told him no, I hadn't.

'Well, you've got to see one some time.'

'Yes, Sergeant.'

'Want to see one today?'

'Well . . .' I did a quick gulp and nodded, anxious not to dither. 'But can I just see a nice, clean, ordinary dead person?'

'Don't you worry. Come with me.'

At the back of the magistrates' court was the coroner's court and beside it the mortuary, an ancient grey stone building with a damp, gloomy entrance hall that echoed at the small-est sound. The sergeant told me to wait and then went off through a door at the end of a passage. I remember thinking how considerate he was, going ahead to make sure every-thing was okay before I had a look.

The door opened again and the sergeant waved. 'All right now, son. You can come in.'

He held the door for me and I walked into the post-mortem room. For one giddy moment I thought I would faint. It was like a butcher's shop. The big white-tiled room smelled of meat and blood and something rotten. On the porcelain tables five bodies were laid out, all of them cut open from chin to crotch. Their scalps had been flapped fore and aft and the tops had been sawn off their skulls. The brains glistened on the tables beside the open heads. The pathologist was still work-ing on a body, his knife slicing easily through soft tissue. I didn't think I could hold on to my breakfast.

Then something unexpected happened. The pathologist looked up and smiled. He called me across.

'It must look pretty bizarre to you,' he said.

I nodded. 'A bit, sir.'

'It's just another branch of investigation. Try to think of it that way.' He waved a hand along the length of the corpse in front of him. 'Every body declares its own history. The signs are all there, clear as the print in a book. All we have to do is learn to interpret the language.'

He began giving me a crisp, detailed explanation of how each of the people on the tables had died. Moving from one to the other, he told me how he had located tell-tale clues in the organs. He pointed to marks and swellings in the arterial structures, all of them clues he had followed to help him arrive at the causes of death.

I was fascinated. I began to understand the order and reason in what had looked, at first sight, like licensed vandalism. I was learning something new and important, and whenever that was happening I could be relied on to keep a level head.

After five minutes I was fine. I could move from table to table beside the pathologist, gazing into the abdominal cavities and scooped-out skulls of the deceased, inhaling the kind of odours that hardly ever reach the outside world. I was still fairly shaken at what I saw, but I was safely distanced from it by the effort to take in what the pathologist was telling me.

Afterwards I thanked the station sergeant. He had been hovering, obviously expecting a different scenario from the one that unfolded. I could see he was disappointed.

3
Vice and Domesticity

When I became a fully fledged constable and began my foot patrols of Camden Town, I understood – and so did a lot of others – that it was important to keep the mischievous impulses alive, even though we were big boys now, required to conduct ourselves in a way that reflected the seriousness of our job. Shenanigans and random outbreaks of silliness were important, because they counterbalanced the patches of ugliness that came with the job.

Just as families did before the days of television, we had to make our own fun. Some mornings at dawn, at the end of a night shift, four or five of us would meet in Regent's Park for a truncheon-throwing contest. One snowy night we got up on the roof of the police station and pelted the duty inspector with snowballs. At other times, with a bit of luck, I could have a giggle on a night shift without any accomplices. One thing I liked to do, now and then, was wind up the duty officer. The one I remember best from that time was a short, truculent Scot called Jock Watt, outwardly fierce but surprisingly benign if you took the trouble to dig down to his humanity.

Inspector Watt regularly trundled along Camden High Street in his Austin Cambridge, a car with an engine sound I always recognised when it came near, usually from behind. By the time he pulled up alongside I was always ready for him, not at all surprised or flustered as he expected.

The drill was always the same. I stopped walking and acknowledged him. He leaned across and put his face to the gap in the window.

'Everything all right?'

'Everything's fine, sir. Nothing to report.'

I took a short step back and saluted him. He nodded curtly, sat back and drove away again, following the one-way system.

If it was a night when I had decided to wind the inspector up, I would resume strolling again at the regulation pace, hearing the engine of the old Cambridge pulling away into the distance. As soon as it was gone I would dart along a back street, then another and another, running like hell, cutting across the route the boss would take until I came out half a mile from where he had just spoken to me.

Then I would brake and start strolling again, still on my beat, a steady reassuring presence. As the Inspector's car came round the corner I would nod to him and salute as he drove past with his mouth open.

In the '60s a police constable was discouraged from arresting a prostitute until he had at least a couple of years' service behind him, and even then there always had to be two officers present to caution the woman or arrest her. The second man was there to reduce the chance of blackmail or coercion.

There was a saying which we all took very seriously: *The three Ps that will cause you trouble are Prostitutes, Property and Prisoners.*

We had a few prostitutes in Camden Town, but mostly they congregated around Euston. All the main-line stations such as Paddington, Euston and King's Cross had a tradition of prostitutes hovering for hire. I knew very little about vice work in those early days, but I was very active on the crime front, apprehending all sorts of villains for a variety of offences, and I had a high number of arrests to my credit. When I had finished my probationer's final exam, which was around the twenty-month mark, I was approached by Dick Turpin, a sergeant on another relief, who asked me if I fancied going out on vice.

I was surprised he asked. Nobody went out on vice work unless he had five or six years' service. Only half a dozen people at any station had ever done vice and I regarded the market as cornered. Inner-London vice teams were usually just one pair per station, a sergeant and a constable, working as buddies.

'I've noticed you're always nicking people,' Dick said. 'You're a very active sort of lad and I think you'd be quite handy at vice work. So what do you say?'

I said I'd love to give it a shot.

In those days we went out for ninety days at a time, and before an officer started his turn on vice he would line up a job to tackle. When we went out on my first turn, Dick Turpin had already lined up the job. It was a case concerning an Irish ponce (a ponce is the same thing as a pimp) who was always beating up his girl and putting her on the streets to earn money. Our task was to follow the ponce for five days, obtain enough evidence to show that he knew the woman was a prostitute, and that he was knowingly living wholly or in part on her immoral earnings. We had to accomplish it all without the ponce knowing he was under surveillance. That was our first job together, and it turned out successfully. We did others, and during those times I got to know Dick Turpin pretty well.

On 7 February 1966, we were out on a job, watching pimps again.

'Amazing, isn't it?' I said to Dick.

'What?'

'The way things turn out. I never imagined I'd be spending my twenty-first birthday doing this.'

He looked at me. 'Pack it in,' he grunted. 'It's not your birthday.'

'It is,' I said.

He shook his head, grinning. 'You're taking the piss.'

I frowned at him. 'It *is* my birthday. I'm twenty-one today.'

Now I could see he believed me. 'Bloody hell.' He shook his head. 'It's my birthday, too.'

'Honest?'

He slapped my shoulder. 'Come on. We can leave the pimps to their own devices for a while. We should be celebrating.'

He took me for a Chinese meal in Camden Town. So there I was, younger than most who had ever done the job, actually working vice on my twenty-first birthday, and being treated to a slap-up dinner by my boss. I should have taken it as a sign.

I had enjoyed the work right from my first stint. It was a greater challenge than it might seem, following someone for five days without him ever seeing me. It was much the same drill when it came to proving that someone was running a brothel: three days of observation were necessary. At the end of the surveillance I had to summarise the notes I had made in the course of the investigation, then put together a report which I would eventually take to the Area Commander, a person the average constable never got to see. I'd have a cup of tea there – bone china, of course – and we'd have a civilised chat about what was going on. Then I would take my paperwork to A Department (A for Admin) at the Yard, which covered Vice and Licensing, then on to the Solicitors' Branch. Finally we would be given a warrant to arrest the person running the brothel. For me it was an intriguing introduction to normally unapproachable senior officers, and a fascinating insight into how the departments at the Yard were run.

From time to time other officers, perhaps suspicious about my sexual proclivities, would ask me why I did vice work. Instead of cooking up a yarn or simply being evasive, I always told them the truth: the attraction, for me, was in the thrill of the chase. Tracking felons, observing them, building the case, then collaring them. It was and is the exciting essence of real police work.

Even though I did relish vice work, however, I was fairly unsettled at that time. I had always wanted to be a detective, the classic kind, and I still did. I wanted to be the wrecker of blags, the dismantler of scams, a taker of big-time criminals. The dream persisted.

I applied to the Special Branch and I was accepted. Almost as soon as I joined I discovered that I had passed the promotion examination to sergeant as a 'competitor'. This meant that I could either return to uniform duty and be promoted very quickly, or forgo my competitive place, become what was known as a 'qualifier' and wait another three years or so before I could be considered for promotion with the branch. To be honest, I found the work at Special Branch bureaucratic, repetitive and completely unexciting. I was relieved to go back to the hustle and bustle of ordinary duty.

Not long after I came back, I was with another Sergeant, John Allinson, when we arrested a girl who had been attracting attention to herself by accosting passers-by in Euston Road. She was obviously very drunk, and we recognised her as a woman we had previously dealt with as a prostitute.

I was talking to her in the charge room at Albany Street when I saw a glint of something on her face. I looked closer, tilting the desk lamp at her. I realised it was stubble. In spite of the blotchy make-up it was obvious, in a strong light, that she had a five o'clock shadow. I asked if she was a man, and that really annoyed her. She called me a couple of names, then jumped on to the charge room desk, took off all her clothes and revealed a body that was convincingly female. However, during the strip, between fits of cursing me and the Metropolitan Police in general, she told us that she had paid £2,000 for a sex change operation in Switzerland. We looked again and we could see she had indeed had surgery. Up to that point I wasn't aware of ever meeting anybody who had undergone the operation.

I told her to put her clothes back on, and John Allinson joined me in a corner for a procedural mutter. We had a problem with charging her, which we had to do, because her arrest was already on the register. The trouble was that under the Street Offences Act the charge of prostitution requires the offender to be a woman. There could be nasty repercussions if the question of our prisoner's gender became an issue.

We decided to call in the Divisional Surgeon, Dr Arnold Mendoza, who later became coroner for North London.

When he arrived he examined our prisoner and told us she was technically a castrated male.

This was no help. What could we charge her with? After some thought and a riffle through the legal books, we considered the charge of *a male person importuning for an immoral purpose*. This was technically correct, but after giving it some more thought and discreetly taking advice, we decided the charge would be inappropriate in this case. In the end, after a lot of discussion with the station officer, we decided to charge her, in her female name, with highway obstruction.

The next problem was, where would we lock her up for the night? We tried to put her in the male cells but she forcibly declined. There were no other women in custody at the time so we put her in the female cells. Next morning the magistrate referred to her as 'Madam', which delighted her. She pleaded guilty, and after she was let off with a warning, we asked her if she would refrain from working on our ground in future, because it caused too many technical problems. She promised she would stay away.

It was an amusing case, but there was a serious undertow. Dr Mendoza told us that at that time, although the sex-change operation was being performed at specialist centres in Switzerland and elsewhere, it was still far from satisfactory, and a large number of patients subsequently committed suicide. The reason for this, in many cases, was that the transsexual's hormonal system would counter the loss of organs and glands by creating – and sustaining – heightened levels of male sexual hormones, including testosterone. This made the patient acutely aware that the body she lived in, although superficially female, now felt more biologically male than ever. The duality and the consequent alienation became, for many people, insufferable, and sometimes they broke under the strain.

On reflection, I think I learned as much about human misery in my time as a vice officer as I did when the protection of children became my main concern.

As a constable I did four tours of ninety days each on vice. Thereafter I was known as a vice officer, because I had served my basic time at the job. I became one of a clique of people around London who knew each other from their work on vice squads at Notting Hill, Kentish Town, Albany Street, West End Central, Caledonian Road, Harrow Road, King's Cross and Paddington.

I was part of an élite. The die was cast.

As Jacky's parents had wished, we waited a few years before we raised the topic of marriage again. After some discussion, and with the blessing of family on both sides, we were married on Jacky's birthday, a Saturday. She was twenty-one and she had just gained a degree in psychology. I was twenty-three, and on the Monday following the wedding I was promoted to sergeant. It was an auspicious start to our married life, or so I believed. I was young then, so my faith in auspices and omens was still intact.

Soon after I went to Bow Street, where I joined a shift with two other young sergeants, John Philpott and John Gillies. John Gillies had married one of the two women officers in my class at Training School. The Division covered the Covent Garden Market and extended into Soho, taking in Leicester Square. The Market was the focus of the station, largely because we were right bang in the middle of it, with the Royal Opera House opposite. That police station is the only one in the country with a white light outside, and the reason for

that, allegedly, is that Queen Victoria insisted she did not
want to see the blue lantern when she came to the opera.

I was at Bow Street for just a month before I was sent on
the Special Course at the National Police College at Bramshill.
This is a year-long national course, funded by the Home
Office, and is designed for officers who have been identified
as high-fliers. Thirty of us were selected from around the
country. The sergeants from the counties had been temporar-
ily promoted; those of us from London were substantive
promotions. Successful completion of the course led to promotion to inspector one year after.

Applicants attend regional selection boards and those who
are successful at that stage go on to the extended interviews,
which last three days. Mine was at Churchill College,
Cambridge. The selection involved psychometric tests, interviews – both in a board situation and one-to-one – and group
exercises. The interviewers were chief constables and external
examiners. One of them was a former ambassador and in my
one-to-one he asked me about vice. He queried my motivation and implied heavily that people who do this work must
be drawn to it for the wrong reasons. Moments later he
remarked that he occasionally stayed at the White House
Hotel in Albany Street. I saw my chance for a touch of redress:
I told him that in those days, the hotel was notorious and fre-
quented by prostitutes.

The course was in two parts, Higher Police studies (strategy of policing – e.g., organisation in public order situations,
major incidents and crime) and general political studies. We
had to pass the equivalent of the County Police Inspector's
Exam, and an examination in general studies. Failure in
either exam would lead to complete failure of the course.
One man from the counties failed and was sent back as a

constable. To drop suddenly from being one of the country's most promising thirty to the rank of PC must have been hell to live with.

When I got back to Bow Street there was no rancour or jealousy from any of my colleagues, even though I had expected at least a little. Life adopted a regulation pace again and I eased myself back into ordinary police duties.

One night in December 1969, I was on late turn in the charge room at Bow Street, talking to my colleague John Gillies. We were interrupted by a young probationer constable from West End Central, off duty and wearing civilian clothes, who had brought in a prisoner.

I went behind the desk, got out a charge sheet and asked the probationer what he had arrested the man for. He said he had been in a cinema in Charing Cross Road when the man came in and sat next to him. After a few minutes, he said, the man had started to rub his leg. Then he moved his hand to the probationer's crotch. John Gillies and I must have looked stunned as the lad went on to tell us that the man had unzipped his fly and taken out his penis.

'I then told him who I was, and arrested him for indecent assault.'

I stared at the probationer. He was perfectly serious and straight faced. I asked him why he let the prisoner go as far as he had.

'Well . . .' The lad frowned. 'I thought I had to get all the evidence I could. I didn't think I had any power of arrest until it had gone as far as it did.'

The logic of it was astounding. That was the training school for you. They extracted common sense from a student and replaced it with learning by rote.

I asked the probationer how he thought the magistrate at

the court next door would react when he was presented with that evidence. More importantly, what would the other officers at West End Central think? What would the wider world make of it?

'What else could I have done, Sarge?'

'Move seats, tell him to fuck off, something like that,' I suggested.

The probationer shuffled his feet awkwardly. The prisoner sat quietly on a bench by the wall, a rumpled onlooker.

'I tell you what I'm going to do,' I said. 'I'm going to let this man go. And I suggest you keep this to yourself, unless you want to suffer for the rest of your service.'

I then used a procedure which was designated *advising the prisoner as to his future conduct*, after which I showed him to the door. He was plainly relieved at the outcome and grateful to be on his way again, free to pester and molest. The probationer had meanwhile disappeared into the night. John Gillies and I took ourselves off to the canteen for a cup of tea and a chuckle.

In February 1970 I was on the move again, posted to West End Central with the now defunct rank of Station Police Sergeant. Six months later I was posted once again, and this time I was promoted, too: on 11 August 1970 I moved to Harrow Road with the rank of inspector.

I had been at Harrow Road for less than a year when I got a radio call one night about a man who claimed he had been robbed by a prostitute. At approximately midnight a sergeant and I drove out to The Artesian, a pub in Chepstow Road. In those days the streets near the pub were notorious for the number of prostitutes who lived and operated there.

A middle-aged man stepped forward as we got out of the car. He wore a dark business suit and spoke politely in a soft

Irish accent. He thanked us for coming and volunteered to tell us about himself. He was married, he lived in Ireland, and he was in London for a few days on business. I could tell from his breath that he had been drinking, but he was not drunk and he told his story coherently.

He said he had just had sex with a prostitute, for which he paid her £20. On leaving the woman's flat he discovered that £80 had disappeared from his pocket. He didn't know how the prostitute had managed it during the ten minutes he had been with her, but he was certain she had stolen his money.

'She saw me take the twenty quid from the wad,' he said. 'I definitely had the money when I was in there and I'm positive it didn't fall out of my pocket after I was back on the street.'

He showed me where the prostitute did business. I checked on the pavement and the path to make sure he hadn't dropped the money, even though I was pretty sure he was right about what happened; prostitutes *do* often steal their clients' wallets and valuables, relying on the men being too embarrassed to report the theft to the police.

I told the man to wait by our car. The sergeant and I walked along to the flat and I rang the bell. The door was opened by a big-bosomed woman in a black miniskirt and a low-cut top. She was somewhere in her thirties. I introduced myself and the sergeant and told her what the Irishman had said. She shook her head firmly.

'No way!' she snapped. 'No way!'

She said the only money she had seen was what he gave her. She suggested that if he really did have more on him earlier, he probably spent it on drink before he got to her place.

I said I wanted to search the flat. She shrugged and showed us in. It was not so much a flat as a bedsitter. Apart from a ramshackle double bed that took up most of the space, there was a chair, a bin, a Baby Belling cooker and a sink. By that time we had been joined by two constables and over the next half-hour the four of us methodically searched every square inch of the place, including the little garden at the back. We found nothing.

'You see?' the woman crowed. 'He's lying, the bastard.'

I was convinced *she* was the liar and I decided to arrest her. When I cautioned her she moaned about the loss of working time, muttered a curse or two, then went outside with us. The businessman was waiting where we had left him. She blew him a kiss.

At the station I took the prostitute to the charge room and called for a WPC, who carried out a full body search. Again nothing was found. But I knew the man was telling the truth about his money – there was nothing fictional about his determination to get it back; no false note in the way he put his case. I was just as convinced the prostitute was lying. The money had to be somewhere.

I stared at her. She stared back. It wasn't just defiance, it was the look of a toe-rag who couldn't hide her sense of triumph at putting one across authority.

Then it dawned on me. Suddenly I was sure I knew, without knowing what made me so certain.

'You know where the money is,' I told her, 'and *I* know where it is.'

'What d'you mean?'

'There's only one place we haven't looked.'

She laughed, a humourless bark. 'I don't know what you're talking about, mate.'

I spelt it out for her. 'I reckon the money's in your fanny.'

'You what?' She feigned shock. 'How dare you! You dirty bugger!'

I asked her if she would submit to an internal examination by a police surgeon. If she had said no, then we could have done nothing, but fortunately she was not aware of her rights and she agreed to the examination, clearly believing she had no choice.

When the doctor arrived I explained what I wanted him to do. He sighed, took off his jacket and rolled up his sleeves. In the medical room the prostitute took off her pants and lay on the examination table. She looked up at the ceiling and took a deep breath, nervous for once at the prospect of being man-handled. The doctor put on a pair of rubber gloves, stood over her and began to poke around.

She howled suddenly. 'Piss off!' She slapped the doctor's arm. 'You're hurting me!'

He started to probe again, taking more care this time. After a minute the prostitute shoved his hand aside.

'Leave it,' she snapped. 'I'll do it.' She sat up, hunched forward, pushed her fingers inside herself and pulled out a wad of notes. 'There. That's what you're looking for.' She handed the money to my colleague. 'But it's not the Paddy's. It's mine.'

My colleague, a fastidious man, went to the sink and washed the eight £10 notes, one at a time. Strictly speaking he was tampering with evidence, but nobody said anything. He put the notes on the radiator to dry.

I went to speak to the Irishman. I told him we'd retrieved his money, and where the prostitute had been secreting it.

'But she denies it's yours,' I said. 'If you want to get it back you'll have to take her to court.'

'I see.'

'Do you want to do that?'

'Yes, certainly,' he replied. 'It's my money and I'll have it back.'

When the prostitute appeared before a judge and jury at the Inner London Crown Court she pleaded not guilty, obviously relying on the Irishman failing to turn up to give evidence. I had my own doubts in that direction.

But we were both wrong. The Irishman arrived wearing the same smart business suit as before, and he got into the witness box and told his story in front of a sniggering court. The defence counsel made him squirm, forcing him to describe in detail the events of the night when his money disappeared. I could see the sheen of sweat on his forehead as he ploughed through the ordeal, but even so, he made a good job of presenting his side of the case.

The prostitute did not take the stand; the jury eventually found her guilty. The court then heard she was in breach of a suspended sentence for a similar offence. The judge sentenced her to eighteen months in prison, wiping off the smile she had been wearing for most of the hearing.

Afterwards I told the plaintiff he could have his money back. I took him to the police room where he signed for the notes, which were in an exhibits bag. He took out the wad of deteriorating tenners and held one curling specimen up to the light. He shook his head.

'How can I use these now?'

I told him a bank would change them.

'What will I say happened?'

'That's up to you,' I said, keeping it deadpan.

4
A Bomb at the Bailey

In 1972 I made my first contact with Spike Milligan. It began in April when my chief superintendent handed me a letter.

'Read that and sort it out,' he said.

I read the letter.

To: The Superintendent,
Police Station,
Harrow Road,
London W2

19th April, 1972

Dear Sir.

I want to report an incident.

On Sunday 2nd April, 1972, at approximately
4.30 pm, I witnessed two women and a man with a
Great Dane dog – the dog defecated on the pavement.

I followed the people who went to Queens Mews.

I wrote to the Westminster City Council and they told me I should report the incident to the Police. As the streets of Bayswater are polluted excessively by this disgusting habit I do hope we can prosecute.

Respectfully,
Spike Milligan

I rang Spike's agent, Norma Farnes, and asked her to tell Mr Milligan I would speak to the people in Queen's Mews. Less than a month later the second letter arrived, addressed to me this time, although he got my name wrong.

To: Inspector Haines,
Harrow Road Police Station,
London W2

16th May, 1972

Dear Sir,
          Milligan versus Dog Shit Case Number 2
On Sunday the 7th May at about 11.30am a large black dog defecated on the pavement, I called the creature and said 'Come here Darling'. I saw that its label bore the address Burnham Court, Moscow Road, and the dog's name was Liz. A fitting Royal name for a debasement of the Royal city.

Would you please prosecute?
Sincerely,
Spike Milligan

Now that we knew with some certainty where the animal lived, I thought I had better go and see the people and warn them they were risking prosecution. That was exactly what I did. Afterwards I popped in to report progress to Norma Farnes at Orme Court, just off the Bayswater Road. As it happened Spike Milligan was there. That was our first meeting and somehow, over a period of months and years, we became very friendly. Norma Farnes became a friend, too, and later she was godmother to my daughter Kirstie.

Spike and I have kept in close touch for over twenty-five years, and he has had an influence on many of the things I've done, socially as well as in the line of duty. Years after our first meeting, it was Spike who helped speed up the formalities when the actor Peter Arne was murdered. Arne, a homosexual who was in the habit of picking up strangers and taking them back to his apartment in Chelsea, was bludgeoned to death in the hallway. The place was such a mess, with blood all over the floor and spattered on the walls, it would have been impossible for us to go into the apartment without disturbing the scene. That meant we could not get in to find the addresses of relatives or friends or associates, not until the forensic team had been and done their job.

Since time is crucially important in a murder investigation, I called Spike and told him what had happened. I asked him to look in the actors' directory, *Spotlight*, and find out the name of Peter Arne's agent. This Spike promptly did, and within minutes we were talking with the agent and getting all the co-operation we needed.

Next day my chief superintendent at Chelsea, Gordon Lloyd, wrote to Spike and thanked him for his help. Three days later Spike wrote back:

Chief Superintendent G. R. Lloyd
Metropolitan Police
Chelsea Police Station
Lucan Place
London SW3 3PB

Dear Super,
Anything to help the police; I have been a police fan
since I was a little boy. When all the others were
shouting out, 'All coppers are bastards,' I used to call
out, 'Some coppers are bastards.'

When Mike Hames phoned me, I am a detective by
nature so much so, before I heard details of the case I
said to Mike, 'This is what it's all about, he's a puff, and
it's a puff murderer.'

Anyway I was delighted to get a letter from the
Guvna himself. Anytime, any place I am always ready
to help the police, they really do a great job.

Love, light and peace,
Spike Milligan

Four months later, Spike again stepped in and gave us ster-
ling support in the aftermath of the Christmas bombing
outside Harrods.

Towards the end of my time at Harrow Road one of my officers, a probationer PC called Roger Williams, was very
seriously assaulted while he was on night duty. He was called
to a disturbance in an Indian restaurant just fifty yards from
the station on the corner of Harrow Road. Inside the place
three young local thugs – Andrews, Smiley and Price – were
causing trouble. Roger was a tall young graduate, quiet and

sweet natured, and when he approached the troublemakers and asked them to leave, his civilised manner must have provoked them further. They piled on to Roger and dragged him outside. Two of them pinned his arms behind his back and the third man hit him in the face with a bottle.

Bryan Boon, the station sergeant, was on patrol that night and was called with others to the scene of the assault. Later he told me he had nearly missed Roger, who had been left in the gutter 'like a pile of rubbish'. Roger needed seventy-two stitches in his wounds.

We all joined in the search and found two of the thugs, Andrews and Price, fairly quickly. Smiley, for the time being, had escaped. Most of us on night duty stayed on into the day shift to look for him. At mid-morning we got a tip-off where he might be found. I went with Detective Sergeant Nicky Birch to an address just off the Harrow Road. Nicky went to the front door, I went round the back. He knocked on the door. Smiley came out of a back window, saw me waiting, and gave up without resistance.

All three were charged with Section 18 Assault, causing grievous bodily harm with intent. The case came up at the Old Bailey on Thursday 8 March 1973. Andrews, Smiley and Price were going to plead not guilty. Roger came to give evidence, accompanied by his father. Shortly before we were due in court I arrived at Harrow Road and saw Nicky Birch in the station yard. I suggested we go in my car, but Nicky said he had already put the exhibits in the boot of his new car, which he had picked up two days earlier, so we got into that and drove off. There was a rail strike that day so the parking meters were suspended and we could park anywhere. We found a spot right outside the court, by the front steps. Our case was being heard in the West Courts, a new building opposite the famous Central Criminal Court with the blind-folded figure of justice on the dome.

At the lunch adjournment, Nicky and I decided to have a pie and a pint at one of the local pubs. We saw that The George and The Magpie and Stump, both adjacent to the court, were full to overflowing, so we walked fifty yards up the road to The White Hart opposite St Bart's Hospital.

A few minutes before two o'clock Nick left the pub; I stayed on, talking to another colleague. After roughly five minutes I looked at the clock and decided I had better get back. I pushed my way through the crowd to the door. As I grasped the handle there was an enormous explosion outside. The sound wasn't so much a bang as a massive growling *whoosh*! I knew it was a bomb. We all did. There was silence for five seconds, then came the shouts and screams. I went outside and saw a huge cloud of smoke and debris outside the Court. I ran towards it, taking my coat off as I went, revealing my uniform. I got to the corner of the road and saw a woman lying on the pavement. Blood was gushing from her leg.

'I'm going to die,' she wailed as I bent over her. 'I'm going to *die*!'

I pressed firmly on the femoral pressure point on her thigh to stem the bleeding. I tried to reassure her, told her she would be all right. Within minutes ambulance men arrived with a stretcher and took over. They hurried her to the hospital a few yards away.

Suddenly I was worried about Nicky and my other colleagues. A PC went with me to the corner where the bomb had gone off. People were rushing everywhere. I helped to get the cordons in place and sent the PC off to find Nicky and to retrieve all our exhibits, which were in the court-room. I was anxious to get them away to safety before anyone tried to

tamper with them. We got the exhibits, but Nicky was
nowhere to be found. We eventually made our way back to
Harrow Road by tube.

It turned out that as Nicky arrived back at the front of the
court, a City Police inspector was rushing around telling
everyone that there was a bomb in the street. He was trying,
without much success, to make people leave The George.
The City Police had called a photographer to the scene and he
was busy taking photographs of a green Ford Cortina opposite the West Court. The Cortina was parked right next to
Nicky's new car.

'That's my car over there,' Nicky said to the Inspector. 'Shall
I go and move it?'

'No,' the inspector said, 'this'll all be over in a couple of
minutes.'

At that moment the Cortina exploded with an orange flash.
There was a deafening roar and a ferocious rush of air that
threw Nicky into the doorway of The Magpie and Stump.
Through a swimming haze he realised his car was completely
wrecked. Apart from extreme shock – he was stunned and his
movements were unco-ordinated – he was physically unhurt.
He crossed the road and tried to help the photographer,
whose leg was terribly injured. The sequence of events was a
blur to Nicky, but after a few minutes during which he tried
to help tend several of the injured, he staggered off and finally
managed to catch a cab. He went to Tintagel House, the headquarters of the Regional Crime Squad, where he saw the
detective chief superintendent, Jim Morrison.

'Best you have a drink,' Jim said, when Nicky had told him
what happened.

They proceeded to kill off a bottle of Scotch, an unwise
move on Nicky's part because his head was scrambled with

the effect of the blast and his body was in the grip of shock; the drink elevated his heart rate, fuddled his wits still further and generally made things worse.

In the meantime, I arrived at Harrow Road where they told me that Nicky had surfaced at Tintagel House. They assured me he was all right. We discussed the events of the afternoon. Four bombs had been planted in central London that day, and two of them had gone off: one at the Old Bailey, the other at the Army Recruiting Office at Great Scotland Yard, off Whitehall. The blasts were timed to coincide with Ulster's referendum on the future of British rule in the province. One person was killed and about 250 injured. The toll would have been much higher if Scotland Yard hadn't acted on a tip-off and defused the other two bombs. One was planted in a Ford Corsair parked outside New Scotland Yard itself, the other was in a car in Dean Stanley Street near the Houses of Parliament.

By this time I felt I had had enough excitement for one day. I decided to drop in on Spike Milligan.

I went down to Orme Court and saw Norma Farnes. She was shocked at my dishevelled state I was in. I told her what had happened and asked where Spike was; she said that he was writing in his room on the first floor. I went up and knocked on the door.

'Who's there?' he called.

'Special Branch,' I snarled. 'Open up, you Irish bastard!'

Spike opened the door. 'Hello, Mike.' He looked me up and down. 'What's happened?'

I told him. He was completely taken aback. He said he was writing a script at the typewriter and had the television on with the sound turned low. He had been half aware of the pictures from the corner of his eye, and he assumed when he heard the bang that it was news footage from Belfast.

'Come away in,' he said. 'You look like a bomb hit you.'

He ushered me inside, sat me down and opened the brandy bottle. He poured two generous snifters and sat with me while I told him all about it. Hours later I made my weary way home, tired but grateful to have been debriefed by my Irish friend.

Our trial at the Old Bailey concluded a few days later. Andrews, Smiley and Price were found guilty and sent to prison for lengthy terms. Young Roger Williams decided he had had enough of the police service and resigned shortly afterwards. I could hardly blame him. To have survived a ferocious attack resulting in terrible injury, then a bomb going off outside a court where he was appearing, and all so early in his career, seemed to me, and no doubt to Roger, to be omens he was wise to heed.

After two and a half exciting and happy years at Harrow Road, I was called up for a career guidance discussion and told that I should now apply for one of the posts advertised in Police Orders at the Community Relations Branch. I was not entirely keen to do this, because I was enjoying myself at Harrow Road, but my superiors told me that the career path demanded I apply. So I applied. In due course I was granted an interview, and I appeared before Commander Kenneth Newman, who later became Commissioner.

He asked me why I had applied. I was tempted to say *because I was told to*, but I played the game and spoke confidently about my ability to contribute to the efforts being made to forge links with the ethnic minorities, and about my experience in the cosmopolitan division of Harrow Road.

I was accepted and went to Community Relations for a three-year posting. I was joined by another inspector, Peter

Lewis, who became a very good friend. Peter had been a station sergeant on the Isle of Dogs and served most of his time in the East End. He later became a deputy assistant commissioner and the deputy commandant at Bramshill.

During my time at Community Relations the Met was determined to build bridges with immigrant communities and minority groups. It was decided that the Community Relations branch needed staff with operational credibility rather than straightforward administrators. This initiative was pushed forward in order to persuade officers of the need to co-operate with – and understand – the different cultures with which they were coming into contact.

At that time, too, John Newing, now Chief Constable of Derbyshire, together with Detective Superintendent Ray Crump, produced a controversial report on 'footpad' crime in Lambeth. The report highlighted the disproportionate involvement of young black men and the worrying fact that the overwhelming majority of their victims were white. I recall that at the time, the report was received in a responsible, non-confrontational way by all sides.

To help put some sparkle into our posting Peter Lewis and I decided to study for a diploma in Management Studies at the Polytechnic of the South Bank. We passed, and the college awarded us our diplomas in the summer of 1976, just as our postings at Community Relations came to an end.

In September 1976 Dad was taken to hospital in Colchester suffering from pneumonia. A complication developed in the form of a deep-seated clot in his leg, and it became clear to us that he was gravely ill. In an effort to reduce the dangerous clot the doctors administered warfarin, a powerful anti-coagulent, but Dad continued to decline. My brother Eric, sister

Pat and I took turns with Mum to sit with him twenty-four
hours a day. He finally succumbed on 27 September. He was
seventy-nine. We buried him at Mersea, dressed in his St John
Ambulance Brigade uniform. On the day of his funeral the
church was packed. I attended in my police uniform as I
knew Dad would have wished. For a long time after he died
we continued to miss him dreadfully. He was a truly good
man and the finest father anyone could have. I never heard
him utter an unkind word against anyone, and I know he was
loved by everyone who knew him.

5
Turbulence at Wembley

After my spell at Community Relations I was posted to Southall by Commander Peter Marshall, who was later to become the Commissioner of the City of London Police. It was a posting I thoroughly enjoyed. I loved the atmosphere of the place and I *adored* the curry houses. After four months, I was given Norwood Green Police Station to look after, with the post of Unit Commander. While I was there a young Sikh boy, Gurdip Singh Jaggar, was murdered on my patch. The killing sparked off some nasty rioting which nevertheless gave me plenty of practice in riot control, *ad hoc* administration and people-handling.

After only seven months at Norwood Green I was promoted to Chief Inspector. I went from Southall to Harrow as Administration Chief Inspector, stayed there for eighteen months, then I was made District Complaints Officer at Wembley. I stayed in that job for under a year, then did a short spell at the same place as Administration Chief

Inspector, waiting for Leo Brighton, the Operations Chief Inspector, to be promoted. When he was, I took his place. The first serious paedophile enquiry I carried out was shortly after I made that move.

One day the Home Beat Officer from the Kingsbury area came to see me. He said a group of parents had talked to him about a man called Ray Eustace who owned a minicab firm at Roe Green. They said he had a Space Invaders machine in the cab office and he encouraged young boys to go in there and play on it for free. He also owned a go-kart which he let boys drive at weekend meetings. He took several lads with him each time and they travelled in a van to tracks around the country.

Recently someone had overheard the boys muttering about Eustace 'messing around' with them; this alerted the adults to the possibility that something unpleasant might be going on. The delegation of parents who talked to the Home Beat Officer were not making accusations. They were voicing a concern.

I ran a check on Ray Eustace and discovered he had a conviction for abusing a ten-year-old boy. It had happened ten years earlier and the conviction was spent, as far as the courts were concerned. In 1979 the theories on criminal recidivism were still developing: we knew practically nothing about serial sex offenders, or the typical patterns of paedophile behaviour, or the ways they have of grooming youngsters. It seemed to me that in the light of his previous conviction Eustace was probably doing, or getting close to doing, things he ought not to do.

I decided to go proactive and have a look at him. I wanted to monitor his behaviour and movements, and at the same time I wanted to identify the lads who were going in and out

of the cab office. I set up an observation point in a flat almost
directly opposite the office and put two men in there. One
had a 35mm camera with a 200mm lens, the other had a pair
of powerful binoculars.

After four days we knew that the same seven or eight boys
went to the cab office regularly. Eustace, a tall, thin, bespec-
tacled man of thirty-five with gaunt features and lank, dirty
hair, travelled to and from the office either in a van or an
estate car, and very often a boy travelled with him. It was
always the same boy, a lad of about sixteen.

But something else was happening. Two West Indian men,
known to the police as burglars, were seen and photographed
several times talking to a couple of the Asian minicab drivers
outside the office. It was obvious that something villainous
was afoot and I assigned the Crime Squad to put the burglars
under surveillance. Shortly afterwards Crime Squad officers
arrested both men coming out of a house carrying a television
set, cameras and jewellery they had stolen from the premises.

The men were kept apart and questioned separately. They
turned out to be working a scam with the cab drivers we had
seen them talking to. Whenever the drivers took punters to
an airport to go on holiday, they passed on the addresses of
the clients to the burglars, who would burgle the unoccu-
pied houses.

The four men were prosecuted and we recovered a huge
amount of property. That was a valuable side issue to come
out of our surveillance of Ray Eustace. We were all gratified
with the outcome, and there was another bonus – the prosecution of the cab drivers allowed me to get close to Eustace
and talk to him. I visited him in his office, because I quite
legitimately needed to look through his record cards. Eustace,
for his part, wanted to co-operate with the police in any way

he could, because it would have hurt his business if local people got the impression he had been mixed up in something illegal.

We soon determined that Eustace had never been a part of the burglary set-up. He continued to accommodate us and help us put our case together, blissfully unaware that he was the subject of an inquiry.

We identified all of the boys who regularly hung around the mini-cab office, and I decided they should be interviewed with their parents present. Nowadays I wouldn't do that: teenage boys are not going to admit, in front of their mothers and fathers, that an adult has made sexual advances to them.

The sessions of questioning were conducted by Stuart Taylor, a police constable with long experience of putting sensitive questions to children and adults in a way that usually elicited answers. But none of the boys said a word against Ray Eustace. Harry,* the boy who spent so much time travelling back and forth with him, was carefully questioned in the presence of his foster mother, but like the others he insisted that Eustace had never said or done anything improper.

The questioning of the boys wasn't a complete waste of time, however, because it threw more light on Eustace's behaviour. We learned that when he and the boys went away to weekend go-karting events, they would all, including Eustace, stay overnight in a single hotel room. The boys would be encouraged to indulge in horseplay, with mock fighting, tickling and wrestling. Although we didn't have any useful evidence to go on, we had no doubt by now that Eustace was up to something, and I began to worry seriously about Harry being so vulnerable.

*The names of victims of abuse have been changed.

Then, by chance, Harry was arrested for possession of a stolen car radio, and he was brought to Wembley Police Station. I heard he was in for a caution, so I got Stuart Taylor to see him and talk to him again, very gently, about his relationship with Eustace. Within ten minutes, with no foster mother present this time, Harry told Constable Taylor that Ray Eustace had buggered him, and had done so regularly for two years.

At last we had grounds for a full and thorough investigation. I got on the phone and spoke to Ray Eustace.

'Mr Eustace? Chief Inspector Hames here. Harry's at the station. I wonder, would you come and pick him up?'

He said it would be no trouble. He arrived less than ten minutes later and was shown to my office on the first floor. He tapped the door and came in, smiling all over his face. He held his hand out to shake mine.

'Hello again Mr Hames,' he beamed. 'How are you?'

I stared at him, stone cold. 'Don't you Mr Hames me.' I stood up and went straight into formal mode. 'Raymond Eustace, I am arresting you for the buggery of Harry Smith. You are not obliged to say anything, but anything you do say will be taken down and may be used in evidence.'

He was a naturally pale man but now he had gone a shade whiter. His Adam's apple went up and down a couple of times, then he muttered something about me getting it all wrong.

'Listen,' I snapped, 'before you start, don't say you didn't do it. Okay? Just stop yourself before you tell me how innocent you are, because later on it'll be hard to retract that.'

He pushed back a strand of dirty hair, staring at me, bewildered at the sudden change in his relationship with the police.

'In any case,' I went on, 'your denials are useless, we know precisely what you've done. We have a statement from Harry.'

I waited a beat to let that soak in. 'Now, say nothing, do you understand?'

I took him down to the charge room where he was entered on the sheet as being in custody. We offered him the opportunity to contact a solicitor but he decided not to.

'I want to interview Mr Eustace in my office now,' I told the Custody Officer.

I took Eustace back upstairs and Constable Taylor came with me. I stared at Eustace, keeping up the stern front.

'I'm going to leave you with Mr Taylor,' I said. 'He's going to talk to you. I'll repeat what I already said. We have a statement from Harry which makes it perfectly clear what you've been doing to him for a considerable time. And I'll tell you now, we've been watching you. Think about all that.'

I left and Taylor went into his humane routine. He played the sympathetic inquirer who seemed sorry that things should have come to this. He used persuasive, non-judgmental language to get Eustace to admit that everything Harry told us was true. Within minutes Taylor came out of my office.

'Mr Eustace wants to make a statement, sir.'

I went in and asked Eustace if he was ready to get it all on paper. He nodded without looking at me. Over the next hour he made a full statement in his own handwriting, without prompting, apart from the occasional 'What happened then?' It was important to have as full and detailed a statement as we could get, to buffer any pressure the defence might put on Harry in court.

Once Eustace was in custody we went to his house and searched it. The place was filthy. We were looking for evidence of buggery, but this was before the development of DNA analysis; we found nothing significant in the way of forensic evidence, certainly nothing that could conclusively prove Harry's story. We took away a tube of KY jelly and the filthy bedsheets, but we knew they would probably yield nothing useful. We were right about that.

Nowadays, armed with what we know about paedophile behaviour, we would look for diaries and other written evidence, for photographs, obscene videos or ciné films. Back then we didn't understand the importance of these things. In the light of what I've learned since, I now know that Ray Eustace was a typical serial sexual offender. He had all the characteristics, including the tactic of singling out a vulnerable target.

Harry was in foster care with no father figure, and we found that other boys often picked on him. He wasn't popular and he was essentially a loner. Ray Eustace worked at increasing the isolation. He not only chose a perfect target, he ingratiated himself with the foster mother to such an extent that she didn't believe Harry's story, and she refused to believe that Ray Eustace was guilty of anything: her response, we now know, was entirely predictable.

Another thing we know paedophiles do is provide amusements for their targets. In this case it was Space Invaders and the go-kart. Eustace also bought the boys food and gave them money for cigarettes. We have learned that encouraging boys to indulge in play-fighting and letting them drink alcohol to ease their inhibitions is also completely typical behaviour among paedophiles, usually as a desensitising precursor to serious abuse.

Harry's foster mother was determined he wouldn't give evidence against Ray Eustace. 'Harry's not going to court,' she said. 'That's final.'

But by this time Harry was an adult. He had just turned seventeen. We didn't need his foster mother's permission to do anything. Nevertheless, I was worried that she might try to send Harry away or find some other way to hamper him so he wouldn't be around to give evidence. I decided not to tell Harry what date he had to appear in court. We knew what time he left the house every day, and on the morning of the trial we waited round the corner until he appeared. He wasn't hard to spot because by that time he had dyed his hair bright ginger.

'Come on, Harry,' I said. 'We're off to court.'

Without his presence as a complainant, we would have had only a statement under caution, which would certainly be attacked, no doubt successfully, by the defence. We had already been notified that Ray Eustace was going to plead not guilty, so I assumed he was banking on Harry not showing.

We stood in the main foyer at the Old Bailey, waiting for our case to be called. Ray Eustace finally arrived. When he came in he saw Harry straight away. His face went the same colour it turned the day I cautioned him in my office. He shuffled away to a corner with his solicitor and counsel. The next thing we knew, he had changed his plea to guilty.

We went into court. Eustace stood before the judge and admitted his guilt. The judge examined the evidence before him, considered it in the light of the guilty plea, and handed down his verdict. I could hardly believe my ears. For seriously and persistently abusing a minor over a period of two years, Ray Eustace was fined £300 and set free.

Shortly after I moved into the new job Alan Minter, holder of the World Middleweight Boxing Championship, defended his title at Wembley Arena against the American challenger Marvin Hagler. The man responsible for overall policing on the night was Chief Superintendent Ben Pountain. I was second in command, in charge of policing the inner arena and the ringside area. The other senior man on the team was Inspector David Hatch. Officers were on duty outside and inside the arena, which was packed to capacity with noisy, boisterous fight fans.

The supporting bill was rubbish. In bout after bout, mismatched boxers with dismal timing shuffled about the ring throwing wild punches at each other and only occasionally connecting. It was dreary stuff and the crowd soon got bored. More and more of them trickled out to the bar. Between the end of the last supporting bout and the start of the big fight, American television created a long gap to let the programme sponsors make their pitch. More spectators left the arena to go and get tanked up. Other fans, already half drunk and brassed off, were chanting and waving Union Jacks. There was an edgy mood and it was obvious the big fight would energise the racists and jingoists in the crowd: Minter was white and British, Hagler was a black American. As the delays piled up so did the tension and resentment. The ingredients for a riot were all there, waiting to boil over.

At these major Wembley bouts it was usual for the Chief Inspector (Operations), who in this case was me, to lead the reigning champion out to the ring, and for his assistant to lead out the challenger. When I finally went to the dressing room to get Minter I could see he was as restless as the crowd outside. He blinked at me moodily as his seconds formed a circle around him. In the corridor a group of constables waited to reinforce the cordon when we came out. We stood by the half-open door and listened as Hagler was led in to booing and catcalls.

I tensed myself, waiting for the champion's fanfare. When it came it was sharp and spectacular, almost a rival event in itself. I glanced at Minter. His look had hardened now. The adrenaline was pumping, he was keen to get into the ring. I led him and his phalanx along the corridor and out into the glittering arena. The crowd roared and the noise of it drowned the trumpets. It was an incredible sound, it resonated in my chest and made the air shudder. I strode briskly to the ringside followed by the huddle of constables and seconds shielding the grim-faced champion.

In Minter's corner I was joined by an old friend, Dennis Pollard. Dennis had once been the British and European Police Light Heavyweight Boxing Champion; nowadays he was a superintendent at Barnet Police Station. I noticed he was in uniform. That evening, he told me, he was Late Senior Duty Officer for S District. That was a long way away, but he was keeping in touch by radio. He had no intention of missing this fight. We sat down to watch.

It seemed like a foregone conclusion. Minter was a fit and hard young fighter, but Hagler was more compact and he had a slow-burning temper in the ring. There was coiled strength in every move he made, even in the way he dipped his head to listen to his trainer. With forearms as big as his biceps and legs like sawn-off oaks he was built to do harm, and he looked like a man who would be hard to damage. As we watched Hagler slip out of his robe and flex his shoulders, Dennis and I reckoned Minter wouldn't last the distance.

At the bell Minter went straight on the attack. He rained down punches on Hagler – left, right, left, right, working up a rhythm, burning his strength in a volley against a man who didn't appear to feel much of it. By the end of round two Minter was sobbing for breath and he was bleeding. In round three Hagler decided to shorten the champion's reign by nine rounds and began to hurt him badly. When the round ended

Minter was dazed and breathless and covered in blood. His trainer threw in the towel.

The place erupted. Men and women screamed foul-mouthed abuse. Bottles, cans and sundry debris were hurled into the ring. The MC appealed for calm but nobody listened to him. Harry Carpenter, reporting for the BBC, was hit on the head by a can of beer as he huddled at the ringside with his microphone, talking on through the barrage and the noise.

We scrambled into the ring. Dennis and David Hatch grabbed Hagler. They got him out through an exit and bustled him along a corridor under the arena to the police room. I told Minter to get behind me and hang on to my shoulders. His seconds huddled round us and we got out of the arena at a fast shuffle, bottles and cans flying past our ears as we went. By the time we got to the dressing-room my uniform was soaked with Minter's blood.

When security in the corridors had been tightened I went down to the police room. Hagler was there and he looked very pleased about winning the championship. He had a gold paper crown on his head.

'Do you want a beer?' I asked him.

'He doesn't drink,' his manager said.

Hagler glared at him. 'Yes I do.'

I handed him a beer and he drank it from the bottle.

We all stayed there and talked for a while, waiting for the chaos in the arena to settle down. When we finally did make our way back to the dressing-rooms one of Minter's entourage, visibly drunk and in full view of journalists, made a lunge at Hagler. We pulled him off and no harm was done, except to the reputation of English boxing.

In due course the British Boxing Board of Control set up an inquiry and they asked Dennis Pollard, well respected in boxing circles, if he would give evidence. He declined, since he shouldn't have been at Wembley at all that night. The Board graciously accepted that giving evidence would not be in his best interests. They decided instead to rely on the evidence of Ben Pountain who was, after all, the chief superintendent in charge of policing on the night of the fight.

Ben's testimony was brief and to the point.

'I know a riot when I see one,' he said, 'and this wasn't one.'

So that was that. Whatever the disturbance had been – affray, clash, fracas or punch-up – it hadn't been a riot, because Ben said so. And as for my blood-soaked uniform, it had to be destroyed.

During my time at Wembley, with the approval of Ben Pountain, I formed a vice squad. I had two sergeants and two constables out on the streets at any one time. They covered the whole range of vice operations: brothels, ponces, cottaging and obscene publications.

The squad had no headline cases, no flashy track record. Vice control is largely just that, control. You keep the nuisance levels as low as you can. I recall at that time we arrested a man called McLelland for dealing in obscene videos. He was supplying the Indian corner shops with the material and I used an Indian undercover policeman to infiltrate the set-up. We prosecuted half a dozen shops for possession with intent to supply. Nothing spectacular, but that kind of case – and in Wembley there were plenty of them – justified the existence of the squad, and kept my vice-cop's antennae in tune.

6
Dunlop

From time to time events showed a tendency to anticipate my career moves. The Dunlop case is a good example. I investigated it a full ten years before I joined the Obscene Publications Branch, and at the time of the investigation I found the case bizarre. Yet it foreshadowed the kind of work I would come to regard as routine.

Police inquiries into the behaviour of John Dunlop began when residents on a quiet street in Harrow complained about suspicious activity at one of the houses on Woodway Crescent. Men, never more than one at a time, called at the house at intervals throughout the day and were shown in. None of them ever seemed to call twice. The neighbours thought something nasty might be going on, something unbefitting an area of moderate behaviour and conservative standards.

As soon as the matter came to our attention we took a look at the electoral roll. Only one person was registered as living at the detached house, a man called John Dunlop. We put the house under surveillance for a week and during that time we saw a number of men knock on the door and be let in. Some of them were young, some were middle-aged. They stayed for varying lengths of time. While we were still watching the place, we had an anonymous tip-off that hardcore pornography was being shown on the premises.

That was all I needed to get a search warrant, because if Dunlop was showing porn films he was technically publishing the material, and that was an offence.

I called at the house one evening with two other officers. The door was answered by a tall, haughty-looking black man in his mid-thirties. He had uncommonly steady, moist-looking eyes with large, very dark pupils. When he spoke he had a distinctive African accent and a slight lisp. Yes, he said, his name was John Dunlop. Yes, he owned the house. What did we want?

There was something menacing in his manner and in the way he used his eyes, glaring and intense, as if they saw past your surface. It made me uneasy, although I tried not to let it show. I told him we wanted to take a look around the premises. He stiffened and the moist eyes narrowed a fraction. This was outrageous, he said. It was a gross invasion of privacy. I waved the search warrant and walked past him into the house. My two colleagues followed.

It was a well-maintained five-bedroomed house. The furnishings were immaculate and it looked as if the place had been cleaned by an army of servants. Mirrors shone and the dark wood of the furniture had been buffed until it gleamed. There wasn't a trace of dust. Dunlop followed us around without saying a word, standing back whenever we stopped, looking offended as we checked everything.

In the sitting room we found a few hardcore heterosexual porn magazines and videos. Gradually we worked our way through the house, and as we did, Dunlop began to complain.

'This is an outrage. Do you hear me? It is an outrage!'

He was getting angry. He had something to hide, and whatever it was, we were getting close.

It turned out that he was hiding letters. In a couple of the rooms we found bundles of them held together with elastic bands. A swift interim examination revealed that they were all from men writing to the same woman, Susannah Adamson, offering her their sexual services.

Under the floorboards in the master bedroom there were more bundles of letters, identically bound, and as we pulled up the floorboards in other rooms we found more and more of the same. Later, we calculated that we had uncovered 16,000 letters written over a period of eight years.

I asked Dunlop what they were and whether he normally used the space under the floor for storage.

'I am saying nothing,' he growled. 'Mind your own business.'

I asked him why the letters had been hidden. He sniffed and said he didn't want to talk to me.

A search of the rest of the house revealed nothing of interest. I decided to examine the haul of letters in more detail at the station. As we carried them out in boxes Dunlop detained me, touching my forearm.

'You have no right to do this,' he said softly, his eyes fixed on mine.

The impression of menace was stronger than before, and I'm sure it was nothing I imagined. I was glad to get out of there.

At the station we went through the letters carefully. They appeared to have been written in response to an advertisement in a contact magazine by an 'attractive blonde' who was 'seeking men for fun'. A number of the replies gave full if occasionally illiterate descriptions of what the writer could do for a woman. One man had traced the outline of his erect penis on a sheet of paper. A number had sent photographs, usually of their lower parts in various states of arousal.

We were able to recognise one of the men, a well-known cop-bashing civil-rights lawyer, because he had allowed himself to be photographed sitting in a chair in a book-lined study, wearing only a smile and an erection. We also found a picture of a very senior civil servant from the Foreign Office.

There was nothing especially illegal in all of this. I told two officers to contact a few of the men who had written letters in recent months to see if we could learn precisely what had been going on. It wasn't long before the officers reported back to me.

'Sir,' one of them said, 'you're not going to believe this.'

It was certainly an amazing story. Men who answered Susannah's advertisement had received a handwritten letter from her, offering them an appointment. When they turned up at the door, nervy with expectation, they were met by Dunlop, who told them he was madame's butler. He explained that his mistress had had to take her husband to the airport at short notice, but she would be back within the hour. In the meantime, would the caller take a seat in the parlour?

Dunlop would then explain that one of his duties was to screen madame's prospective lovers to ensure there were no health hazards. Could he inspect the visitor's penis?

At that point in the interview process a number of men left. Those who stayed and submitted to the inspection were then

told that madame insisted on a further check: was the caller
able to prove that he could sustain an erection?

Quite a few men left at that point, too. For those who consented to the test, Dunlop would put on a pornographic
video. As the caller watched and stimulated himself manually,
Dunlop would ask if he needed help. That was another point
at which more men would leave.

A number of those who reached that stage, however,
allowed Dunlop to help. While he did so he offered to fellate
them as well. For the ones who passed beyond this stage,
Dunlop would suddenly stop what he was doing, take off his
trousers and lie on the floor with his legs raised. He would
then ask if the aroused visitor would like to sodomise him.

Detailed statements from a number of Dunlop's visitors
helped me to crack the code of a meticulously organised chart
he had designed. In addition to keeping every letter, he had
made a record of each resulting encounter. Men's status in the
chart depended on what they had allowed to happen. Callers
got points according to which category they were in: there
were separate grades for those who left after being asked to
expose themselves, those who left after being asked to create
and sustain an erection, those who allowed themselves to be
masturbated, those who took up the offer of oral sex, and
then, in the supreme category, those who buggered Dunlop.

According to the chart, roughly half of the visitors had left
at the first or second stage. Over three-quarters of those who
remained had had some form of sexual contact with Dunlop,
but amazingly, over a period of eight years, almost a thousand
men had actually buggered Dunlop. He had even inserted
little comments beside each conquest: very good, not bad, disappointing.

Another extraordinary feature of the case was that Dunlop

had handwritten 16,000 letters to prospective visitors, all of them in a painstaking, ornate copperplate. This was obviously the creative project of his life, the sole focus of his drive and his only form of work. He appeared to live off an inheritance, so he was free to direct his considerable energy to deceiving men into having sex with him.

I presumed that since Dunlop was rather ugly, he didn't see any future in trying to pick up men in the usual way. A few officers speculated that he didn't advertise in homosexual contact magazines because anyone who responded would show up expecting gay sex, and so Dunlop would run the risk of a more crushing rejection. My own view was that he only wanted to have sex with straight men. Years later I learned that seducing male heterosexuals is a common fantasy among gay men.

I had to face the problem of what to do with Dunlop. Some wag suggested we charge him under the Trades Descriptions Act. A few people believed that as the activity fell within the definition of consensual sex, I should drop the case. But I believed, and I still do, that it's a duty of the police to protect people from deception and exploitation. What Dunlop did was wrong: men had been lured to his house to meet a woman and they were seduced into having sex with a man, if not quite against their will, at least against their original intentions.

The men we interviewed who had gone all the way with Dunlop felt ashamed of what they had done, but they blamed themselves. I conducted several of the interviews and they nearly all showed me the same baffled reaction – they could not understand their behaviour. I asked them all why they had had sex with Dunlop and the majority said they had absolutely no idea, it was a mystery to them and it was something they had never done before.

Several men spoke of Dunlop's powerful personality, his
daunting combination of overt charm and suppressed
menace. Several of the men, who were from all walks of life,
broke down and cried as they confessed what they had done.
Some of them were retrospectively angry and I could see that
Dunlop's behaviour might easily cause a violent reaction.
Neighbours had told us they often heard shouting and swearing coming from the house. There was also the potential for
blackmail, although we found no evidence that Dunlop had
ever tried to blackmail anybody.

We discussed the case extensively in the office, but at the
end of it all I still wasn't sure how to proceed. Then, going
through the letters again, I realised that several of them were
from men who would have been under twenty-one at the
time of their meeting with Dunlop. When I checked against
the chart I discovered that several of those under twenty-one
had actually buggered Dunlop.

We interviewed five of them under caution – one was only
seventeen – and they confessed to what had taken place. We
told them that if they gave evidence against Dunlop we would
ask the Director of Public Prosecutions to treat them as witnesses and thereby avoid any necessity to prosecute them. All
five agreed. So Dunlop's fastidious hoarding of the correspondence was his undoing. He could never claim that he
didn't know the boys were under age, because they had told
him so in their letters.

Some months after our first raid, when we had put
together our case, we went back to Dunlop's house. We
watched him go in, then we went to the door and knocked.
We waited and knocked again, several times, but there was
no reply. A constable broke a side window and got in through
the lounge. He opened the door and we all trooped in. We

found Dunlop in the kitchen. He was panting softly, glaring at us, saying nothing.

A search of the house revealed that in the meantime he had started up his hobby again. There was a fresh collection of letters and the beginnings of a new chart. We took him to the station and charged him. He didn't admit or deny anything. He kept quiet, apart from occasionally glaring at me and saying, 'This has nothing to do with the police.'

When Dunlop appeared at St Albans Crown Court in September 1980 he was tried by Judge Anwyl-Davies, a man with a reputation for harsh sentencing. He was known to the police as Animal-Davies. Dunlop's chances of an acquittal were slim; he jeopardised them further by sacking his counsel and repeatedly asking to be taken down to the cells. He pleaded not guilty to several counts of buggery and gross indecency, but he would not speak in his own defence.

The jury took about ten minutes to convict him. Judge Anwyl-Davies rounded off the occasion with an eloquent summary of the defendant's nastiness: 'By deceit you enticed young men to your own house for heterosexual relationships,' he said, staring straight at Dunlop, his voice level and toneless. 'By dissimulation you prevented them from leaving. By loathsome and abominable persuasion, and by playing on their inexperience of the world and their youthful ardour for feminine companionship and association, you forced them to have criminal connection with you to gratify your own carnal lust. Little wonder that Parliament set an age limit under which the law forbids homosexual relationships. For all I and the jury have heard in this case, there is only one proper course which can be taken, and that is that you shall go to prison for three years.'

For a while afterwards the term *loathsome and abominable persuasion* was popular in our office.

Inevitably the case made me wonder about the stability of sexual orientation. It was plain that every man who went to Dunlop's house went there in direct response to heterosexual enticement, *ergo* they expected to have heterosexual sex. Surely no one could have pinpointed a straighter bunch of men?

But facts are facts. Whereas half those men left Dunlop's house at the first whiff of homosexuality, the other half stayed and went some way down the line. It might be argued that men who responded to that kind of advertisement could scarcely be characteristic of the heterosexual male population. You could also argue that they aroused themselves in front of Dunlop with the clear intention of passing a test that would bring them heterosexual sex, and that the prospect of sex with the fictitious Susannah was enough to override any qualms they had about engaging in homosexual behaviour. But that is hardly believable.

People will draw their own conclusions about the solidity of people's sexuality. To quote a remark somebody made at the time of the trial: 'A lot of men, when they get aroused but can't find an outlet with a pulse, will have sex with a warm scarf.'

Years later, when I had moved to another station, I was asked to go back to Harrow to help with another investigation into Dunlop's behaviour. This time he had been charged with indecent assault and had been taken into custody. The local police wanted me to supervise the search of his house. Predictably, we found another pile of letters.

If any of Dunlop's correspondents, including the civil-rights lawyer (he left at an early stage) ever read this, they should know that their secrets are safe. Once Dunlop had been convicted we gathered up every single letter and every photograph and destroyed them.

Looking back on the case, I wish we had kept the documentation and handed it over to a department of psychology for evaluation. The subsequent report would have been far more useful, and certainly more credible, than the surveys of male sexual behaviour that have cluttered the professional journals for the past fifty years.

In the second week of August 1981, the chief superintendent at Wembley called me to his office. He said he had great news for me. I was to be promoted on Monday of the following week, and I would be posted to the Cadet School at Hendon as the officer in charge – that is, the headmaster.

That was not quite what I had hoped for. I told him so. I had visions of being the deputy at one of the busy Inner London Divisions like Paddington or Kilburn or some similar place. I had never imagined myself looking after a few hundred seventeen-year-old cadets. This was not the kind of police work that I knew and relished. But naturally I did as I was told.

When I arrived at the school the first person I saw was Percy Gill, who had been one of my reporting sergeants when I was a probationer at Albany Street. He was the sergeant in charge of the accommodation at the school. There were about three hundred cadets of both sexes, all of them on holiday at that point, since the terms mirrored those of state schools and colleges.

'What's it like, Percy?' I asked him.

'Not enough discipline,' he said.

We had a long discussion about the ins and outs of running

the place, then I met my deputy, Chief Inspector Dan Glen. He was an accomplished yachtsman, quiet and firm, and a comprehensively nice guy. So that was one bonus. I was heartened, too, when I found that there were a number of staff members who had been cadets with me in 1962. Peter Bucknole was an inspector; he joined on the same day as me and had been in the same house, Trenchard. He was now the housemaster of that quarter of the school. There were also Mick Yates and Ian Bevan, constable instructors. At least I wasn't going to be among strangers.

By 1981 Ashford, the mansion in Kent where the second phase of training used to be conducted, had been disposed of: it's now a Regional Training School. So by the time I arrived cadets were moved from Hendon directly to the third phase and into Cadet Centres dotted around the capital.

I decided I would adopt a persona that did not sit easily with me, i.e., the hard-nosed disciplinarian. This was no idle whim. It is vital that young people are given a lead in a disciplined environment, and it was not so long since I had been a rookie that I didn't remember how easily and often a police cadet gets into trouble. They are young, bursting with energy and victimised by their own wayward hormones. One of the physical training instructors told me the male cadets were 'all ribs and prick'. It's essential their natural exuberance is productively channelled: to give an effective lead in that, and to give myself a recreational excursion out of character, I decided I would play a textbook martinet, perhaps lightening the harshness with a touch of humour. The drill instructors agreed with my choice of front and we set about constructing my image and reputation.

It was not long before my resentment about this posting gave way to admiration for the work done by the staff at

Hendon. They moulded their charges' characters and tough-
ened their self-confidence with devotion and extraordinary
patience. They turned the most raw, diffident, cack-handed,
mollycoddled young people into rounded, confident men and
women to whom circumspection and a flexible temperament
were second nature. The cadets wound up as people who
could be self-reliant without the impulse to put themselves
first. At passing-out parades gratified parents always
remarked on the changes.

There was a former army major whose son had been quite
a trial to me, a lad who was always in trouble. Several times I
bawled him out in my office, and two or three times I threatened to sack him. However, I had seen the likeable and
potentially strong character shadowed by the gangling, unfo-
cused youth I regularly carpeted. He made it to the end of the
course and his father said that he was absolutely in awe of the
change he detected in his son. I saw that same cadet nine
years later, when he had become a detective sergeant, and I
was proud of both of us.

The cadets were trained in searching techniques and were
available to the regular force to help find evidence at the
scenes of crimes. I discovered they were brilliant at doing
this and, in my opinion, they had better powers of concentration and doggedness than their older colleagues. This
could have been a reflection of the team-building skills and
the encouragement of the staff who goaded them on to suc-
ceed.

I went with them on search projects on two occasions. The
first was in response to a telephone call from Norman Brown,
the detective superintendent in charge of the scene at the
house of horrors in Melrose Avenue, Cricklewood, where the
serial killer Dennis Nilsen had lived. Nilsen had moved to

Muswell Hill, where he was arrested when police were alerted to the smell of decomposing flesh; then his terrible past began to unfold. He had lived at Melrose Avenue for several years and it was here that he had carried out many of his murders. He dismembered his victims, boiled them in pots and made various attempts to erase evidence of their having been there. Norman wanted the cadets to search the garden and the open space behind the house at Melrose Avenue. I took thirty cadets, including eight girls. They conducted a meticulous and intensely patient fingertip search without much need for supervision. There is no certainty of how many people Nilsen killed, but it must have been more than a few: immediately the cadets began searching, they began to find bones. There was a spot in the garden where Nilsen had obviously had a bonfire, and they found pieces of smashed-up skulls there. With their customary grim humour, the cadets nicknamed the spot 'the skullery'.

My second outing with them was on the afternoon following the IRA bomb explosion in Regent's Park, in July 1982. The bomb went off under the bandstand while the Band of the Royal Green Jackets were playing. Several people were killed and many were injured. We were called in to help the Anti-Terrorist Squad to search the park and recover evidence. When I arrived with fifty cadets I briefed them as well as I could about what they were going to deal with, and I tried to prepare them for the terrible things they would see. I kept the briefing as dispassionate as I could.

It was a scene of absolute carnage. There were limbs and chunks of bloodied flesh in all directions for a distance of 100 yards from the bandstand. There was a crazy jumble of chairs, hats, tree branches and people's clothing. The cadets formed a line across the park, then they knelt, and began a fingertip search with exhibits officers right behind them. It was like a giant Hoover moving across the crime scene. They crawled through pools of congealed blood, holding their hands up when they found anything and passing it back to the officers with their plastic bags. The search took a couple of hours but afterwards the scene was completely cleared. The cadets also performed a sweep of the bushes at the side of the park and found more evidence, including a leg from one of the dead. None of them showed any sign of distress. They acted impeccably.

Towards the end of my time at the school I visited Spike Milligan, who had a one-man show running in the West End. He offered to bring his performance to the Cadet School and to contribute the entry charges to the Metropolitan Police Widows and Orphans Fund. Naturally I took him up on the offer, and he brought with him Gerard Kenny, the American singer and songwriter. We filled the Simpson Hall at the school and the evening was a roaring success. Afterwards I presented Spike with a ceremonial sword inscribed with the Metropolitan Police Coat of Arms and he was lost for words. Well, almost.

In April 1983, I was delighted to be offered a three-month stint at Kensington Division while an old friend, Michael McAdam, attended the Intermediate Command Course at Bramshill. I would then transfer to Chelsea, the adjoining division, on the retirement of the incumbent. I was going to be a real policeman again.

The cadets are no more, because their training was seen as an expense we could do without – maintenance of the corps was put at £6 million a year. It was argued that the service had plenty of recruits, and in any event, the emphasis was increasingly on recruiting people who had seen a bit of life. I do not believe that someone who is twenty-two or twenty-three, and has worked in a bank or has had some other job between school and joining the police, is necessarily a more mature prospect than a young person who has been the subject of firm but enlightened discipline, and who has learned, early on, what it means to be part of a functioning team.

This is my biased view, of course. But having experienced the system at both ends, and knowing how powerful an impact the corps had on my life as a shy young man, I am convinced that the Police Service is the poorer for the loss.

7
Policing Paddington

By 1983 the most obvious and certainly the most severe casualty of my fast-moving career was my marriage. What had once been an idyllic refuge had become, by stages, the casual partnership of strangers with different directions in life. Love had not been so enduring after all, and now all we shared was an emotional desert. Jacky and I had two lovely daughters: Kirstie was born in January 1972, and Laura came along in August 1976. The girls were a blessing and they continue to be. They were never a substitute or a consolation for what had been lost, and we never wanted them to be that, so Jacky and I decided to put the process of divorce in motion at approximately the time I left the cadet school.

I was at Kensington and Chelsea while the divorce went through its various stages. I was living in a small, not-very-nice ground-floor flat in West Harrow. We sold our three-bedroomed detached house in Pinner. Jacky bought a semi-detached house within sight of the other place, so that our girls could stay at the same schools and have the same friends as before. I saw them every weekend. It was a civilised, amicable arrangement, and Jacky and I have stayed friendly since.

The divorce was being finalised at the time of the Harrods bomb. Days after the explosion the decree nisi was delivered to me, followed in due course by the decree absolute. All of a sudden I was single again. It felt strange.

I met Jacqui Clarke on the 'B' District Burglary Squad. 'B' District covered Kensington, Chelsea and Notting Hill. Jacqui didn't work for me – that squad was really for people who wanted to be detectives, and it came under the authority of the detective superintendent. While I was at Jane Arbuthnot's funeral, Jacqui left a note on my desk at Chelsea Police Station: the note asked if I would give her a ring. She put a Scotland Yard number at the bottom, as she had been seconded to the Yard to help investigate the bomb incident.

I rang her and said I was calling in response to her note. She said, 'Yes, I thought you looked so sad and I was a bit worried about you. Would you like to have a drink?'

We had spoken to each other before at various events, but we hadn't been out together or gone for a drink on a one-to-one arrangement. So we met, had a drink, and I learned that Jacqui's father had died a few weeks before, so she was a bit low, too. Our meeting was really a mutual support event and we did cheer each other up. Afterwards, the relationship deepened rather quickly.

I had appeared on my first promotion board on 11 May 1984. What happened, I gathered, was that the powers-that-be felt I had shown enough initiative, energy and leadership at the time of the Harrods bomb to justify putting me straight up for promotion. It was around that time, too, that a vacancy had arisen at the Obscene Publications Branch; the man who was there at the time, an old friend called Peter Kruger, was being promoted to chief superintendent, with a posting to Harrow Road. We had a chat. Everybody knew I was interested in going to the Obscene Publications Branch, so I suppose I was considered to be a contender. Peter said they would want three years from me as a superintendent in that post. That created an awkwardness, because everybody was talking about me soon being promoted to chief superintendent. I would not have the time to put in at Obscene Publications. I remember thinking, rather wistfully, that I would never get to work on the Dirty Squad after all.

The meeting in May was not the roaring success that I and some others had hoped. The promotion board members reported: 'Hames is nervous and rather defensive in some of his replies . . . At 39 he has obvious potential, but needs more time and on this occasion there are others with far stronger claims. No change of duty is recommended.' That was what one calls 'a run'. But it did mean, I suppose, that I was on the path to promotion.

It was suggested to me that I ought to put in for the Intermediate Command Course, which is designed for superintendents from all over the country who are actively seeking promotion. So from 25 June to 21 September 1984 I was at the Police College at Bramshill on that three-month course. Just a week or so before I started the course Jacqui and I decided to live together. Quaint as it might seem, the Police Service requires couples to apply for permission to cohabit. I suppose, looking at it now, that a superintendent applying to live with a constable was rather a strange application.

I was sent a report in response to the application which said, in essence, that it would be 'improper and unwise' for the two of us to cohabit while serving on the same district. It was a stuffy response which did not take account of the facts, because Jacqui had been away on her detective's course, which meant she had not actually worked on the same district as me for at least three months.

The commander's actual recommendation to Mike Huins, the Deputy Assistant Commissioner (DAC), Personnel, was that since Miss Clarke was due to be appointed a detective constable on 2 July and posted to 'V' District, Kingston, he recommended that from 6 July permission be granted for us to live together at Jacqui's Whiteleaf address. From that point on I would be attending the Intermediate Command Course, so the two of us certainly wouldn't be working together.

When I went on the ICC I was told I would be going back to Chelsea, and I still felt a need to be there. I suppose it was a need arising from team dependency, and the proper discharge of grief. We were all still coming to terms with the incredible trauma the division had suffered, and I felt it was important to help people through the healing stages.

But then I was told that I would be posted. I told Mike Huins that I was annoyed at being shunted on, especially as it was happening at the very moment I was expecting to return to Chelsea. I actually made the point explicit and said, 'I suppose this is because I'm living with a constable.'

'No, Mike,' he said, 'I can promise you it has nothing to do with that.' I didn't believe him at the time, though.

In the event, I was posted to Paddington Green Division. It's the busiest police station in Western Europe, so I had been catapulted from a very quiet police station to one of the busiest imaginable. It was a prime posting, and in the end I didn't feel so bad about it.

Jacqui and I were married in September 1985, at St Luke's

Church in Chelsea, and we went on honeymoon to Italy and
Yugoslavia. We bought a house in Laleham, near Ashford in
Middlesex, and as far as I could tell, we were fine. I was very
happy.

Brothels provided some of my biggest headaches at
Paddington Green, and occasionally there were complica-
tions. One day we had a tip-off that two West Indian girls,
specialists in sado-masochism, were peddling their services
through a parlour they had opened in a basement flat at
Balcombe Street in Paddington. An investigation was set in
motion. We kept the basement under surveillance for four
days and in that time we determined that it was indeed a
brothel. So a raid would be in order.

I led the raiding party of vice officers and uniformed constables. In the flat we found whips, chains, manacles, studded
belts, leather gags and custom-made torture racks. In the
living room there was basket of unwashed knickers which the
girls were selling to punters as a sideline. Also in the living
room was a naked, wistful-looking man chained up in a
corner. This was a character we came to know as Brian the
Pervert.

Brian was a dental technician by trade and a masochist by
impulse. For no wages at all, he regularly travelled to London
from his home in Wales to work as a servant to the girls at the
brothel. He answered the door to customers, cleaned the
place, fetched and carried and did everything else a domestic
menial would do. The job suited Brian, because what he
craved more than anything was to be an entirely subjugated
slave. In exchange for doing the girls' bidding he was abused,
beaten, shackled and generally treated like dirt, all of which
he loved. One of the girls had branded her initials on the

inside of each of his thighs, using branding irons designed
and fashioned from dental metal by Brian himself. When we
told him he would be charged with assisting in the management of a brothel he looked huffy; it didn't suit him to be
characterised as a person who *managed* anything – submis-
sion was his thing, after all.

I was in the hallway while officers searched other parts of
the flat, securing the evidence. The bell rang and I opened the
door. A man in a pin-striped suit was on the step, holding a
fine leather briefcase. He smiled and I smiled back. He made
to come in and I let him.

'Is Victoria here this afternoon?' he asked, his voice hushed.

'Yes, she is,' I said. 'But so are we.'

He frowned. 'Sorry?'

'I'm afraid you've walked into a police raid.'

'Oh my God.' Even in the gloomy hallway I could see him
going pale. 'I – I'm a Member of Parliament.'

It occurred to me he could have been cagey about his identity. He could have said nothing about it and given a false
name when he was asked. It wasn't as if he had committed
any felony, and for all we knew he could be dropping in for
afternoon tea.

He then went ahead and dug himself in deeper.

'The fact is,' he said, getting out his Commons pass, 'I'm a
minister.'

He wasn't anybody I recognised so I assumed he was a
junior minister. I looked at his ID and gave it back to him. His
hand was shaking.

'Do you realise what you're doing, nipping down here for a
quick thrashing?' I said. 'Have you ever thought about the risk
to your reputation? Your career? And what about all the other
implications?'

He didn't need a lecture. He knew there was still a Cold War on, and closer to home there were journalists ready to destroy the likes of him for plain spite. Maybe, like a lot of people in positions of power, he got a special kick from transactions that had the potential to ruin him.

I told him he was a prat and said he could go. He scampered off and I considered the episode closed, until I'd had time to think about it. Was there, I wondered, somebody who should know, officially, about the encounter with the Cabinet minister? I couldn't be sure that no one else already knew; I could imagine what the press would make of me letting him go like that without saying anything: 'VICE COP'S COVER-UP FOR KINKY CABINET CRONY!'

If I didn't make a report I would leave my back clear for knifing. If, on the other hand, I mentioned the MP's visit in an official report, it would get leaked – that was a certainty. It was too juicy to be left alone.

I decided my official report on the raid would carry no mention of the MP's untimely trip to the brothel. Instead, I contacted an acquaintance who had direct links to upper levels of the government, a man of solid discretion with an endless capacity for keeping secrets. I told him what had happened.

'It needs to be reported,' I said, 'but I don't think it's the business of anybody but the Prime Minister.'

He said okay, he would alert Mrs Thatcher by the most direct route. I learned later that only one other person, a senior Tory, knew of the incident before Mrs Thatcher. I never heard what action the Prime Minister took.

An unusual bonus from the brothel raid was a big, beautifully crafted wooden cross which the girls used as a whipping-gibbet for their clients. I was anxious we should keep it after the case and put it in the CID museum at Hendon, where it stands to this day. Looking at it, you can't help wondering how many well-connected souls, from what lofty positions of power, have clung to its crossbeam and taken their punishment like men.

One morning a girl, very obviously a prostitute, staggered into Paddington Green Police Station and asked to see someone from Vice. Barry Jones went down and spoke to her. She was shaking with fear and appeared to be in great distress.

'How can I help you?' Barry said.

She began to cry. Barry got her a tissue. In a shaky voice she told him she could not stand any more of the treatment she was getting from her ponce.

'What's he been doing?'

She pulled back her sleeves and revealed parallel scars running the length of both arms. The ponce, she said, had made the cuts with a Stanley knife.

'I've got a little kiddie,' she said. 'Lives up north with my mum. I support the baby and my mum and myself, or I try to. But he keeps taking my money off me. And every now and then he just beats me up, for no reason at all.'

Barry took some details. She was Valerie Craig, nineteen years old, from Huddersfield. She had been on the game for about a year. She told Barry she worked the streets mainly in the Paddington area, but lived with her ponce in a flat in New Cross.

'What's this charmer's name?' Barry asked.

'Victor Noicely.'

'Afro-Caribbean?' (All but one of the pimps in Paddington at this time were Afro-Caribbean.)

Valerie nodded. 'He came down here from Fartown, near Huddersfield. His street name's "Vicious".'

'Does he run other girls?'

'Him and four other blokes, all from that part of Yorkshire, they got a string of eight girls between them.'

'And do they all work the Paddington area?'

'That's right.'

Barry asked for details of how the ponces operated their girls. Valerie gave him what she could, and although it helped create an insight into how the business was run, she was essentially a slave and not privy to the finer points of the business, if there were any. Barry asked her if any of the other girls knew she had come to the police. She said no, she had come on her own initiative. She added that she was sure the others would talk to us, but only in secret, because they were literally in fear of their lives.

Barry called me down at that point and I joined in the discussion with Valerie. It was clear we had to give the matter our immediate attention. The priority was to protect the girls, but at the same time, we would have to move very carefully. The dilemma in cases like this is that a ponce cannot be arrested solely on the word of any of his girls. A prostitute giving evidence against him would be torn apart in court. In fact, without other evidence, a prosecution would not even be mounted.

So Valerie had to be told to go away and carry on with her life. She was given no instructions. If she were told to carry on being a prostitute and lead us to her ponce, we could be accused of setting him up. In truth we had to consider the possibility that she was doing just that – what if she had made the cuts on her arms herself? Noicely could have been a rival or an enemy of her real ponce, and she could have been told to set him up. As I have mentioned, prostitutes make the best informants, but they can also be the most dangerous. In this case, we were sure that Valerie's information and her motive – terror – were genuine, but we still had to exercise the appropriate caution.

It was hard telling a person so vulnerable and scared that she had to leave. We suggested that she go back home and put her life in London behind her.

'If I did that he'd only find me, and then I'd be for it.' She looked at me. 'He's capable of murder, that one. I'm sure of it.'

All I could tell her, before she left, was that we would deal with the matter. I thanked her for coming.

I put Barry Jones and Stewart Taylor on the job. It took them four weeks to find and identify all of the ponces, to locate their home addresses, establish their lifestyles and figure out which girls each of them was living off. A point worth mentioning here is that if a man actually lives with a prostitute the onus is then on him to prove that he is *not* living on the earnings of his partner.

On the evening the surveillance ended we decided we had enough evidence against all of the ponces; we also decided we would arrest them that same night. With the exception of Noicely, they were all taken into custody while the girls were actually working on the streets.

Noicely was the prime target, but he had gone up north for a few days. We had no idea when he would come back. We knew that he had a house in Huddersfield so I sent a team there to see if they could find him. They called in the help of the local constabulary to swell their numbers, and the team worked under the command of one of my inspectors, Andy Bamber, a man I wanted to introduce to vice operations.

Local officers soon located Noicely and he was arrested

coming out of a nightclub. His house was searched and the team took possession of a lot of property, including jewellery, which would call for further investigation. Our team snatched a few hours' rest at the local police station before bringing Noicely back to London. As the senior officer, Andy Bamber took the prime sleeping position – on the police station snooker table.

Noicely was charged with living on immoral earnings and with committing grievous bodily harm on Valerie Craig. He was remanded in custody. We spoke to the girls and per-suaded them all to make statements, but at that stage they refused to give evidence. They were terrified.

Valerie decided to stay at the Kensington Hilton hotel near Shepherd's Bush Green in conditions of secrecy. She refused protection and carried on earning her living in the West End. Somehow her hiding-place was discovered and one night her room was burned out. This development badly frightened her.

Noicely kept applying for bail and, in spite of our strenu-ous objections, bail was finally granted by a judge in chambers at Knightsbridge Crown Court. One of the condi-tions of bail was that Noicely went back to live in Huddersfield.

The team continued to investigate the origins of the prop-erty they had seized at Noicely's house. They also sought out more witnesses to his offending behaviour. Evidence emerged that he had committed robberies and burglaries – enough evidence, in fact, to have him charged. One robbery was on a prostitute who had refused to work for him. In reprisal, he had torn the rings from her fingers.

During the time he was on bail in Yorkshire, he grabbed a girl off the streets, dragged her into a garden and raped her.

He was tracked down and once again he was arrested and charged, this time in Yorkshire.

It was agreed between the Crown Courts in London and Leeds that the entire case be transferred to Leeds. Noicely was now charged with rape, robbery, burglary, living on immoral earnings and GBH. Meanwhile the other four ponces were given custodial sentences in London.

Noicely applied for the indictments to be split, as he was entitled to do, and plans were made to conduct four trials, with sentencing reserved to the end. By this time, with the other ponces locked up, we had persuaded six girls to give evidence against Noicely.

Barry stayed in Leeds for the duration of the trials. We escorted the girls up to the Hilton hotel at Garforth two at a time. For ease, we booked the same two rooms and the manager was fully aware of the situation. Barry got on quite well with him and they often sat down together for a drink in the evening. One night, the manager told Barry he was in a rather difficult position, and did not quite know how to put it.

'Just spit it out,' Barry told him.

'Well, it appears that your young ladies, your witnesses – they're, well, they're *entertaining* people in their rooms.'

'What, men, you mean?'

'Clients would be a better word,' the manager said.

He went on to explain that the first two girls' entrepreneurial flair had come to the fore and they had picked up one or two regular clients, who were being passed on to the next pair of girls as they appeared. The girls could easily be found because the room numbers were always the same.

Barry had a very sharp word with the girls and told them their business dealings would stop at once, before the

Metropolitan Police became party to a charge of brothel-keeping.

During a lunch break in one of the trials, Barry and the prosecuting counsel remained in the court for a few minutes discussing some detail or other. As they left the courtroom they were attacked by a group of seven or eight West Indian men in the corridor outside. Counsel fell to the floor and was punched and kicked. Barry managed to stay upright, but took quite a few kicks and punches as well. The men then ran off. This kind of ambush was entirely unprecedented in the experience of any of us.

The clerk was told immediately and so was the judge. As the court reassembled, the men came back into the building. Barry could hardly believe it. As they made their way brazenly up to the public gallery, a plan of procedure was quickly hatched between Barry and the court officials.

When the court came to order Barry was called to the witness box and took the oath. He then gave direct evidence of what had gone on outside the court an hour earlier and pointed out the assailants where they sat in the public gallery. Meanwhile, police and court security staff had crept into the court and surrounded the suspects. They were all arrested and taken straight into the dock. The judge sentenced them to immediate imprisonment for at least the duration of the trial. As a demonstration of the contempt a criminal and his associates had for the authorities, that attack on Barry and the lawyer had to be one of the most outrageous ever.

At the end of the four trials, which lasted six weeks, Noicely was found guilty of all charges and was sentenced to sixteen years' imprisonment. This was reduced to twelve years on appeal.

Valerie went back to Yorkshire and sporadically kept in

touch with Barry. When we were at the Dirty Squad in 1991, she telephoned him in a panic. One of the girls in the Noicely case, Christina Requina, had been found murdered in the Manchester area (there was nothing to suggest Noicely was involved in the killing). Her body had been cut up and the pieces crammed into a black plastic sack. Valerie was again in fear of her life. We put her in touch with the Murder Squad and gave them all the information we had about Christina Requina's life in London five years before. Her murderer has never been caught.

Prostitution has been around for as long as there have been men and women. It is a form of trade, subject to marketing vagaries, and it is usually considered to be unsavoury, and by some downright evil. So what do we do in a civilised society to counter this unpleasantness in our midst?

The police attitude is generally relaxed. Contrary to general opinion, police officers are open-minded and relatively liberal when it comes to dealing with prostitutes. Familiarity is the main reason. As with so much else, prostitution fails to excite strong emotions once the shock element has dimmed. On the other hand, the police may appear hard and unfeeling if a whore is killed: *she chose to work in a high-risk business where she knew the hazards*, the argument goes, *so where's the room for pity*? At the same time, the police will hunt down a working girl's killer as vigorously as they would go after any other murderer.

A tremendous amount of criminal activity tends to surround anything that is in major and persistent demand, and that obviously goes for sex. And therein lies the big social problem. It is easier and demonstrably less dangerous to make money from prostitution than from drugs, and that might be

counted an incentive to getting involved in the trade, but
the business of operating whores is considered by 'proper'
villains as being beneath their dignity. In recent times, a
distinct racist slant has excluded prostitution from the range
of work opportunities open to lawless entrepreneurs. Any
self-respecting villain will explain that pimping and brothel-
keeping are suitable occupations for Maltese (e.g., the
Messina family from the 1960s to the 1970s), Cypriots (they
had a fairly serious grip on the trade in London during the
1970s), and blacks (e.g., the Yardies in the 1980s). But in
spite of its low rating with the status-conscious criminal,
prostitution is still big business, and it is difficult to police.

What would happen if we were to decriminalise the trade?
In fact it would not be impossible to do that. It is not a criminal offence to be a prostitute, but a clutch of necessary laws
are in place to control exploitation and coercion. There are
also statutes to protect the quality of life of people who want
to go about their business without being harassed by prostitutes' punters, and who don't want their peace disturbed by
the to-and-fro of customers and the other nuisances associ-
ated with the trade.

Suppose we legalised brothels. Where would we put them?
The Soho Society would have something to say about a designated red-light district on their turf. So would any other
local committee or community group.

In any case, decriminalisation offers no practical improvements. The crimes that surround prostitution – murder,
frequent rape, blackmail, robbery, theft, drug trafficking, kid-
napping and slavery – are all serious, and they would not
cease if brothels were legalised. Throughout the rest of
Europe there *are* legalised brothels, yet all the crimes listed
above flourish in those countries.

The expertise of criminal gangs in organising sex for sale is growing, alongside the escalating violence towards the women, now that East European Mafia gangs are involved. Disputes between pimps are getting more vicious, too: recently a Ugandan who had been running a prostitution agency in London was tortured to death, then his body was burned and left in the deep freeze of a butcher's shop in Wembley.

If we are to keep the lid on vice-related crime, then it has to be permanently monitored, the participants must be targeted, and there must be an agreed level of police response.

One obvious way of monitoring vice-related crime is to watch the prostitutes and their pimps, and note who their associates are. If they operate away from your line of vision, there are always other ways of finding out what is going on. For instance, if a hotel register shows that people keep booking in for an hour or two in the afternoon, it is usually safe to assume the place is being used by prostitutes and their punters.

In the summer of 1986 we began watching a four-storey hotel in Bayswater where we reckoned, after preliminary surveillance, that upwards of a dozen prostitutes were servicing clients every day of the week. When we decided to raid the place, it was to be the start of a blitz on the practice of using Paddington hotels as brothels. We wanted publicity for the campaign; we wanted the message brought home to pimps and madams and prostitutes, as well as the general public, that we were going to wipe this category of vice off our patch.

I got the *Sunday Mirror* interested. The arrangement was that we would take one of their photographers with us when we did the bust. We slated the raid for Saturday 2 August, but circumstances changed our timetable. The day before we were due to raid the hotel a punter from Pakistan arrived with a prostitute and went with her to a room on the top floor. Once they were inside the room they were joined by a friend of the prostitute. It was an ambush. The pair tried to rob the man, and in the struggle that followed he fell out of the window. He fell three storeys and landed on top of the front-door portico. The impact broke his pelvis.

An ambulance was called and so were the police. When we heard about it in Vice I decided we'd better bring our raid forward before our whole case fell apart. I rang the *Sunday Mirror* and told them to send their photographer to the hotel in Bayswater as soon as they could, then we all rushed down there ourselves. We arrested ten or eleven prostitutes who were still in the hotel. The woman who owned the place, a Russian, was arrested and charged with managing a brothel; so was her partner in the venture, a Polish woman who worked as the receptionist.

The *Sunday Mirror*'s crime reporter, Chris House, took me aside while the girls were being rounded up.

'We've got a sort of a story here,' he said. 'Brothel right in the middle of Bayswater and so forth . . .' He shrugged. 'It's not exactly news though, is it? I mean, how am I going to sell this to the editor? As it stands it's just a titchy piece for the bottom of page seven.'

'Listen . . .' I kept my voice low and confidential. 'Just as a matter of interest, the woman running this place is Russian. For all you or I know, it could be a spy house.'

Chris's eyes lit up.

'Another thing,' I said. 'The Russian embassy's just round the corner.'

'Hey . . .' The eyes got still brighter. 'You're right.'

Chris was delighted. He slapped my arm and hurried away.

On Sunday there was a front page splash – VICE COPS RAID SPY

BROTHEL – in the *Mirror*. Inside, under the heading 'IRON CUR-TAIN WOMEN HELD AT VICE HOTEL' there were pictures of the hotel, with a shot of police officers talking to a prostitute on the steps. Chris House's story told of a major spy probe being conducted after two East European women were discovered running a brothel in the heart of London's diplomatic community. The startling implications of the case were revealed when vice officers led by Detective Superintendent Mick Hames raided the hotel on Friday afternoon.

'*When the two madams revealed their nationalities,*' the piece went on, '*MI5 chiefs were alerted . . . A Whitehall source said, "The security services are investigating to find out if the brothel was used for espionage or blackmailing VIPs."*'

The article went on to describe dark diplomatic limousines driving slowly past the hotel while the raid continued, the drivers staring anxiously into the foyer. '*As we left, we saw a Mercedes that had been there for about half an hour. We saw the number plates as we drove past – it was a diplomatic car.*'

Further down the page was an inset story headed 'HOW THE KGB USE THE HONEY TRAP', all about the methods the Russian secret police used to set up their sex-for-secrets operations.

It was all rubbish, of course, and a damned good laugh into the bargain. We got our publicity and Chris House actually won an award for his story. A while later I saw him at a function in the City. He waved and came across.

'Mickey,' he said, squeezing my shoulder, 'that brothel story was one of the best I ever had.'

'You reckon?'

'Definitely. We got sex, violence, espionage, international intrigue . . .' He grinned. 'It had everything in it but the royal family!'

*

Another measure that came into operation during my time at Paddington was the Sexual Offences Act 1985. Under Section One of the Act, police can take action in one or all of three instances:

1. When the manner or circumstances of a woman being solicited is likely to cause her annoyance.
2. When a person persistently solicits a woman or a number of women.
3. When a prostitute is solicited in a way that is likely to cause a nuisance to other people in the vicinity.

At first, we thought this anti-kerbcrawling legislation would be a useful new tool in the job of deterring punters. We had always thought it was unfair to target the women and take no account of their customers – after all, if there was no market on the street, the problem would be drastically reduced.

But we hit problems straight away. Persistence and annoyance were hard to prove. Annoyance is difficult to establish at any time, and prostitutes are not likely to complain about punters soliciting them. As for persistence, that usually only happened when a punter was trying to negotiate a price. The places where we had the biggest problems with kerb-crawlers were the very areas where the prostitutes paraded in large numbers, so it didn't take much persistence on a man's part to get the price or the service he was looking for.

Proving 'nuisance' was another hardship for the police. A man in a car stopping beside a prostitute and making a deal with her would not usually create much of a nuisance for other people. What annoys people living nearby is that transactions of that kind tend to happen in large numbers and all the time. It is a continuous traffic. Another annoyance is the fact that trade in the popular red-light spots tends to start early, often before noon, and it goes on throughout the day and into the early hours of the morning. The prostitutes and the men coming to the district to hire them abuse the sur-roundings: they urinate in the streets and in driveways and in private gardens. Residents are regularly threatened or shouted down when they try to complain. So there is a problem, but getting evidence to uphold prosecutions in those situations takes a considerable time, and on most occasions it's just too big a job for the manpower available.

Most of the cases that we did forward to the Crown Prosecutor were eventually stamped *no further action*. Men were kerb-crawling all right, but the Act's terms of reference made it nearly impossible for us to take effective action.

In 1989 a conviction for kerb-crawling was actually upheld on appeal to the High Court. The evidence put forward to the magistrates' court was that the accused man's behaviour was 'likely to cause a nuisance'. Although there were no people in the vicinity at the time, the magistrate took into account the police officers' local knowledge of the region and the fact that the area in question was residential. On that basis he decided that it was reasonable to assume that the behaviour was likely to cause a nuisance, as the officers claimed.

Turning down the appeal, Lord Justice Woolf said, 'The offence created by Section One of the Sexual Offences Act of 1985 deals with conduct which was notoriously known to be able to cause nuisance in residential areas. The procession of cars stopping to solicit women for the purposes of prostitu-tion can be highly offensive conduct in a residential area. In my view it is the clear intent of the section that where con-duct of that sort takes place, which is likely to cause grave offence in the locality, the offence should be regarded as being established.'

That judgement helped considerably in the short term: in 1990 the level of prosecutions went up to nearly 1,500. In 1993, however, it fell back to about 850.

The legislation has never been as reliable or as useful as we thought it would be when it was first framed. The plain fact is that organised community action, with residents demonstrating and driving kerb-crawlers off their streets, has been far more effective than Section One of the Act ever was.

8
Arresting Boy George

Paddington Green's six-man Drug Squad, led by a fireball detective sergeant called Dave Leader, was as successful in percentage prosecutions as the Central Drug Squad at Scotland Yard. The team made relentless war on the drug scene, using a strategy aimed at breaking down the lines of supply. In a single year Dave's squad made record hauls of cocaine and prosecuted an entire top-level gang of Colombian pushers in Holloway. Dave's speciality was catching dealers and then turning them, getting them to collect evidence that would help corner the next villain up the line. Dave was so good that almost every week we went to the Deputy Assistant Commissioner for permission to make arrested dealers into participating informants.

One day Dave came to me and said, 'It's about that pop singer, Boy George.'

'What about him?'

'We know he's on heroin and we're pretty sure we know who his dealer is.'

The accumulated intelligence on Boy George was the outcome of Dave's investigations into the activities of a drug
dealer called Steve Luben and his girlfriend, Ginty Feiner,
who lived together in a basement flat in Westbourne Terrace.
As information on Luben built up, it became clear that he was
a specialist – he supplied drugs to people in the pop music
industry. When that aspect was put under scrutiny, along
came reliable information, though not yet proof, that Luben
was supplying Boy George.

'So how do you plan to proceed with this?' I asked Dave.

'We want to raid the singer and one or two of his associates,' he said.

I had no argument with the plan, but I decided that as
second-in-command at Paddington I had better lead on this
one, since it could be contentious. Dave got the necessary
warrants and after a briefing we split into two teams. I took
my group up to Boy George's mews house at St John's Wood
while the others went to the family home in Hampstead
where his brother lived. At the mews house we sledge-
hammered the door and bundled in. The first thing that
struck me was the smell of stale air and unwashed bodies. In
the sitting room we found an uncommunicative American
girl. There was no trace of Boy George. We didn't find any
drugs, either.

Meanwhile the brother, Kevin O'Dowd, had been arrested
with a curious-looking individual calling himself Marilyn,
who was also a singer. Both men were charged with possession of heroin. There was still no sign of Boy George. In his
autobiography, *Take it Like a Man*, George reveals that at the
time the arrests were taking place, he was in a country retreat
in Essex, doubled up with sickness and cramp, undergoing
the worst stages of heroin withdrawal.

Dave Leader and I went to see Richard Branson at his houseboat on the Regent's Canal. At that time Boy George and his band, Culture Club, recorded for Branson's Virgin record label, and it was well known that Branson took a personal interest in the welfare of his artists.

It was a civilised meeting with none of the them-and-us atmosphere that these encounters can sometimes generate. I was sure Branson knew where Boy George was, but I had not gone there to winkle the information out of him.

'Don't tell me where he is,' I said. 'Just tell me what you know about his circumstances.'

We had picked up a rumour that Boy George was being treated for heroin addiction. I needed to know if that was true before we pushed any harder to find him, since a statement made by anyone suffering from narcotic withdrawal would be useless – better to wait until his chemistry was stable and he was in a balanced frame of mind.

Branson said he understood that George was receiving treatment for his addiction. I asked him if he was sure that information was reliable.

Branson looked at me squarely. 'I'm sure,' he said.

In that case, I thought, we should let as much time as possible elapse before we picked him up.

'It would be a good thing if we could talk to him as soon as he's over the worst of the withdrawal,' I said.

Branson said he thought that made sense. I thanked him for his time and we left. I had no idea how long we could put off making an arrest. There was pressure from within the system to get a result, and the media were getting restless. All I could do, I supposed, was keep bluffing as long as I had to.

In the meantime Steven Luben had been arrested. We had enough evidence to prosecute him for possession, but if we were going to shut him down we would need hard testimony about his dealing in drugs.

Three days passed and word got to me that the Home Secretary was demanding to know why we still hadn't arrested Boy George. I threw up a couple of smokescreens and kept on playing for time. Finally Richard Branson called and told me that Boy George would surrender to police the following Saturday morning. Branson was also able to confirm that George was prepared to show us the house in Bayswater where his drugs supplier lived.

By now the reporters and photographers were staking out Paddington Green Station, and they were the last thing we needed. I called up my old pal Ben Pountain, who at that stage was chief superintendent at Harrow. I asked him if I could borrow his nick on Saturday the 13th.

'What do you want it for?'

'We want to bring in Boy George,' I said. 'We have to do it in secret. The plan is that we can have a few hours to talk to him, then we'll take him out and he can show us where his peddler lives. If we try anything like that from Paddington Green, we'll have the press all over us. I'd sooner they didn't know George is out of hiding until we've done all the necessary.'

Ben agreed to let me use his station. First thing on Saturday Dave Leader went off to Brentwood in Essex to arrest George, who had been staying with Dr Meg Patterson, who was treating him for his drug dependency. When they arrived at the station George came in looking very pale and ill. He had brought Dr Patterson and his business solicitor with him. I motioned them to chairs and watched how shakily George moved. He was carrying a small wooden box with wires leading from it to clips on the lobes of his ears. This, I was informed, was an electrical discharge apparatus, a key part of Dr Patterson's treatment for heroin addiction.

I was anxious about George's level of fitness, so I called the Divisional Surgeon and some time later he came to the station. He examined George and declared him fit to be interviewed, and fit to be held.

When we tried to get down to the questioning, however, there was a snag. The solicitor wasn't keen that George should say much, even though George himself was prepared to make a clean breast of everything. The reason for the solicitor's uneasiness was a million-dollar advertising contract between George and the Japanese whisky manufacturer Suntory. Built into the contract was a morality clause, which would be breached if George were to be convicted of any drug-related offence.

In the end George brushed aside the solicitor's objections, because he was determined to talk to us. We took a statement from him under caution and he gave such a clear and precise description of the dealer's house that we had no need to take him out to identify it. By then, of course, Steve Luben and his girlfriend were in custody.

On the strength of George's statement that he had bought and used heroin, we charged him with possession. That was the only time, in my experience, that an individual was charged with possession of a drug when no drugs were found on his person or at his home.

By the time the formalities were completed the press had found us – not just the papers but radio and television, too. ITN were set up outside the front door of the station. I went out and made a brief announcement: 'I can confirm that George O'Dowd has today made a statement to the police and has been charged with possession of heroin. He has been bailed to appear at Marylebone Court on the 29th of July.'

Back inside the station I asked George if he wanted us to smuggle him out the back way.

'Oh, no,' he said brightly. 'I'll meet my public. I'm happy to do that.'

I could see he was relieved to have unloaded the weight. For our part, we were distinctly charmed. Interviews with drug addicts are hardly ever occasions for delight on either side, but this had been very different. From the start of nego-tiations between myself and Richard Branson we had shared the plain wish to satisfy the law and at the same time cause his client a minimum of distress. George himself was a reve-lation. He was witty and courteous, a genuinely nice man who had made the ghastly mistake of experimenting with heroin and getting addicted. In accepting therapy and in sur-rendering himself to the police, he wanted to undo as much of the harm as he could.

Some time later George spent two days in the witness box at Knightsbridge Crown Court, giving evidence at the trial of Luben and Feiner. He explained to the court how Luben had gone with him on tours abroad and had acted as his personal supplier of drugs. Luben and Feiner were eventually found guilty and sentenced to four years' imprisonment. In our view, without George's evidence they would not have been found guilty.

On 29 July at Marylebone Court George was fined £250 for possession of heroin. In his autobiography he reveals that as he stood there listening to the magistrate he was high on methadone and had a hash joint in his pocket. Outside the court there were dozens of young people screaming and waving banners. George relates that among them was a girl with £16,000 in her handbag. She had re-mortgaged her house in case he needed money for bail.

Shortly after George was fined, Suntory tried to sue him for loss of face. He lost the million-dollar advertising contract, and was banned for life from Japan, one of his biggest markets.

On the evening of 6 March 1987, I was at home with Jacqui when the telephone rang. It was Mum. She sounded agitated. 'Have you heard about the terrible disaster on one of the Channel ferries?' she said.

I said no, I hadn't.

'Then go and turn on the television. They're talking about it now. Young Sue was on it.'

'On the ferry?' Sue was my niece. 'Do you mean she was on the ferry, Mum?'

'Yes. Switch it on.'

I turned on the TV. BBC news was reporting the sinking of the Townsend Thoresen ferry *Herald of Free Enterprise*, outside the port of Zeebrugge in Belgium. Right there on the screen was Sue, my brother Ken's daughter. She was being interviewed as a survivor. It was an incredible shock, and the weirdest coincidence that she should appear just as we switched on. She looked cold and bedraggled, wrapped in a blanket and shivering as she spoke. She was telling the interviewer that her boyfriend, Bob, was still missing.

That night the phone lines buzzed as we contacted my relatives to try to find out what was happening. Ken was working in Germany at the time and was already heading for Zeebrugge.

We got the story piece by piece. Sue and her fiancé had been travelling back from Germany. They were in the restaurant of the 7,951-ton *Herald* when it left Zeebrugge at seven o'clock, bound for Dover. A few minutes later the vessel keeled over and sank, leaving a third of the hull still above water. Sue and Bob were holding hands when they were hit by a wall of water and thrown apart. Sue went one way and was forced to the surface. Bob went the opposite way and was trapped in the restaurant.

It had been a nightmare. Survivors spoke of the constant screaming as the ship went over, people hanging on to fixed furniture to keep from falling into the freezing water, seeing others slowly lose their grip and drown. The disaster happened so fast there was no time for the ferry to send an SOS, but Dutch and Belgian ships and helicopters were soon at the scene picking up survivors. Two hundred people died in the water that night. Sue's fiancé Bob was one of them. His body was recovered a few days later.

Underlying my shock was a terrible uneasiness. The sensation was familiar, even though it had been years since the last time I had felt that way. Somebody has called it spiritual concussion; I'm sure it was an element of shock, something that had the power to alter me and my colleagues in the aftermath of the Harrods bomb. Until that moment, conscious of Sue's dreadful loss, I never thought I would feel that kind of agitation again. It was terrible, and I know now that it is a permanent thing, one of trauma's offshoots that can be revived by shock.

And I was going to feel it again, sooner than I could have imagined.

I moved to the station at Ealing in 1987, by which time my wife Jacqui was a detective at Kingston. When the Crimestoppers office opened at the Yard, her DI at Kingston moved there and asked if Jacqui would like to work alongside him. She said yes, and was promptly transferred to the Yard.

Shortly afterwards an advertisement appeared in the Police Review, inviting applicants for the job of co-presenter on BBC TV's *Crimewatch UK*. Jacqui applied, she was auditioned, and she got the job. Her first programme went out on air on 15 March 1990. I was very proud of her.

Over a period I had developed a rather painful curiosity about paedophile networks. The accumulating intelligence suggested they were larger and more numerous than we had believed, and far from being the product of campaigners' fevered delusions, they constituted a real and burgeoning horror at the heart of society.

Networks become apparent in any number of ways. Very often they are uncovered by accident, or through the detection of a single abuser. On one occasion the quirks in the baggage handling system at an airport led to a successful operation and the conviction of a number of paedophiles both in the UK and abroad. As is the case with so many networks, nearly all the paedophiles involved had jobs which brought them into contact with children in one way or another.

One day in 1988, just before the enactment of the Criminal Justice Act which made it an offence to possess indecent photographs of children, Leonard Jeans, a school nurse who lived in Notting Hill, flew into Gatwick from Amsterdam. He had been there with his nephew visiting a teacher, Chris Wiseman. Jeans and Wiseman were both paedophiles.

Jeans's suitcases did not arrive at Gatwick with him. They went instead to Heathrow, where Customs officers opened them. Inside they found a quantity of indecent photographs of boys. It was a weekend, so Customs called out the duty reserve officers at the Obscene Publications Branch, who on this occasion were Keith Driver and Terry Bailey.

At that stage, Jeans didn't know his luggage had been opened, so he had no reason to expect a visit at home from Keith and Terry, who produced a warrant, raided his house and seized a large number of videos, photographs and a pile of letters. They took the haul back to the Yard for examination.

Among the seized videos they found one in which Jeans had been filmed indecently assaulting a boy at the school where he worked. Jeans was arrested. It transpired that the film had been taken by another of his friends in Holland, a professional photographer called Fred Vivjer. Jeans had told the headmaster that Vivjer was willing to take photographs around the school as part of a promotional movie and was given permission to do so. Vivjer's real motive was to join Jeans in his abuse of boys at the school.

Leonard Jeans was charged with indecent assault, taking indecent photographs and importation of obscene material. He was sentenced to eighteen months' imprisonment.

The authorities in Holland arrested Fred Vivjer, the schoolteacher friend Chris Wiseman, and another youth worker. Terry went to Utrecht and saw where Vivjer lived. He had a caravan called the Pink Panther, parked on the edge of a river, and inside the caravan were a number of furry Pink Panther dolls. Terry recalled that Jeans had a number of photographs of boys taken with these dolls. All three men were subsequently prosecuted in Holland for indecency with children.

Meanwhile, in the UK, Keith and Terry were sifting through the rest of Jeans's property. They found several letters from a man called John Shannon, a retired schoolmaster who lived in Rugby, and another, Ted Robinson from Nottingham. It was evident that all three were swapping indecent photographs and videos. The officers went to Rugby to interview Shannon, but he was away on holiday in Portugal. On the strength of the letters they had found, Keith and Terry obtained a warrant and broke into Shannon's cottage. They found that he had barricaded the top floor, and it was difficult even to get up the stairs. It appeared that Shannon had shut the door to a bedroom, barricaded it, then put a lot of boxes and furniture and other heavy, bulky obstacles in the way as he retreated along the landing and down the stairs.

Keith and Terry moved the furniture and boxes out of the way and eventually got to the door, which had electric wires attached to it. Cautious investigation revealed that the wires were not connected to any electrical outlet. They finally opened the door and found Shannon's treasure: under a blanket on the bed there were approximately one hundred videos.

The tapes were taken back to the screening room at the Obscene Publications Branch, where the first few were examined. They contained footage of boys who were clearly foreign, committing sexual acts with each other in the back of a camper van.

The next move was to put out an All Ports Warning on Shannon, who was stopped soon afterwards at Portsmouth. He was travelling back from Portugal in his camper van which turned out to be, not surprisingly, the one that was used in the videos.

Terry and Keith went to Portsmouth to interview Shannon. They were not in a position of strength, because all they had as evidence were videotapes showing sexual acts committed abroad. Since they had no evidence of crimes committed in the UK, and because at that time it was not an offence in

Britain to possess obscene photographs of children, Shannon
had to be allowed to go on his way.

Meanwhile the pile of tapes taken from the cottage was
still being examined, with Mick Platt, one of the sergeants in
the office, sharing the workload. The breakthrough came
when, at the end of an apparently innocent tape of a television
programme, there was footage of a young boy, apparently not
foreign this time, being sodomised by an equally British-look-
ing man.

Keith and Terry took off for Rugby, armed this time with
much stronger evidence. They demanded that Shannon tell
them who the boy was. Shannon said he didn't know, but he
was obviously shaken by what had been discovered and he
gave them the name of the man in the film, Alan Bowler,
whom he believed lived in Birmingham. Shannon admitted
that he had operated the camera while the boy was being
sodomised.

Strictly speaking, photographs of child victims should not
be published. Nevertheless, the decision was taken to issue a
photograph of the boy on the tape and have it published in
local newspapers in the Midlands, with a caption saying that
he was being sought as a witness.

A woman in Walsall saw the picture and recognised the
boy as her next-door neighbour's son. It turned out that
Bowler had made friends with the family through a working
men's club. In thoroughly typical paedophile fashion, he had
groomed the parents to the point where they had no hesitation in allowing him to take their two boys away for
weekends. Bowler took them to Shannon, who violated them
and even lent them to another abuser, Douglas Brookes, who
also lived in Birmingham.

Shannon was charged with making the videos and aiding

and abetting the abuse. He pleaded guilty and was sent to prison for eighteen months. Bowler also pleaded guilty to a number of charges and was sentenced to eight years in prison. Brookes pleaded not guilty but Bowler gave evidence against him; he was eventually found guilty and sent to prison for three years. Without Bowler's declaration Brookes might have gone free, because the only other witnesses were the abused boys themselves, and defence counsel would have torn apart the testimony of mentally retarded children.

The role of the photographs, videos and letters as evidence was crucial in this case, just as it has been in many other cases. We can despise the abusers' reasons for hanging on to their stashes, but many a hoard of pornography has helped take an active paedophile out of circulation.

Hoarding was one of Shannon's compulsions. Apart from the videos that were found in his bedroom, he possessed what we considered to be the most extensive collection of scrapbooks of children that has ever been seized. There were twelve A4-size books containing an amazing assortment of lithographs, photographs and even cartoon depictions of young people. There were pieces of birthday cards, cuttings from catalogues, and curling, discoloured black and white photographs, many of them showing boys innocently swimming naked in rivers. These would have been taken some time in the 1950s: the era could be pinpointed from the haircuts and the skinny bodies – there were no hamburger joints in those days. Shannon probably took the photographs himself when he was a schoolmaster. By stages the hoarded images descended into obscene and degrading photographs of children. Carefree smiles and laughter faded to pained squints and puzzled expressions, the haunted looks of children realising there was something wrong with what was happening to them. This collection was Shannon's pride and joy and had been amassed over at least forty years. The judge ordered it to be forfeited. I would bet the loss hurt Shannon as much as the prison sentence.

This case highlights the reality of abusive networks. Rather than the image conjured by the rather misapplied word 'ring', the true pattern is more like a spider's web, with the connections going out so wide, and branching so sharply and in so many directions that they are impossible to follow. The Shannon case is also a clear indicator of the international nature of networks. It provides an argument, if one were needed, for a national and international proactive approach to the policing of these men and their criminal cliques.

Towards the end of 1988 the chief's post at the Obscene Publications Branch was advertised. I saw this as my chance, at last, to do the job I felt I was cut out to do. It was a post that combined proactive operations with the opportunity to influence and drive forward a logical agenda on the investigation of child abuse. The prospect of doing the work was tremendously exciting, and I knew I was one of only a handful of superintendents in London with the career profile to handle the job. I knew, too, that there would be very few applicants, because the job would not appeal to the faint-hearted, or to officers with an eye on the highest ranks in the service – there was an odd, persistent impression among many officers that the job would put a brake on promotion. That was silly. John Smith, the Deputy Commissioner who was later knighted, and John Hoddinott, the Chief Constable of Hampshire who was also later knighted, had both at one point in their careers been in charge of the Obscene Publications Branch.

I applied for the job and was interviewed by Neil Dickens, commander in overall charge of Territorial Operations at the time, and Detective Chief Superintendent Tony Kilkerr, the man who had exposed the corruption in the Dirty Squad in the 1970s. The interview seemed to go well, but in the event the job went to Les Bennett, a superintendent on my district and a friend of mine whose daughter was in the same class at school as my younger daughter, Laura. Les had no experience of the field and I was puzzled by his selection. I was terribly disappointed, too. Nevertheless, when I saw him at a senior officers' lunch on the day the decision was announced, I swallowed my disappointment and congratulated him.

I was not unhappy at Ealing, in any case. It was a big and busy division and the team in management were an amiable crew. The chief superintendent was John Purnell, with whom I had been a friendly rival when I was an inspector at Harrow Road and he was an inspector on the corresponding shift at Paddington. John was awarded the George Medal for Gallantry during his Paddington days when he chased the Balcombe Street bombers and came under fire. At Ealing we took similar approaches to our work and occasionally, it is fair to say, we tried to do each other's jobs, which now and then led to friction. But by and large we got on, and the congenial atmosphere at Ealing soon got me over my disappointment at not getting the Dirty Squad job.

In the middle of 1989 John was posted away to run the Training School. His place at Ealing was taken by Stewart Higgins, a former Clubs Office man who had served in the Dirty Squad. To some of the staff he appeared stiff and uncommunicative, but I knew Stewart Higgins to be a warm and kindly person with immense talent.

Not long after he arrived at Ealing, in August 1989, I had a call at home one evening from my brother Eric: he told me our mother had been rushed to hospital in Colchester. She had suffered a heart attack. I told Eric I would get there as fast as I could and would meet him at the hospital.

Literally one minute later, as I was getting ready to leave, the phone rang again. It was the Station Officer at Ealing Police Station to tell me there had been a major incident at Ealing West railway station. An express train had come off the rails and ended up on the platform.

I phoned Stewart Higgins, who lived just five minutes from my house at Windlesham. I told him about both messages and said I would go to the station and collect him on the way. He told me to go straight to Colchester, but I felt I should deal with business first, and besides, Mum was in hospital and was being looked after.

Stewart and I went to the scene of the accident, which was a thorough mess of broken masonry, tangled steel and smashed railway coaches. The express train had struck a concrete sleeper which vandals had put on the track close to Hanwell station. The train careered along for nearly a mile before it jumped the tracks and smashed into the platform at Ealing.

Incredibly, no one was killed. Seven people including the driver suffered minor injuries and were taken to Ealing Hospital. I waited until the emergency services had done their stuff, then I went on to Colchester.

At the recently opened Colchester District Hospital I got a blank look when I asked where I could find my mother. She was not on their list of admissions. Great, I thought, these new places were always the same, all chaos and palaver until they got used to the latest information-retrieval systems. I waited, not very patiently. A couple of telephone calls were made and the receptionist was finally able to tell me that instead of being brought to the Intensive Care Unit at this hospital, my mother had been taken directly to St Mary's, which caters for geriatric cases. She had been put on an ordinary ward there.

I rushed to St Mary's and found her. Eric was sitting by the bed. Although Mum was seventy-six and had been suffering from angina, she had had no previous heart attacks. When I demanded to know why she was not in the ITU, the nurse said they hadn't been able to get her in there because there was no room.

I suppose I got stroppy. This was my mother, after all. I insisted she be given the best care, and I kept asking questions about the treatment she was getting. I told the nurse in charge of the ward that the family would stay with Mum twenty-four hours a day, in relays, as we had done with my father.

Shortly after I arrived, the medical staff put my mother on a brand-new heart monitor which had just been donated to the hospital by voluntary subscribers.

Our sister Pat caught the next flight out of Auckland, New Zealand, with her youngest daughter Joanne. They arrived two days later. We had been told that there was extensive damage to Mum's heart and that the prognosis was not good, so we were concerned that the shock of seeing Pat might give Mum another attack. There was the possibility, too, that seeing so many loved ones around the bed would give her the notion she was extremely ill, which of course she was.

Jacqui stayed with me on my segments of the vigil. Between us we sat continuously with Mum until one evening when she had another severe attack. She died on the morning of the following day, 16 August, which was Eric's birthday and the anniversary of the death of Elvis Presley. There was no chance that any of us would forget that date.

Mum's funeral was obviously a sad affair, but I could not help thinking that she was with Dad, as she had wanted to be. I felt no shock or spiritual distress as I had felt after the Harrods outrage and the Zeebrugge disaster. This was the sadly inevitable, and there had been time to prepare myself for Mum's leaving. At the service Jacqui recited the words which had been read by Mike Thwaites at Jane Arbuthnot's funeral. They were by Canon Scott Holland and began, 'Death is nothing at all . . .'

Mum was laid to rest with Dad in the beautiful island cemetery at Mersea, with the sound of skylarks and curlews singing across the marshes.

In November there had been a change of commander at Territorial Operations. Dick Monk was now the man in charge. I heard a rumour that he was going to make changes, and that the job of head of the Obscene Publications Branch might come up again. Sure enough, on 24 November, applications for the post were once more invited. I was determined to have another shot at it and within days my application was in. Stewart Higgins supported me, although he said he would have preferred me to stay with him at Ealing.

The advertisement had invited interested officers to discuss the job with Dick Monk prior to interview. I went to see him. He was very encouraging, and I arrived at the Yard for my second attempt with genuinely high hopes. I was interviewed by Dick and by Sally Hubbard, a chief superintendent in one of the Territorial Operations sections. It was a lively and searching session which I thoroughly enjoyed, and I left feeling that I had done well and had not let myself down on any crucial issue.

A few long days passed. Then it happened. I was told I had the job.

This was it, I thought, *this was it*! This was my career summit, the high ground I had wanted for so long. At last they were handing me the opportunity to make a difference.

PART TWO

9
The Dirty Squad

The office of the Obscene Publications Branch was on the seventh floor at New Scotland Yard, one storey below the Commissioner. We were at one end of the floor, next door to the Public Order Department, who were responsible for assembling manpower to police demos and ceremonial events, and the Firearms Department, a civilian-run team that controlled the issue of gun licences.

As I already mentioned, the Dirty Squad was headed by Commander Dick Monk, whose responsibilities covered crime policy and courts as well as us. He was a great supporter of the branch where, unlike any other department, the superintendent was responsible directly to the commander. This was probably a throwback to the time when the uniformed branch took over the Obscene Publications Branch, and the line of command was shortened to bring it under the tight scrutiny and control of the most senior ranks. From the commander, the line upward was deputy assistant commissioner, then assistant commissioner.

Dick Monk and I had coffee together at 7:45 practically every morning, and we used the time to talk over policy and departmental detail. I was responsible then for policy in relation to things like cottaging – i.e., gay men hanging about in public lavatories to make sexual contacts – and indeed everything connected with the policing of public morals. Not quite so often, but often enough, Dick and I would meet again in his office at 7:45 in the evening. Invariably he would ask me if I wanted a drink, and invariably I would say yes. Dick would lean into a cupboard for a moment, then turn sharply and throw a glass at me. I came to expect this, but it always startled any third party who happened to be there. The drink on these occasions was always Famous Grouse whisky, and the talk was usually about what had been accomplished that day, compared with what we had set out to do.

In those days it was vitally important for me to have direct access to my Commander. Quite apart from the fact that we always got on well, I *needed* contact with him as much in operational terms as I did in matters of policy, for he was a thoroughly reliable sounding-board. Increasingly, we were doing trail-blazing work, work which no other force in the country was tackling, and because my Commander's support went deep I could go out on a limb when I had to, knowing that I had a safety net.

Unfortunately, in 1991 Dick applied for the post of Assistant Chief Constable at Devon and Cornwall, and he got the job. After he left, I had very little support from above. I found that I was rudderless, and it was a while before I managed to readjust.

My deputy at the Obscene Publications Branch was

Inspector Stuart Baker. We had been cadets together and subsequently Stuart was at the Clubs Office, so he was experienced in vice work. He was, and is, a knowledgeable, efficient officer and a loyal friend. His style as an administrator was always unhurried and laid-back, but he knew how to get people working hard. Having said that, I have to admit that all the staff were self-starters: we had to do no more than point them in specific directions and equip them with the tools to do the job in hand. Stuart was promoted to chief inspector within the branch – his post was variable – but he was warned that if he wanted to make the rank of superintendent before he retired, he ought to go to Division. The jump in rank would be most significant in terms of pension, because the pay difference is substantial: chief inspectors get overtime, superintendents do not, and obviously their pay reflects this.

In early 1991, after serving with me for a year, Stuart Baker decided to follow the advice he had been given and we advertised for a replacement. The post was open to uniform or detective inspectors; Stuart and I held boards for the half-dozen or so applicants who survived the paper sifting. Finally we decided to appoint Bob McLachlan, a young detective inspector working at Notting Hill who had already shown an interest in the kind of work we did. The decision to appoint Bob was a tremendous success and he rapidly immersed himself in the complex mix of work that made up our remit.

I knew over half of the rest of the personnel in the office, having worked with them in the past. Jack Jones, a personal friend, had worked with me at Paddington and was one of the undercover officers in the famous Cynthia Payne case. Although he had been at Notting Hill for most of his service, this was his second tour of duty in the Obscene Publications

Branch. The first time his partner, a sergeant, had died of cancer. This second time, by a nasty irony, Jack's wife had cancer, and she died while he was still in the branch in 1993. Jack was always serious, as many Welshmen can be, and also industrious and a fanatic for accuracy. He was a fluent Welsh speaker and indeed had hardly spoken any English until he was eleven. He had played the organ in chapel as a boy and later, as an adult, he performed in an Eistedfodd. On his desk in the office he kept a number of toy furry sheep. When his back was turned, or when he was out of the office, his colleagues often rearranged the sheep into predictably obscene tableaux.

Terry Bailey, large and bluff, was another Notting Hill stalwart, one half of a pair who had been doing paedophile investigations for a couple of years. Terry was outspoken, self-confident, hardworking, and a straight dealer with everyone. He is another good friend.

Mick Platt, Terry's sergeant, was the most relaxed man in the office. He fell asleep every time he went to autogenic training, which I will talk about later. Mick was a highly experienced vice man, and he was at pains to make sure he was never filmed or photographed while he was working. His reason, plain and simple, was that he did not want his neighbours to know what he did for a living. He remains an intensely private man with a gentle, firm approach in his handling of witnesses and suspects, and he has rightly been described as a consummate professional. Mick was and is a lover of horse-racing, like most of the people in the office, and when I was there he was always coming up with winning systems. He was a great fan of Tony Stafford, the *Telegraph*'s racing correspondent, whom he would study with ferocious concentration, then go out and make complicated ten-pence bets. He now works for the

Missing Persons help-line, tracking people in the West End of London. He is one of the best friends anyone could have, and I'm happy to say he is one of mine.

Carmel McKee, a woman sergeant, had worked on my vice squad at Paddington. She was a very short Geordie girl, a devout Roman Catholic who posed as a prostitute on a number of occasions during her time at Paddington. Carmel was critical and could well hold her own with the lads, even though she wasn't a drinker or a swearer. After I had been at Obscene Publications for roughly a year, Carmel joined a Child Protection team in Ruislip.

Bernie Meadon, older than I and substantially bearded, was Stuart Baker's deputy and, from time to time, acting inspector. He was also a hugely experienced vice officer and had run the King's Cross clean-up operation. He knew the law on Obscene Publications and all of the related cases in detail. Bernie was dry, taciturn and loyal. He retired a year before me and went to work in security in the City. I still see him at our racing trips.

My personal office was on a corner of the building. It was larger than the space usually authorised for superintendents because there had been a civilian senior executive officer in there when I arrived. This man was responsible for the Dirty Squad's civil staff, and for the supervision of the masses of pornography and other property at our store in South London. Following a review of the work of the civilian staff, it was decided to do away with his post. I was therefore left with plenty of room to work, and host large meetings and briefings. This was in marked contrast to the working environment of the rest of the department.

The main Dirty Squad office, along the passage from mine, housed the sixteen police officers and ten civilians who made

up the staff. The overcrowding was appalling. Desks were
packed together in blocks of four and six and it was hard for
someone to push back a chair without bumping into the
person behind. The noise level rose at times to a noisy babble
and phone calls were often conducted with the phone at one
ear and a hand over the other. The number of bodies per
square metre violated the Health and Safety Regulations, but
at that time the police were exempt, so it was all right to treat
personnel like battery animals.

The viewing room, where seized videotapes were continu-
ally being screened, was in fact a big cupboard which, for
most of the time, was stiflingly hot, even with the door wide
open. Along one side was a shelf unit with TV sets and tape
machines; on the end wall were two banks of three screens
each, with video machines below. All of the video machines
were old models, with the recording facility removed. Two
ordinary TV sets sat on top of the banked sets, permanently
switched to terrestrial stations showing cricket, racing or
anything else that would distract the viewers, whenever
necessary, from the awfulness on the screens below. Sometimes
we would find programmes like *Blackadder* or *Fawlty Towers*
on tapes seized from suspects and they would be screened as
well.

Civilian staff organised the grouping and documentation of
the videos and magazines, and they viewed them. Run-of-
the-mill pornography was classified by the nature of the acts
depicted, and records were made on file pages prepared for
the purpose. Tapes that featured children, whether indecently
or not, would be referred to the investigating officer for analysis. In these cases we regarded the material as scenes of crime
as well as evidence: we went to great lengths to identify the
victims, the suspects and their surroundings.

A day's work on the videos was always tiring and often emotionally traumatic to the personnel involved, but the atmosphere in that cubby-hole of flickering screens stayed relentlessly cheerful, with plenty of good-natured banter and occasional noisy outbursts of shared disgust.

The eventual 'feel' of our big family was of an elite squad, but with no triumphalism. No prima donnas, either. If there were flare-ups they were trivial, caused by caffeine overdoses and irritations like smoking or too much noise. Always, at the back of everything we did, there was the sense of being pioneers with a steady need to learn more about what we were doing.

Everyone in the branch was learning as much as they could about paedophilia. Dick Monk and I eventually became Trustees of the Faithfull Foundation, an organisation that sought, among its other objectives, to rescue the treatment programme for sex offenders at the Gracewell clinic in Birmingham from abandonment. We joined the foundation because we detected a need to address offending behaviour and learn more about the nature of the offenders.

Just before I arrived Dick Monk had successfully negotiated an increase in the number of officers dealing with paedophiles from two to six; the strength of the Branch was thus increased from twelve to sixteen, plus the civilians. I started to involve almost everyone in paedophile enquiries. Four were left to investigate adult porn for a while; that number was later cut to two, then even they were given work related to child protection.

We were busy all the time, always up to our ears and finding ways to take on more. There was endless sharing of information about suspects and their habits, and as profiles

filled out and took firm shape, new information was recorded
to substantiate or replace the existing material. Everyone in
the squad prepared meticulous reports; they were all very
skilled at this and their work was commended by the Crown
Prosecution Service and by counsel, who would quote
directly from case material prepared by members of the
squad. We conducted intensive programmes of research into
organised and ritual abuse, computer pornography, the for-
mation and structure of networks of paedophiles, and the
Children of God sect. On top of all this were the practical
matters of ongoing investigation, informant handling and
dawn raids.

Busy as I was, there was always room to squeeze in a little
more. In May 1991 a new Interpol committee was set up,
called the Standing Working Party on Offences Against
Minors. I was nominated as the UK police representative,
together with Dr Frances Lewington from the Metropolitan
Police Forensic Science Laboratory, and I was elected Chair of
the Law Enforcement sub-group. This gave me the opportunity to meet and start to work with colleagues from around
the world, and we rapidly formed a specialist network. We
exchanged information about individual paedophiles and
their methods, and, wherever necessary, we lobbied for
change in the laws of the member countries. It was agreed in
particular that we should encourage all nations to pass laws
banning the possession of child pornography. We also cam-
paigned for measures to clamp down on child sex tourism
and the prostitution of children. My friends in the US
Customs Service, headed by Don Huycke, the National Child
Pornography Program Manager based in Washington DC,
were to prove particularly helpful on the international stage.

This was no talking shop. It was a platform for executive

action and continues to grow from strength to strength. In 1999 Bob McLachlan was elected Chair of the Working Party, a post in which he makes sure that the drive does not slacken.

Working parties and committees aside, our day-to-day life in the Dirty Squad could have stood comparison with a bee-hive, maybe even an ant-hill. I had never in my career known such a variety and intensity of work to be carried out under one roof. We were able to mingle street-level policing with dozens of other activities and projects. We pioneered research and information on the global problem of child abuse which actually unfolded as we worked; we put together new ways to investigate, particularly in relation to the interviewing of suspects, while we worked with, and educated, other police officers throughout the country.

We lectured and attended conferences, we lobbied for changes in the law both nationally and internationally, and we fought to protect our work against factions hell-bent on destroying or deprecating it, from whatever motives. We strove hard to educate the public in a way that was responsible and did not patronise them. And we enjoyed occasional surges of social life, which usually took the form of squad lunches, where we could let down our hair and do some therapeutic bitching among ourselves. As a treat, we sometimes went to the races.

An especially memorable member of our team was June Saffhill, one of the civilian staff who preferred to be called by her long-standing nickname, Ferret. I first met Ferret at Paddington, where her job was to organise and collate the daily influx of information to the station. A plodding approach would have kept the job afloat and she could have made a career out of being a specialist filing clerk. But Ferret had flair and a capacity for hard work, and on top of that she was a natural for the job. She made it special. Among her talents was a knack for spotting things other people missed, such as patterns of behaviour, unlikely coincidences, odd changes of habit.

She had no need for a computer. Instead, she had a row of filing cabinets full of typed and handwritten cards that catalogued the appearance, traits, tastes and track records of scores of local villains. The cards were updated as soon as new information came to hand. Nothing escaped Ferret's attention and nothing was considered too trivial to be included. She recorded criminals' preferences in clothes and jewellery, she detailed their unwitting habits (lip chewing, nose scratching, fidgeting), she even noted the positions of their gold fillings, if they had any.

On one occasion Ferret made a point of 'carding' a fifteen-year-old boy called Eddie, who had been charged with indecent exposure. She had a hunch, based on trends she could detect in her files, that the boy had an embryonic compulsion; she believed he had been caught at an early stage in the growth of his deviation and that in time he would become a serious sexual criminal. Less than a year later Ferret saw a rape report from a neighbouring police area; at several points the details matched her notes on Eddie. She checked the records and found that he was actually in a residential home in the north of England. In spite of that she was still convinced he could be the rapist. She called the home and learned that on the weekend of the attack, Eddie had been allowed to go home to London. Ferret alerted the appropriate departments. Eddie was subsequently convicted of rape and sent to prison for seven years.

By the time I met Ferret she was in her early fifties. She was a self-possessed woman from Muswell Hill who had left school at fifteen and had never obtained any formal qualifications. In spite of what might have been considered an educational handicap, she had always found challenging jobs in areas that nowadays would be reserved for graduates. She developed a phenomenal memory during years when she worked at the Foreign Office and at the Ministry of Defence, engaged on projects where some information was so sensitive it could not be written down, and so had to be memorised. She told me she had changed jobs and become a civilian worker with the Met because she liked to get home in the evening to her husband, Stan. She was fed up being on call in the Foreign Office at all hours, usually to open locked files so that ministers could answer late-night questions in the Commons.

Ferret's skills were wide-ranging. Whenever a suspected pimp was in the cells at Paddington there was invariably a problem with identification, because pimps have changeable identities and usually more than one street name. The solution was to send Ferret down to make a positive identification. She always put on an overall before she went into the cell area. As disguises go it was flimsy, but the overall did a perfect job of making her look like a tea lady. The pimps never realised what she was up to and they ignored her, but one hard look at a face was enough for Ferret to nail an identity.

At that time, as already noted, the vast majority of the known pimps in Paddington were Afro-Caribbean. It was simply a demographic fact of the period. One official visitor to the station passed through Ferret's lair and noticed that the pimps' wall had only one photo of a white man in a sea of black faces. The visitor remarked that it was an obviously racist state of affairs. Ferret wearily denied it. 'What d'you want me to do, dear?' she asked. 'Stick up some pictures of my family to balance things out?'

Ferret was a formidable drinker, the kind who could put it away in quantity yet seem hardly to touch her glass. In that regard, as well as in her personality and background, I always thought she resembled Connie in John Le Carré's *Smiley's People*. It was common for police officers to take her along to the pub to celebrate arrests where she had played a part, including the ones where she did surveillance work – another of her skills. Sometimes on these drinking sessions Ferret would lose track of time and would telephone Stan at two in the morning, telling him she would be back in time for *News at Ten*.

Police officers found Ferret easy to talk to and a number of them treated her as a confidante. In most cases she displayed a motherly warmth and was protective of her 'little soldiers', as she called them. She would even voice grievances on their behalf to senior officers, many of whom she despised, especially if they were the kind who used rank like a battering ram. Once, in a pub, Ferret cornered an inspector who had been giving one of her favourites a hard time. The inspector belonged to a class of officers known at the Yard as 'seagulls', because of their habit of swooping down without warning, shitting on somebody and then flying off again. Ferret's condemnation of the inspector was swift, stylish and stinging. The incident showed a fine disregard for authority that was endearing to many of us, but it did nothing to help her career. She was good at her job and always gave more than people expected, but her civilian bosses never promoted her beyond a minor grade.

At that time Ferret's dearest wish, so she said, was to die at her desk at Paddington and have her coffin carried out of the building by eight pimps, for cremation in a nearby park. A crucial part of her wish was that after the pimps had put the coffin on the pyre, and had lit it, they should perform an act of outstanding civic decency and throw themselves on the fire beside her.

Contrary to her wishes she did not die at her desk in Paddington. Scotland Yard spotted her talents and in 1987 she was invited to become the collator of the new nationwide Paedophile Index, working in the office of the Obscene Publications Branch.

The police had been slow to recognise the extent of the paedophile problem and were slower still to combat it with special resources. When Ferret arrived she made up for lost time. She worked from scratch, building up a comprehensive record of paedophiles and their networks, starting with the seventy-six names on the membership list of the Paedophile Information Exchange, known as PIE. By the time I took charge of the Dirty Squad in 1989 the Paedophile Index carried several hundred names. When I left in 1994 Ferret had added two thousand more.

Over the years at Obscene Publications she supplemented her distaste for pimps with a loathing of paedophiles. In my time as chief, approximately ten paedophiles killed themselves during or after investigations into their activities. While neither I nor most of the other members of the Dirty Squad felt any regret at their passing, we didn't exactly rejoice either. Ferret, on the other hand, was once or twice heard to murmur, 'More PIE in the sky, my dears. More PIE in the sky . . .'

Ferret always took time to think over a problem or a dilemma, and there was more than a hint of forethought one day when she was asked if she believed, as some people did, that paedophiles should be castrated.

'Oh, I think so, yes,' she replied, nodding. 'From the neck down, preferably.'

If you spend your days tracking paedophiles you can begin to believe you see them everywhere. Before long, Ferret's suspicions were on a hair trigger. In 1992, when I organised an exhibition at the Houses of Parliament to illustrate and explain the work of the Obscene Publications Branch, I made sure we included magazines and excerpts from films seized by the branch, so that MPs would see the kind of material in everyday circulation, and would therefore approach legislative proposals with reasonably informed minds. Ferret, who helped run the two-day exhibition, noticed that a couple of the lords were coming back for a second viewing and, in her wary opinion, were loitering far too long by the child-pornography section. At one point she tapped my arm. 'Just look at that one,' she muttered. 'He's dribbling. I'll *swear* he's dribbling.'

Not all of Ferret's time was spent on paedophile matters. She was the collator for the branch's other areas of activity, and the work certainly broadened her understanding of human frailty. When she first went to Paddington at the age of forty-nine she had had to ask someone what a lesbian was. Now, a decade later, no area of sexual deviation was unknown to her. Even her ears developed a sensitivity to perversion. Sounds from the video viewing rooms of animals being violated grew so familiar that Ferret could identify a species without seeing the screen. Occasionally, however, she was wrong. On one occasion she heard an odd strangulated noise and looked up.

'Would that be a duck?'

The video officers were viewing was one that had been seized during Operation Spanner, of which more later. The sound Ferret heard, an officer explained, was a gagged man howling as a nail was hammered through his foreskin into a plank.

'Thank God,' Ferret sighed, carrying on with her notes. 'I thought it was an animal.'

Ferret found most adults-only perversions either pathetic or amusing. Infantilists were especially droll. She cherished a photo of an RAF sergeant dressed as a baby, wearing a nappy and bib, with a dummy in his mouth. The pencilled note on the back said *Nanny has just given me a three-pint enema and I'm waiting for the result.*

Another favourite picture was of a man wearing a yellow oilskin coat, a matching waterproof hat, a snorkel and flippers. He was a sado-masochist advertising for a partner willing to submerge him slowly in a swimming pool and pull him out just before he drowned.

The Amputees Club also made Ferret smile. They were not, as one might expect, a mutual-help outfit, but a group of deviants who preferred to have sex with people who had lost limbs.

As Ferret approached retirement she said the only perverts who worried her now were the gerontophiles, who are sexually attracted to old people. In spite of her fears I am sure she has spent her retirement unmolested. I'm also certain that at the Muswell Hill branch of the Royal British Legion, where she and Stan go for an occasional quiet drink, no one knows what extraordinary things the unassuming Mrs Saffhill used to do for a living.

10
Villains and Casualties

When I went to the Obscene Publications Branch, Jacqui and I made a joint and amicable decision that she would ask for a transfer, since it would not have been right for both of us to be in Territorial Operations (TO): she was in TO12, I was in TO13, and although she did not work for me, we nevertheless shared the same Commander, Dick Monk. So at the end of July 1990 Jacqui went to work at London Airport, a couple of months before our fifth wedding anniversary.

On Sunday 5 August 1990, I was at home with Jacqui when I had a call from John, the son of my older brother (technically my half-brother) Ken. Young John, known as Tiny because he is 6 feet 5 inches tall, was a sergeant in the Met at that time. I could tell straight away from the tone of his voice that something was wrong.

'It's Dad,' he said. 'He died at ten o'clock this morning.'

The news had been telephoned to John by his stepmother

Mum and Dad on their
wedding day in 1944.

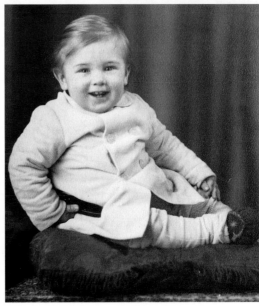

Studio portrait of the author,
aged eighteen months.

The author and his brother Eric playing cricket on the beach at West Mersea, *circa* 1952.

The front page of the *Evening Standard* after the IRA bomb at the Old Bailey, 8 March 1973.

TERROR BOMBS BLITZ LONDON —SCORES HURT

ayhem in the boxing ring at
embley Arena, following the
feat of Alan Minter by
arvin Hagler in September
79.

author at his desk while
erintendent in charge of the
tropolitan Police Cadet
ool, Hendon.

The scene of the Harrods bomb, Hans Crescent, 17 December 1983.

A confrontation with a prostitute at a hotel brothel in Paddington, August 19
The author is accompanied by Barry Jones of the Vice Squad.

EXCLUSIVE on-the-spot report

IRON CURTAIN WOMEN HELD AT VICE HOTEL

By CHRIS HOUSE
Sunday Mirror Crime Reporter

A MAJOR spy probe was under way last night after two Iron Curtain women were discovered running a brothel in the heart of London's diplomatic community.

The women—a Russian and a Pole—were seized along with 15 prostitutes when vice squad officers, accompanied by a Sunday Mirror reporter and photographer, raided the hotel in Bayswater.

When the two "madams" revealed their nationalities MI5 chiefs were alerted.

A senior officer said: "We were astonished to discover such an unlikely pair running a sex-for-sale operation.

"They were both highly intelligent women who had become friends when they were students together in the Soviet Union."

A Whitehall source said: "The security services are investigating to find out if the brothel was used for espionage or blackmailing VIPs."

The hotel—owned by the Russian woman and only a few hundred yards from the Soviet Embassy—was raided last week.

Kisses

The Pole, Alicja Lewicka, is an economics graduate from Warsaw University. She was the "receptionist" at the brothel.

On Thursday, she slipped out of Britain on a boat from Tilbury after being fined £300 for managing a brothel.

Lewicka was allegedly on a ten-week holiday in Britain and was staying at an address near Kew Gardens.

For two months undercover vice officers from Paddington Green kept observation on the four storey hotel.

The raid was the start of a blitz on London hotels being used as brothels.

Officers said the Bayswater brothel was the first to be hit because it was so "outrageous."

Police discovered that at least ten of the hotel's 18 rooms were being used by prostitutes who were charging up to £50 for sex.

Each client had to pay £10 to Lewicka, before being allowed up to the rooms.

In three days, 90 men, including a dwarf, visited the hotel.

Plans to raid the brothel were hurriedly brought forward after one of the girl's clients fell out of a fourth-floor window.

The man landed on a first-floor balcony—breaking his legs, arms and pelvis.

As the officers searched the hotel, they found packets of contraceptives in the bathrooms.

In a narrow, cramped twin bedded room a young Asian-looking girl and her boyfriend were questioned.

She denied being a prostitute, but her boyfriend was warned that he could be charged with being a pimp.

During the three hour operation, Mercedes cars were repeatedly seen driving up and down the street, their drivers peering into the hotel lobby.

Punter

Two girls, tarted up and wearing leather, walked into the hotel and asked for a room.

A plain clothes cop asked them if they were regulars and how much they were usually charged.

They replied: "£15 for the room and £8 for each punter."

Instead of getting a room, they were introduced to Detective Superintendent Mick Hames, the officer in charge of the operation.

Photographer Geoff Garratt took a picture of them being questioned and one shouted obscenities and both ran from the hotel. The police did not bother to chase them.

As we left, we spotted a couple of cars parked near the hotel, their drivers watching the building—obviously regular customers.

A Mercedes had been there for about half-an-hour. As we drove past we noticed the number plates—it was a diplomatic car.

ce to face—Police and a prostitute on the steps of the hotel   Picture: GEOFF GARRATT

Police keep watch outside the hotel

How the KGB use the honey trap . .

E KGB are expert at setting "a honey trap"—a sex-for-rets operation.

hey use attractive girls to : their unsuspecting victims revealing confidential information. Diplomats, business-and computer experts are main targets.

ten rooms are bugged and et cameras take pictures of a in compromising posis. The Russians are eager et their hands on vital information as well as : secrets.

oney traps" are rare in the West but behind the Iron Curtain they are used regularly by the KGB.

British businessmen—even tourists—are warned before they go to the Soviet Union about the trouble they can "get" into if they are not careful.

The pretty maids inside Russian hotels are quite often members of the KGB—just waiting for the right person to come along.

An intelligence source said: "It's the oldest trick in the espionage book—and the Russians are specialists at it."

● A Civil Service union yesterday attacked an "insane" Defence Department decision to hire private agency typists as "an open invitation to the KGB" to plant girl spies.

Civil Service typists, who are subject to the Official Secrets Act, are to be laid off to make way for the agency girls in order to save money.

A report of the raid on the brothel, by Chris House of the *Sunday Mirror*.

The publicity wall in the vice office in Paddington in late 1986.

A copy of the 'Unwanted' poster distributed outside New Scotland Yard following the Operation Spanner trial at the Old Bailey.

UNWANTED

**SUPERINTENDENT MICHAEL HAMES
HEAD OF THE OBSCENE PUBLICATIONS SQUAD**

**SHATTERED LIVES, OPPRESSED
COMMUNITIES, INNOCENT DEATHS**

*THE OBSCENE PUBLICATIONS SQUAD IS NOT MERELY
ENFORCING THE LAW BUT TRYING TO EXTEND CENSORSHIP*

"Operation Spanner" cost an estimated £3 million. It was supposed to target a large-scale vice ring involving snuff videos. In fact, the only result was the conviction of 14 gay men for consensual sexual activities that harmed no one and a legal precedent which now criminalises ordinary sexual behaviour - such as love bites.

The attempt to ban the book "Modern Primitives" failed. However, book shops are now effectively restrained from stocking works dealing with variant sexual practices because the police are using their powers of seizure under the Obscene Publications Act so frequently and indiscriminately.

Media hysteria was created and public attitudes hardened when Hames attacked safer sex educational materials, including "The Gay Man's Guide to Safer Sex". This is a dangerous step towards further restrictive legislation and potentially extends the domain of the "*obscene*" into essential HIV-prevention information.

The OPS use the threat of prosecution to restrict the free distribution of literature and suppress variant sexual cultures. Their operations feed the media's appetite for scandal, and the resulting moral panic is used to justify their continued existence. Europe survives without these draconian laws.

FIGHTING ON . . . Det. Superintendent Mike Hames' grim task is to protect youngsters from abuse   Main picture: PAUL WILLIS

The man with the worst job in Britain

By PETER HOOLEY
Whitehall Correspondent

VETERAN detective Mike Hames and his team are in the frontline in the battle against child sex abuse. Their job tears so hard at the emotions it sometimes makes them weep.

Hames, a father of two teenage girls, tries to remain detached, but as he plays one of the homemade porn videos seized with terrible regularity, he becomes angry.

In his office, as an obscene film unfolds on a bank of six screens, he says: "Many abusers try to justify themselves by saying they love children, but just look at this."

A little girl of no more than eight is pictured being subjected to unspeakable abuse by a man wearing a bracelet.

The camera pulls back and her pleading, frightened look is frozen in the frame. It is unmistakeable and simply says: "Please God, help me."

Detective Superintendent Hames, the 16 detectives and 11 civilians who make up the Obscene Publications Department, work from New Scotland Yard, dedicating themselves to tracking down child abusers and protecting youngsters from them.

Hames, who kept the mods from the rockers on Brighton sea front as a rookie in the Sixties and is married to a policewoman, says of the videos: "To call it kiddie porn makes it sound innocent and is missing the point. These people don't love children, they hate them.

"What we see on film is callous, illegal and the most serious sexual assault of a child which will almost certainly wreck the rest of their lives."

HAMES works an 11-hour day and his men travel the country in their search for what they call "hands-on abusers". The office is full of good-humoured banter from men united in a common task.

Outside, often working undercover, they act on intelligence culled from every legal source.

They work closely with counterparts in the U.S. and Europe and have compiled a paedophile index which has topped 3,000 names and grows daily.

Hames, 44, says: "We are on the side of the angels. Nobody disagrees with what we do, which is catch abusers and protect children.

"Not everyone wants to do it, and we all get ribbed that we must be perverts because we're surrounded by porn all the time.

"It's when you tell people it involves children and is not the breasts and bums stuff you see at the rugby club that they walk away from you in horror."

Hames knows what he wants from his staff. "I'm not interested in zealots, I just want the best detectives that I can get.

"The quality I insist on is that ability to know themselves pretty well because it can be a very heavy scene.

"It is among the most difficult jobs in policing because you're not dealing with bank robbers but with the whole range of human emotions."

Pornography is at the heart of child abuse, according to the profile of the typical paedophile that police and psychologists have built up.

Once, a paedophile was perhaps an isolated schoolmaster in a boys' boarding school with few sharing his terrible secrets.

Now, he is on an undercover American computerised porn mailing list and can fax material to other men with the same sick obsession.

"The first thing to face up to is that these people, invariably men, fantasise about having sex with children, whether boys or girls," Hames says.

"Once they have made that decision, they invariably start on a journey towards becoming a hands-on abuser which may take years."

They start collecting scrap books of cuttings which may be as innocent as a child model in a knitting pattern advertisement. Slowly, the progression turns towards porn magazines and the photographs and videos of children they seduce.

"One thing which helps us is that paedophiles hardly *ever* throw any of this material away," says Hames.

"They simply hide it, either in their homes or at work, and when we find it we get a vital identification breakthrough into a network of police inquiries."

Every one of the 2,000 hours of videos seized in raids are viewed by police because often the offending material will be hidden in the middle of a soft-porn tape.

Hames is adamant that child abusers need treatment in prison to rid themselves of their obsession. "You can't hang abusers or lock them up for ever, but when in prison they are segregated with each other for their own protection on Rule 43."

"They sit round feeding off each other's fantasies, and when they come out they tend to re-offend."

He is concerned that the furore surrounding allegations of Satanic or ritualised abuse in Nottingham and Rochdale will only serve as a distraction from the real problem.

A recent study from 39 out of 52 police forces revealed 2,000 known child victims of 186 paedophile gangs in the last three years.

IN ONLY five of those cases were there any allegations of Satanic or ritualised abuse, and the Obscene Publications Branch has not come across one case.

"Entrenched positions are dangerous things and I cannot say it doesn't exist, just that there is not one scrap of evidence for it that I know of," says Hames.

"But I am anxious that we should not lose sight of the real dangers and I would urge all parents to take a keen interest in the adults which their children mix with outside the home.

"Often when a sex abuse ring is uncovered, parents who never suspected their youngster's involvement feel a terrible sense of guilt after their initial outrage subsides."

But by then, as Mike Hames says, it's too late.

The *Daily Express* profile of the author in October 1990.

Captured by two of the UK's most prominent investigative TV journalists –
Esther Rantzen and Roger Cook.

The author and his wife Caroline on their wedding day, March 1996.
Spike Milligan was best man.

from the villa in Spain where the couple lived. Ken had been by the swimming pool when he became unwell and died soon after in his wife's arms. He had been waiting for a heart by-pass operation and we all knew his condition was serious. Even so, this was a terrible shock.

I had a hurried discussion with John and we decided to go out to Spain at once. I booked a scheduled aircraft from Heathrow to Alicante via Madrid that afternoon. We boarded the plane at approximately three o'clock and when we landed at Alicante we hired a car at the airport. We arrived at Ken's house in Moraira at 8 P.M. We were met by his widow, Mary, who tearfully told us that Ken had been had buried at five o'clock. We were astounded.

It appeared that the undertakers were anxious to dispose of the body quickly, because of the heat. The doctor had issued a death certificate, so there was no need for an autopsy and therefore no reason to delay the funeral. The arrangements were minimal: a few expatriate friends were informed, the body was washed and fitted into a coffin and was then uncer-emoniously slotted into a hole, roughly twelve feet above the ground, in the wall of the local cemetery. No priest was pres-ent; the friends simply said a few words of remembrance.

The three of us went to the cemetery immediately and saw the coffin up there in its slot, the varnished wood visible through the gap which would remain open for a few days. John and I felt devastated, unable to take our leave of Ken properly, but there was nothing we could do. I glanced at poor Mary standing there, forlorn, staring up at the wall. That morning Ken had been at her side; now, before sunset, he was gone from her, without ceremony, without even the time for Mary to accept that he had died.

*

Work at the Dirty Squad continued apace. A case we dealt with around the time of Ken's death underscored the fact that some paedophiles abuse children for many years, before a simple investigative fluke brings their world down around their ears. The case began with a tip-off about a young man called Steven Heaver, a known villain with a substantial amount of form. The informant said Heaver was dealing in adult and child pornography from his flat in Brixton. Two officers from the Dirty Squad went down there with a warrant and searched the place. They found what they were looking for, and when they questioned Heaver he gave them the names of a couple of dealers. One was in Nottingham, the other in Cheshire. The man in Cheshire, Heaver said, had a penchant for abusing mentally retarded children. When we called on him we found a quantity of photographs that he had exchanged with a man called Charles O'Rourke in Greenford, Middlesex.

That was how we came across O'Rourke, a man who had been abusing children for twenty years without coming to the notice of the authorities. We only found him because he had exchanged material with a paedophile in Cheshire.

Two officers went round to see O'Rourke. When he opened the door they introduced themselves. One of the officers, Sergeant Keith Driver, said he could see the man's whole world fall apart. He showed them into his kitchen, where they learned a strong lesson about searching. Without being coerced or even asked, O'Rourke showed them where his collection of pornography was kept. He got down on his knees on the floor and pulled back part of the wooden apron that ran along the bottom of the kitchen units. Behind it was his stash. Not many police officers would have thought of looking under the units, or even unscrewing a panel to look for evidence.

O'Rourke had pictures and diaries going back twenty years. The first child he abused was an eight-year-old boy, Gareth, a neighbour's son in Greenford, who used to ride up and down the street outside O'Rourke's house on his bike. O'Rourke began chatting to Gareth, and eventually invited him into his house. Soon he was sexually abusing the boy, and he continued to abuse him until he was sixteen. At that point O'Rourke moved away to Harrow, but later he moved back to a different part of Greenford and lived in the house where our officers visited him and later arrested him.

We eventually located Gareth, the first boy O'Rourke had abused. He was now a grown man of twenty-six, married with two children. When our officers visited him at work and he realised who they were, he burst into tears. He told them that for years he had felt he was living with a nightmare. It was a relief for him to talk to the police. When he went home that day he told his wife everything, and later he told his parents. Until the Dirty Squad officers approached him he had bottled everything up and had told no one.

Keith Driver said that when he met Charlie O'Rourke, the man was totally out of control. He had business cards printed with his name, address, and a drawing of the 'Charlie' cartoon character he had, by horrible irony, created for BBC Television. He would spend a lot of time in amusement arcades and public parks. In the arcades his standard ploy was to stand next to a machine where a boy was playing and hand over a pound when the lad's money ran out. He would also follow children home from school and start talking to them and handing out the visiting cards. He would invite the children round to his place to do housework and then he would give them pocket money. He often introduced himself to parents and let them know who he was, using his small fame as a lever to ingratiate himself and show how solid and genuine he was. One mother and father would not let their son go round to O'Rourke's place, or let him take the child out for the day, and O'Rourke wrote two indignant letters telling the parents they were denying their child simple freedom, and that they had no right to stifle a young human being's enjoyment of life in such a fashion.

At Isleworth Crown Court the evidence of O'Rourke's first victim helped send him to prison for four years.

Charles O'Rourke had found an ingenious nook to conceal his pictures, but there have been stranger hiding places. Shortly after the O'Rourke case we handled a job that began in Thames Valley. A young girl claimed that she had been serially abused by a man in East London. One of the addresses where she claimed she had been abused was a house which, our inquiries revealed, was owned by a man called Cedric Sands.

Squad officers made a few searches and discovered that the man in East London had been found not guilty of a previous allegation of indecent assault. We also learned that at one time, Cedric Sands's car had been stolen, and when it was recovered indecent photographs of children were found in the glove compartment. Added to the information we had from the girl, that was enough to justify warrants to search both men's addresses.

At the East London address we found nothing incriminating. We went to Sands's house, which was a dirty, untidy place; we searched it and found a couple of indecent photographs. Our group instinct was that there had been a clear-out: there were empty shelves and drawers adjacent to others that were crammed full, and even whole cupboards appeared to have been recently emptied out. So, since there was very little in the house, there might well be a lot somewhere else.

As we carried on searching, a man who was lodging at the house approached a couple of our officers and told them that he had been planning to come and see us. He said that since he had been living at the address he had not been very happy with what was going on.

'What do you mean?' Keith Driver asked him.

'Well, it's just occasional things, you know? A couple of weeks ago a bunch of blokes came into the house, put some stuff into lots of plastic bags and took them round the corner to where Sands's brother lives. They took some to the church where he's an organist, too.'

I went with several officers to the church and found three sacks full of child pornography in the vestry.

'Listen,' I said to Sands, looking as indignant as I could, 'as a communicant member of the Church of England, I take serious exception to you hiding your filthy pictures in a vestry.'

He muttered that he was sorry.

Further investigation turned up the fact that Sands was one of the two official photographers at the Eureka Naturist Club. Both of them were paedophiles. We found a vast collection of child pornography in various forms which belonged to a number of men who attended the Eureka club. We could not ascribe all the material to individuals, there was just so much – nine sacks of it in all.

Some material *could* be pinpointed, however. There were videos and photographs of Sands performing sex acts on young boys. In all of the shots Sands wore white socks. No one ever found out if there was a reason.

We searched the address of the other photographer and found more child pornography there. Ultimately both he and Sands were prosecuted and pleaded guilty to taking indecent photographs of children; a charge of indecent assault against Sands was dropped.

On a Saturday morning just before Christmas, around the time when my girls were due to visit, I came downstairs and found Jacqui standing in the sitting room, looking out of the window. She looked different.

I said, 'Are you all right?'

'No,' she said. 'I'm dreadfully sad.'

Suddenly I felt it again, the uneasiness, the shadowy agitation, 'spiritual concussion'.

'Sad?'

'I'm really, really depressed.'

My heart sank. Every instinct told me this was bad, this was the worst I could imagine. I had been going along thinking everything was all right, then in that moment when she spoke my life was changed. I had no doubt what was wrong.

'Have you got somebody else?'

She said no, she hadn't. She said we should leave it and talk about it after Christmas. Then, after Christmas, it became apparent that she was determined to end the marriage. She left me the following April.

I was quite simply devastated.

This would have been a profoundly disturbing development under any circumstances; from the standpoint of someone in my job, it had an especially unpleasant angle. Doing horrible work of the kind I was doing, I needed stability in my home life and support at work. Now, suddenly, I had neither. My wife had left me, and I had just lost my

Commander and most important mentor, Dick Monk, who had gone to the Devon and Cornwall Constabulary. I was adrift, and I'm still not sure how much it showed.

But life went on, as it had to. Eventually our home was sold. I bought myself a place in Pinner, a lovely, almost untouched 1930s detached house. Feeling slightly better about my material security, I then worked on my emotional stability the only way I knew how. I threw myself into my work.

11
Operation Spanner

Operation Spanner had already been running for two years before I joined the Obscene Publications Branch. The investigation into widespread and extreme sado-masochism had its beginnings in 1987, in Manchester, during a routine seizure of videos. Sergeant Ken Lee and his partner were given a tape by a man who, according to an informant, was a child pornographer. The man was a strange individual who lived in a room laid out to look like a child's bedroom, complete with a dummy of a small child sitting at the table. There were several child pornography videotapes hidden in the room.

The man wanted to make a deal. He produced a tape from a cupboard. 'Never mind me,' he said, tapping the tape box, 'you ought to have a look at this bunch of weirdos.'

He put the tape in his VCR and switched it on. The video showed one man slitting open another man's penis with a scalpel. It was a direct and brutal act of violence and the police officers were quite shaken. Before they left the man handed over another tape which he said contained more of the same, and he gave them the addresses of a few of the people involved. The investigation had begun. The first tape viewed by Ken Lee and his partner, long since officially labelled 'KL7', is now something of a milestone in the recent annals of British crime detection and legal argument.

Ken Lee and his partner made calls at the addresses the man had given them, and the resulting accumulation of tapes and testimonies formed the nucleus of the case. Later, they contacted the Metropolitan Police and asked members of the Obscene Publications Branch to check on spin-off addresses they had obtained as a result of their own further investigations. The calls in London and in the suburbs produced several more tapes and photographs.

A meeting was then called by the Manchester Police. They asked Met officers to attend, along with officers from Whitchurch in Shropshire and a few other places where inquiries had spread. Inspector Stuart Baker from Obscene Publications at the Yard attended with Sergeant Dick Langley and PC Lenny Yeoell. The purpose of the meeting was to work out who was going to oversee this far-flung investigation, and what kind of co-operational strategy could be organised. Eventually it was agreed that the Metropolitan Police should lead the whole investigation. It was also agreed at the meeting that Ken Lee and his partner would work for a while in our office at the Yard, familiarising our officers with what they had learned about the case so far.

My predecessor but one, Ian Donaldson, was put in charge of the case. Straight away he went to the office of the Director of Public Prosecutions (DPP) and explained the daunting levels of work that were necessary to mount such an investigation. It was essential, Donaldson said, to have some

accessible authority to oversee the inquiries and to advise
officers on the kind of evidence they needed in order to build
a case. The DPP appointed a senior counsel to handle the
work, and from that point forward the office of the DPP co-
ordinated the whole inquiry, which was now officially called
Operation Spanner. (An internal rumour claimed the job was
called 'Spanner' because when you looked at the evidence,
your nuts tightened.)

Stuart Baker supervised the investigation with a squad of
four – Lennie Yeoell, Dick Langley and the two men from
Manchester. From the start the investigation was sheer slog.
Police made arrests at numerous locations on the basis of
faces and felonies on the tapes; further arrests were based on
testimonies from people already arrested. Gradually the links
between individual offenders became clearer, although it
would have been easy to believe the S&M ring had no limits.
The police, it seemed, could have gone on extending their
inquiries indefinitely to friends of friends.

Stuart Baker, Lennie Yeoell and Dick Langley sustained a
vigorous programme of raids at dozens of addresses up and
down the country. As more people were raided the amount of
seized material grew to mountainous proportions. The list of
names and addresses made a formidable database. Slowly, the
true proportions and implications of the case became clear.
What the investigators saw, reviewing the material, was a
well-chronicled history of depravity stretching back over a
number of years. The tapes showed, moreover, that in the
midst of many hours of recreational sadism and suffering, a
training programme had been in progress. Boys and young
men of sixteen, seventeen and eighteen were introduced to
sado-masochism in stages; the violence could be seen getting
gradually more severe until, by the time the men were into

their mid-twenties, they were engaging in very hard S&M. The degree of violence in the films could be graded by date, and it culminated in scenes of almost unbelievable torture and suffering.

A priority in building the case had been to identify the individuals on the original tape KL7 – the man cutting and the man being cut. In other areas the team had been making good progress, but in the KL7 episode, to quote Stuart Baker, 'We didn't know who owned the dick, or who was cutting it.'

What they did know was that the man cutting the penis had a very distinctive forefinger. It was deformed, probably as the result of an old fracture, and in addition all his fingers were unusually long. The tape was shown to police in various parts of the country, and each time it was shown, attention was drawn to the cutter's distinguishing finger. As clues went it was slender, but it was the only one the team had to work on and they put it forward at every opportunity.

A week after visiting Southampton to check on an address and to show KL7 to the local police, Stuart Baker had a call from the DS at Southampton.

'Did you see *Panorama* last night?' the DS asked.

Stuart said he hadn't.

'Well, your man was on it.'

'What man?'

'The one with the deformed finger.'

The programme had carried a feature about gay men and gay weddings, and the DS had spotted the telltale finger when a close-up of a groom's hand was shown putting on a wedding ring.

So Stuart Baker, Lennie Yeoell and Dick Langley went hot-foot to Shepherd's Bush and the offices of *Panorama*. They spoke to a receptionist, who was extremely helpful. She

showed them into a booth and arranged for the previous
evening's programme to be screened for them. They watched
intently and sure enough, there was their man. They saw his
face, they saw the deformed finger as he handled the ring, and
they even saw his name in the credits. It was a name that connected with an address already in their possession.

Then the programme director came into the booth. He
wanted to know what the officers were up to. Stuart told him.
The director said he wanted them to leave. They did as he
wished. There was no need to linger, since they now had
what they had come for.

The two men on tape KL7, Lucas and Atkinson, were eventually arrested and questioned. Under questioning Atkinson
broke down and revealed that since early boyhood he had
only been able to experience sexual pleasure and orgasm
when severe pain was inflicted upon him. In one of the tapes
he is shown having a tube with spikes on the inside placed
over his penis; he had in fact made the device himself, to
masturbate with. It transpired that as a young boy, Atkinson
had been raped numerous times, extremely violently, by staff
at the children's home where he was raised.

Now that so many police were involved in so many places,
new tapes were appearing daily, all of them gory and brutal
and featuring men who were by now familiar to the investigators. In several instances the violence shown in the tapes
amounted to grievous bodily harm, which caused several
police officers and psychologists to worry that the tapes were
edited versions of 'snuff movies' – films alleged to show genuine acts of violent murder. Most people who saw the tapes
were convinced, in any case, that such reckless and escalating
violence, left unchecked, was bound to lead to someone
getting killed. The police already knew that devotees of S&M

sometimes get more than they bargained for. Two male masochists, members of the same gay sports club in London, died in separate incidents in 1988 and 1989; one, a clerk, asked to be beaten up by men on Hampstead Heath and forgot to tell them when to stop. The other, a senior Bank of England official, was found floating in an East Anglian river. He had been choked to death.

When I took charge of the Dirty Squad the case was nearly ready for court, and over a period I acquainted myself with the details. The preparation of the case had been formidably arduous. The huge pile of videotapes at the office had to be viewed in their entirety, then a written commentary had to be prepared for each one. Whenever a prosecutable act was performed on the screen, the relevant number on the tape-counter was written down and followed by a description of the act and a note of who performed it on whom. All of this took an incredibly long time.

The ringleaders had all been identified and charged and the voluminous case papers covered several shelves. I spent many hours acquainting myself with the case, but the undoubted hero on the organisational side was Lenny Yeoell, who worked almost full-time on Spanner and displayed amazing dedication and attention to detail.

Details leaked back from the interviews and often the information was depressingly familiar, especially to the personnel of Obscene Publications. Colin Lasky, for instance, one of the nucleus of regulars on the Spanner tapes, was a former schoolteacher with a previous conviction for buggery on a boy, for which he had been sentenced to five years' imprisonment. He was a paedophile and in this case he was being charged, among much else, with possession of indecent photographs of a child.

Then there was Cadman, the odd man out. He was an ice-cream vendor, the humblest calling in a cast list that included a missile designer, a lawyer and a civil servant. Because of the nature of his job, Cadman had contact with children, and he could beguile them and lead them away whenever he wanted. His exclusive speciality was boys around the ages of eleven and twelve. That hideous talent had been his entrée to the S&M circle.

Kelly, another of those interviewed, was brought into the circle when he was young, and he had been systematically debauched by the group. Cadman started the ball rolling by playing 'master-slave' bondage games with the youth, then Lasky was introduced to Kelly, and Lasky became Kelly's master. As time went on, Kelly became a master in his own right – at the age of seventeen.

Kelly had been to a house known as Parkside in Whitchurch, where two of the other men who were questioned, Wilkinson and Grindley, held parties. They had a torture chamber where guests and hosts dressed as Nazi officers, among other things, and indulged in sado-masochistic orgies. These were generally videotaped, and anyone attending the parties could have a copy for the price of a blank tape. Most of the eventual defendants had been to these parties.

Lofthouse, a married man, lived in Norfolk at the time he was identified on tape. Under questioning he told our officers that he first met another of the Spanner regulars, a lawyer called Christopher Zimmerli from Hampstead, while they were both loitering with intent in a public lavatory. Zimmerli was a Swiss national who worked for an international corporation. His job gave him limited diplomatic immunity, but we were still able to arrest and charge him.

In the opinion of several police officers, Roland Jaggard, a missile designer for British Aerospace, was probably the most dangerous man within the group. He seemed to be driven by powerful sadistic impulses, and had a fascination with blood. The cutting of Atkinson's penis on tape KL7 was done at Jaggard's suggestion, and he operated the camera. There was conjecture among police officers about what might have happened on that occasion if Jaggard had been left alone with Atkinson; part of the reason for so much speculation was the fact that in Jaggard's house the police had found dozens of photographs of penile mutilations, all of them extreme and grotesque.

A time came when we had to draw the line and assemble our material into a finished case. By the time we stopped investigating new names we had interviewed eighty-two potential defendants, a number of whom could have put us in touch with even more. We then had to decide who were the main offenders, the nucleus of the circle. In the end sixteen men were charged.

In December 1990, three years after inquiries began, the defendants stood in the dock at the Central Criminal Court in London. They included a forester, a care assistant for the mentally disabled, two restaurateurs (one of them a lay preacher), a former fire officer, a computer operator, a retired finance officer, an antiques restorer, a tattooist, a porter and a former pig-breeder. Their average age was fifty. They were described in the schedule of indictments as men who, for many years, had gathered together to commit acts of violence against each other and against other persons who were induced to join them. It was added that the acts of violence occurred in many places in England and Wales, as far apart, for example, as Whitchurch in Shropshire,

Pontypridd in Wales, Stechford in Birmingham, Bolton in Lancashire, Evesham in Worcester, Cambridge, and the London area.

At the beginning of the trial, Judge Rant wanted to see all the video evidence before he listened to counsel. However, when the screening reached the moment of the penis being slit in KL7, the judge ordered the VCR to be turned off. He then hurried from the courtroom looking decidedly ill. When he came back he apologised to the defence.

'I am only human,' he added, 'but it won't affect my decision in law.'

The Spanner inquiry had found no deaths. We did uncover drug abuse; we found production, possession and distribution of child pornography, and an instance of a teenage minor being corrupted by two of the defendants. Most of the evidence, taken from the videotapes, centred on the hideous games the men played. There were savage beatings, the finance officer being especially active in that department. An unidentified participant was branded with a hot wire to the sound of a Gregorian chant. Genital torture was practised – for example, sandpaper was rubbed on the head of the missile engineer's penis; the computer operator nailed a co-defendant's penis to a board; a screaming man had a wire and then a finger pushed down his urethra, while another had his scrotum pinned to a plank. The fire officer carved his initials on the lawyer's buttocks with a Stanley knife and the forester did much the same to a man identified as James Phippen. In some cases both the torturer and his victim were charged with the same offence; thus the missile engineer was accused of torturing the fire officer's genitals, and the fire officer was accused of aiding and abetting him. In a taped session described by the prosecution as the worst the investigators had encountered in the entire investigation, Lucas was seen using a scalpel to cut the penis and scrotum of a man called Johnny Atkinson, causing blood to flow freely. A few of the charges related to keeping a disorderly house, which meant providing the premises where activities took place; there was also a charge of bestiality against the farmer, Donald Anderson. The bulk of the charges, however, related to assault or bodily harm, since the prosecution lawyers decided these were the most appropriate charges in the circumstances.

Because the activities at the heart of the case were recorded on videotape, the only defence was to claim that they were not criminal acts. If everyone consented, how could anyone be guilty? Before the trial began, defence counsel put that proposition to Judge Rant. He rejected it. In his written ruling he said,

> I must, of course, have regard to the important matter of individual liberty. Liberty, however, is not to be confused with licence. Society expects its members to restrain themselves from indulging in undesirable activities, and in my judgement the exercise of what can only be termed cruel practices (as opposed to playfulness) can only be categorised as undesirable.

Faced with Judge Rant's decision, the defence advised their clients to plead guilty, which they did. No jury trial took place. Instead the prosecution stated its case, being careful to remind the court that it is already established in law that consent by the victim is no defence to an assault which occasions actual bodily harm.

The defence then made pleas in mitigation. Anne Worrall

QC, appearing for Lasky, spoke of acts which, however distasteful to those who viewed the videos, were enjoyable to those taking part. Judge Rant replied that he found it hard to accept that 'any sensible, intelligent, mature man' would feel he should indulge in such conduct. 'If something is plainly unacceptable, then surely, that is a matter that I am entitled to take into account, am I not?'

Worrall suggested that there might be things 'disgusting to those of us who have a normal sexual outlook' which society might condone when they were done in private. Criminal law, she said, was not concerned with moral standards.

'It's not a question of morals,' the judge retorted. 'It is a question of sheer common sense. How can any intelligent, sensible man think that it is acceptable to slit open another man's scrotum with a scalpel?'

In passing sentence, Judge Rant reinforced remarks he had made earlier. 'This is not a witch-hunt against homosexuals. The unlawful conduct before the court would result equally in the prosecution of heterosexuals or bisexuals . . . Nor is it a campaign to curtail the private sexual activities of citizens of this country.' The judge added that 'much has been said about individual liberties and people's rights to do what they want with their own bodies. The courts must draw the line between what is acceptable in a civilised society and what is not. In this case, the practices clearly lie on the wrong side of that line.'

The forester and the care worker were each sent to prison for three and a half years. The computer operator and the ice-cream vendor – the two involved with the teenager – were each given four and a half years. The missile engineer and the lay preacher were sentenced to three years; the finance officer, thirty-three months; the pig breeder, a year. Of the seven remaining, four were given suspended sentences, one was fined, one put on probation and one given a conditional discharge.

Immediately after the trial the homosexual action group Outrage staged a public protest outside Scotland Yard, and it was directed solely against me. Not for the first time, I was accused of carrying out an anti-homosexual campaign, even though it had been made clear that the thrust of Operation Spanner was against violence, not sexuality, and that I was well aware, as were all my officers, that violent criminal behaviour is not the prerogative of any particular sexual group. Leaflets carrying my picture under the heading UNWANTED were distributed to passers-by while fifty protesters waving placards and chanting 'Hames out! Hames out!' had to be kept back behind a barrier. The leaflet accused me of shattering lives, oppressing communities and causing innocent deaths. It said I was behind a new legal precedent that criminalised ordinary sexual behaviour, and that I had targeted people innocent of any crime other than offending the sensibilities of a bigoted minority.

I never expected anybody to love me for the job I did, but I felt this was going a bit far. My team at the Dirty Squad thought the incident was hilarious and they jokingly threatened to show solidarity with the mob outside.

Later that day, in the company of other speakers, I was scheduled to address a national conference of the Women's Institute. As I got up and began to speak, a bunch of skinheads with moustaches suddenly stood up at the back of the crowded hall and began shouting, blowing whistles and using football rattles to drown me out.

The audience, who were mostly delegates of the WI from regions throughout Britain, were terrified at the uproar. The chairwoman sidled up to me while the racket was going on and asked me what she should do.

'There's only one thing you can do,' I told her. 'Call the police.'

Afterwards, when the police had restored order and the protesters were gathered in a huddle outside the hall, I went across and had a word. I asked what was the matter with them, interrupting a meeting like that and upsetting all those women.

They mumbled and shuffled their feet.

'We don't agree with what you done,' one of them said. 'Prosecuting innocent men. It wasn't like they done anything wrong, was it? It was in private and they was consenting.'

I waited till the mutters of 'Yeah, right, right,' fizzled out, then I asked if any of them knew even a few of the details of the things that went on between these men they had decided to defend so noisily. Nobody replied. One or two shook their heads, a couple of them shrugged.

I told them a little of what had gone on. Their bland expressions changed. They looked at one another.

'Jesus Christ!' their spokesman stared at me. 'You kidding, or what?'

'I promise you, I'm not kidding.'

'Aw, bloody hell, that's horrible . . .'

Later, six of the convicted men appealed. It took over a year for the case to reach the appeal court, which upheld the convictions. In delivering judgement the Lord Chief Justice, Lord Lane, pointed out that 'the satisfying of the sado-masochistic libido does not come within the category of good reason'.

A final appeal was made to the House of Lords. After lengthy deliberation by five of the law lords, the convictions were again upheld. In summing up his reasons for dismissing the appeals, Lord Templeman said, 'Society is entitled and bound to protect itself against a cult of violence. Pleasure derived from the infliction of pain is an evil thing. Cruelty is uncivilised.'

12
Investigating Ritual Abuse

Since the 1980s, reports had been reaching the police of people allegedly witnessing or having been involved in extreme sexual and physical abuse during rituals based on Satanism and black magic. There was talk of human sacrifice, torture, the forceful administration of drugs, the eating of human flesh and faeces, the drinking of blood and urine. Some allegedly verbatim witness statements and victim accounts began to appear, and these were held up by certain factions as proof of the widespread practice of ritual satanic abuse.

The presence of demonology at the core of specialised crime is not new. Satan has been an excuse for bad behaviour since records began – 'the Devil made me do it'. As shallow reasoning goes, the notion of the Dark One overwhelming a human spirit is simple and convenient, and it doesn't trouble the intellect with the idea that there might be territory intermediate to good and evil.

For much of my time at the Yard I was under pressure from different lobby groups to fall in with their particular viewpoints on ritual abuse. There were people telling me they had evidence of ritual sacrifice and hellish torture; they quoted accounts of murder and sexual abuse of the most extreme kind. Numerous conferences on the subject of widespread satanic practices were being addressed by 'experts'. There were worldwide reports that the phenomenon of ritual abuse was being disclosed to law enforcement officers and to psychiatrists – to everyone, in fact, concerned with the care of the vulnerable. It would have been too easy to get drawn into this maelstrom and align myself and my department with people who were driven to the conclusion that these nightmare scenarios were true. I resisted.

On the other hand, we were not ready to dismiss the subject out of hand. We had to stay objective and be prepared to listen to people in distress. I spent hours with psychiatrists and therapists who described the information in their possession. I even met some of the unfortunate people who were in unthinkable mental anguish and I listened to their nightmarish stories. On one occasion I went to a hotel in Croydon with the now eminent interviewer, Martin Bashir. There we kept an appointment with a woman and we both tried hard, without success, to make sense of the garbled story of Satanic barbarity she tried to tell us.

In another case, I invited officers from a northern force to London, where they took a lengthy statement from a woman who alleged that on many occasions she had been raped in devil-worship rituals, and had more than once been impregnated as a result. The foetuses, she claimed, had been aborted and killed. She also said that murders of adults had been committed in her presence. This case came to nothing, but it was necessary to investigate the complaint properly, for the woman was clearly in extreme distress. Whatever the element of fantasy in her statement to the officers, it was hard to escape the conviction that some real horror lay underneath the embroidery.

In 1990 reports were reaching us of the difficulties some police officers were facing when they tried to investigate cases of alleged ritual abuse. There were serious management problems centring around the extremes of officers' reactions to such cases. One half of the office would get immersed in the subject and believe everything they were told; the other half would dismiss the allegations as nonsense. Arguments between the two sides only hardened the polarisation of opinion. I don't exaggerate when I say that the tensions of the 'belief, non-belief' issue, combined with the strains of interviewing the victims and listening to their stories, often led to sickness and severely low morale.

I managed to get the Commissioner's authority to examine the phenomenon of ritual abuse with a view to issuing guidelines to investigators. I appointed Sergeant Keith Driver and two assistants to speak to police forces around the country, and to look at a range of cases and record the experiences of the officers who dealt with them.

Typical of the cases in Keith Driver's report was the story of Tessa, a fifteen-year-old ward of court with a low mental age who ran away with another girl from the children's home where they had been living. In a nearby town they called at a number of addresses, looking for people they had met at the home. The people who answered the doors were generally hostile to the girls, but at one or two places strangers invited them to come in. They finally accepted the invitation of a man who seemed kind and friendly. He gave them coffee and sandwiches, then made sexual advances towards them. He eventually performed oral sex on both girls.

Later, the man took Tessa to a flat where a young mother lived with her three children. Two other teenagers, a girl and a boy, also lived there. The girl, who was the sister of the young mother, told Tessa the children were on the 'at risk' register because their mother could not look after them. Tessa gathered that the children were also the subject of a custody battle between the separated parents.

On Tessa's second evening at the flat they all took part in a spirit-communication session with a ouija board, after which the children's mother tried to hypnotise Tessa, but failed. The mother then told Tessa to take off all her clothes, which she did. A lighted candle was placed against her pubic hair, singeing it.

Tessa was hidden in the flat for several days, sleeping in a wardrobe to avoid being found by the woman's mother, who regularly visited the flat to check on her grandchildren. Tessa was too frightened to leave, because the others had threatened her and told her a policeman was watching the flat from across the road.

During Tessa's stay at the flat she was subjected to a number of severe beatings by the young mother and the two teenagers. In the course of the beatings they attacked her with a hammer, a shoe and an electric carving knife. Tessa did not know of any reason for the attacks, although there was a dispute over money allegedly missing from the gas meter. There was no evidence to suggest that the beatings were part of any occult or ritual activity. Tessa mentioned that she and her abusers had smoked a small amount of cannabis, but there was no suggestion that any of them were ever seriously under the influence of drugs.

Tessa's case is one of a number used by various factions to substantiate claims for the existence of ritual abuse. In one of the summary lists, the case is described as the 'torture of a fifteen-year-old-girl during ouija board sessions'. In a presentation to senior police officers by an alleged expert, it was elevated to 'a case of child torture at a ritual conducted by a black magic occultist'.

The story of Tessa also appeared in a list of six others that was circulated among professionals and non professionals. It was claimed that the list reflected investigations that had resulted in convictions, and that the case details were based on testimony which gave clear evidence of ritual activity. In this particular list, Tessa's story is described as 'a case of a fifteen-year-old girl being subjected to grievous bodily harm during satanic rituals'. The list goes on to describe how a teenaged boy was ordered to cut and carve the girl during the rituals, which also involved the placing of lighted candles on or around the victim's vagina. It suggests that, because the people were convicted of assault, the jury accepted the explicit details of the satanic rituals.

In another case featured in the report, a sixteen-year-old girl, Gloria, told police that she had been raped and indecently assaulted by the man who lived with her mother. Gloria was in care at the time she made the allegation. She was the second of four children, and her mother's partner was the latest of a number of men the mother had lived with after separating from her husband. The eldest daughter had gone into care earlier than Gloria, following a suspicion that she had been sexually abused by the first of the mother's boyfriends. The mother had also claimed that she herself had been sexually abused as a child by her father.

Gloria claimed that her mother's boyfriend had an interest

in the supernatural and that he had drawn a pentagram, in chalk, on the living-room floor. She said that she and her brother were made to stand inside the pentagram while the boyfriend chanted and spoke of ghosts, of other worlds and of strange missions. She said he put plastic gnomes on the tips of the pentagram and drew parallel lines on the floor, saying that the spirit world and the living world were in parallel. At other times he burned toys, Gloria said, because he claimed they were possessed by evil spirits.

Gloria claimed that this man regularly had sexual intercourse with her, and often performed oral sex on her. Furthermore, she was made to lie on the pentagram and insert the handle of a hairbrush into her vagina, with the boyfriend and her mother looking on. Gloria further alleged the boyfriend had taken her to a special place in Epping Forest, which was never identified, where he raped her.

The mother and her boyfriend were arrested and the police searched their home. They found a number of books on the supernatural, two gnomes, three 'mystical' pendants, a decorative sword and notebooks containing supernatural – though not at all sinister – stories, written by various members of the family.

The mother and her boyfriend denied Gloria's allegations. The boyfriend admitted that he drew the pentagram, but he insisted it was at the request of Gloria who was, he claimed, deeply interested in the supernatural. Gloria's brother, also in care, provided some corroboration by confirming that he and his sister were made to stand in the pentagram; he said it was done in order to determine whether they were evil. His mother's boyfriend, the boy said, talked to them of other worlds and of voodoo. There was never any suggestion that the brother had been sexually abused.

The officers investigating the case considered the evidence to be weak. There was no corroboration of the allegation of sexual abuse. Gloria had begun to run away from home at the time she alleged the offences happened, and although a medical examination showed that she was not a virgin, she had a number of adult friends with whom she was thought to be sexually active.

The mother and her partner were charged, but the case was eventually dropped after numerous delays caused by the boyfriend suffering recurrent bouts of illness. Gloria appeared to lose her resolve and finally withdrew her allegation.

A third illustrative case from Keith Driver's report concerns a woman called Alison and her sister Cora, both active members of the Salvation Army who had been raised by a devout Salvationist father. A short time after marrying a man called Peter, Alison became disenchanted with her faith. Cora and her husband Donald, the parents of three girls and one boy, also began to lose interest in the Salvation Army – this started a few weeks after the newly-wed Alison and Peter came to live with them.

Peter and Alison developed an interest in witchcraft and black magic. So did Cora, apparently coincidentally. Donald, Cora's husband, did not share their interest. While Donald was away working, Peter, Alison and Cora began to indulge in rituals and perform small ceremonies connected with devil worship.

Some time later Peter and Alison moved into council accommodation of their own, but the rituals and ceremonies between the three of them continued. They obtained black ceremonial clothing and bought the trappings for a Satanist altar, which included various black cloths embroidered with symbols, a goblet, a dagger, candles, candlesticks, candle-holders, a witch's wand and cap, and a black mirror. The altar was usually set up in the dining room at Cora's house.

Cora's children were present at some of the ceremonies, including the initiation of their aunt Alison before the satanic altar, which consisted of her swearing an oath of allegiance to the devil, sealed with blood from her pricked thumb. At first the children were light-hearted about the ceremonies, but eventually their interest in the occult became more serious and they began taking an active part in the rituals. Following one ceremony, Peter took on the role of Lucifer while his sister-in-law adopted the personality of a black witch. During this time Peter and Alison bought some of the adornments for an altar and created one at their own house, although it was not as elaborate as the one at Cora's place.

Peter and Alison eventually had a child of their own, a son, and in due course they found themselves a babysitter. She was Betty, a sexually active fifteen-year-old with an extremely troubled background. Betty was attracted by Peter and Alison's interest in black magic; before long Peter had recruited her and she was primed to become an initiate. At the ceremony Peter recited satanic prayers and dripped hot wax on Betty's naked breasts and stomach, making the shape of an inverted cross, which is the symbol of the Antichrist. Betty then had to swear an oath of complete allegiance to the devil in his incarnate form – none other than Peter.

Following the initiation Betty had to submit to a number of ritual acts, including the 'five-fold kiss', where Peter kissed her on the forehead, mouth, each breast, and pubis. He also made the sign of the inverted cross on her chest with a dagger, without injuring her, and inserted newly extinguished candles and the blade of a dagger into her vagina.

Soon there were frequent black masses at both houses,

where sexual intercourse formed a regular part of the ceremony. Peter told Betty she should submit to him as often as he
demanded, because it would give her 'the power of Celeste'.
Alison played a central part in all these activities, including
lesbian sexual acts and buggery, which Peter described as 'the
passing of the power of Isis'. Sexual acts soon formed the
core of all the rituals.

On one occasion, near the end of Betty's involvement, Peter
heated the blade of the ceremonial dagger in a candle flame
and placed it against the top of her leg, while Alison held her
hand. Peter described the consequent burn as 'the mark of the
devil's children'. The wound did not heal properly for a long
time and left a permanent scar.

Soon after they met Betty Peter had told her to recruit some
of her friends into their black magic circle. One of these, a
thirteen-year-old girl, at first refused to join, but changed her
mind after Peter threatened that something evil would
happen to her parents. All the new initiates were similarly
threatened. The thirteen-year-old was initiated in much the
same way as Betty, and was also indecently assaulted, albeit to
a lesser extent. She was also given gifts of jewellery and make
up. In a ritual similar to the one where Betty was burned,
Peter placed a heated pendant against the top of the girl's leg,
causing her to cry out in pain. The injury in this case was not
severe and it healed quickly.

The daughters of Donald and Cora were sexually assaulted
during some of the ceremonies. The assaults were always
instigated by Peter, but he was readily supported by Alison
and Cora, who remained present throughout. The action
usually took the form of Peter having sexual intercourse with
the eldest daughter and indecently assaulting the other
two. These three girls were being separately sexually abused,

outside the context of satanic worship, by both their father and mother.

Even the seven-month-old son of Peter and Alison had been used in some of the ceremonies, again at Peter's instigation. The boy was masturbated and fellated and involved in group sex with both parents and the fifteen-year-old girl.

One girl recruited by Betty was so shocked at what was going on that she told her parents. This eventually resulted in a police investigation. The other girls who were involved denied any knowledge and no corroborative evidence was found.

Betty then went into care, amid rumours of her involvement in black magic rituals. Her mother went to the social services and told them of her concern over the girl's involvement with Peter and Alison. Betty was examined by a child psychiatrist who initially dismissed her stories as childhood fantasy. Eventually it was realised that she may have been telling the truth. Because of the psychiatrist's fear of violating a professional confidence, Betty was persuaded to repeat her allegation to her social worker, so that the police could become involved.

In the meantime Peter and Alison had moved to another area and were believed to have already targeted a girl to replace Betty.

Following Betty's disclosures the other girls started to overcome their fears of Peter's death-threats and began coming forward with their stories. All the offenders were arrested. Their black magic trappings were seized, along with a quantity of books on the occult and numerous pornographic magazines. Various admissions were obtained and the accused were convicted of the offences they had disclosed.

Following the arrests in this case, the police believed the

offenders might try to defend their behaviour by claiming to be under the sway of a recognised system of belief. The officers involved carried out research, aided by academics and clerics, in an effort to establish whether the ceremonies conducted by Peter were indeed part of some recognised occult religion. They also read the seized literature and many other publications referred to in them. In the end, no particular religious belief could be found to fit the activities indulged in by Peter and his cohorts.

In spite of their extensive research the police believed, without a trace of doubt, that Peter had used his knowledge of witchcraft to lure young girls and persuade them to indulge in sexual practices for his own gratification. This belief was reinforced by Peter's sexual abuse of children outside of any ritual or occult context. Records showed that he had been convicted of indecent assault on a three-year-old girl for whom he was babysitting, and he had also indecently assaulted a thirteen-year-old girl to whom he was distantly related. He and Alison were excluded from a naturist club because of Peter's alleged 'unhealthy' interest in the young girls there.

Keith Driver's report contained details of a further thirty-seven cases, many of them involving the ritualised abuse of children. In Keith's summing-up on the research project, he said that no evidence was found in any of the cases to support the more extreme allegations, such as human sacrifice, torture, or the eating of human flesh and drinking of blood. He added that it would be impossible to prove that these acts have never taken place in the context of an occult ritual. But even allowing for the existence of that kind of behaviour, there was nothing within the existing bodies of evidence to suggest that it would be anything other than a rare occurrence.

It was also true that no evidence was found to support other extreme allegations that were made, including the eating of faeces and drinking of urine. These particular acts are recognisable features of the sexual behaviour of some individuals and groups; they would not of themselves indicate ritual abuse.

As for suggestions that there is a widespread conspiracy of people involved in the ritual abuse either of children or adults, Keith's research again came up with no evidence. However, he did find a lack of cohesion in the way that intelligence about people who are considered a risk to children was collated and distributed. He felt that the system would benefit from an examination of existing procedures and the development of a co-ordinated intelligence strategy.

The report found that the most seriously complicating factor in any investigation of this kind was a misplaced belief in the widespread existence of ritual or satanic abuse. The misconception was founded, to a large extent, on the uncorroborated testimony of alleged victims, supported by unsubstantiated theories, and reinforced in many cases by a Christian fundamentalist belief in a satanic conspiracy. None of the detailed arguments put forward has ever been confirmed by authoritative research. They would appear to be an amalgamation – and often exaggeration – of four factors: one, the effects on victims who have been genuinely abused; two, the methods used, mainly by paedophiles, to entrap and abuse children; three, the practices indulged in by sado-masochists; and four, the activities of people who have taken up, or have an interest in, alternative systems of belief.

In the light of so much misinformation, the report concluded that it was vitally important for investigators to hold on to their objectivity. People claiming to be knowledgeable on the subject of ritual abuse had to be treated with caution. They and their theories must not be accepted at face value. Their involvement, in whatever form it took, had to be closely monitored at all times.

In my own experience, the only limits to the abuse that human beings will wreak on each other are the extremes of fantasy that exist in the minds of the abusers. There is no *evidence* that there is a worldwide, or even a large-scale network of 'satanic abusers', but it would be wrong to dismiss all allegations of ritual abuse as fantasy. It would be dangerous, too, because things may be nowhere near as crazy or far-fetched as they sound. A young child, for example, may tell about being abused by a clown; abusers do sometimes dress up, both as part of their fantasy and to disorientate the victim.

It is counter-productive to fall into the trap of either believing or disbelieving the allegations of 'victims'. Law enforcement officers *must listen*. They have to retain objectivity and examine each piece of information patiently, working towards a conclusion rather than jumping to one. An investigator always has to remember that at the heart of an allegation there may be acts that did take place, but they may be distorted or rendered unbelievable by misinformation. Many genuine victims will exaggerate their claims, often because of mental illness as a result of abuse, or an over-intense desire to impress and convince the investigator.

A sad reality of ritual-abuse cases is that where 'victims' make confused, sometimes contradictory and bizarre allegations, it is unlikely the case will reach a criminal court, even if the officers can find enough evidence to support a case of abuse. Why? Because the defence would have a field day with the prosecution case. They would pile ridicule on mockery as they impugned the plaintiff's sanity without even having to argue the case. It is sadly true that if a victim starts to talk about ritual abuse, and there is mention of daggers and amulets and the other trappings of witchcraft, then the investigator can't help but see any hope of a case dwindle to dust.

If anyone doubts there are people who methodically plan the most ghastly crimes – ritualised or otherwise – against children, they should acquaint themselves with the case of a man who was arrested in Europe with a large suitcase with holes in it which was designed to carry a very young child. The interception of messages between the man and his accomplices had already led the police to his apartment, where they found a gun. The man's plan, mercifully discovered before he could carry it out, was to put a small living child into a glass tank of water. He would then pour piranha fish into the tank and film the result.

13
Caring for the Team

In January 1991 we made a seizure of child pornography which was truly chilling. Two London Underground train drivers, Richard Mercer and David Barry, were stopped in the green Customs channel at Gatwick Airport. They had arrived on a flight from Amsterdam and although they had travelled together, and Mercer had paid their fares, they went through Customs some distance apart. Both men were questioned and searched. Mercer had nine video cassette spools hidden in the lining of his jacket and Barry had nine video cassette housings minus their spools. The spools were fitted to the casings and the tapes were screened. All nine films depicted pornographic action involving young children.

The two men had visited a notorious Amsterdam video outlet, the *City Shop*, owned and run by a Dutch national, Outse Devos. He would allow customers to watch child porn videos, pick out the ones they wanted to buy, then tell them to come back in three hours, by which time he would have copies of the selected tapes ready. Devos also offered an exclusive advisory service for customers who wanted to get the tapes safely through Customs. He or his assistants would demonstrate how to make the tape into two separate units; alternatively, the tapes could be wound back-to-front on the spools so that if they were played by Customs, they would show as blanks.

The method of evasion adopted by Mercer and Barry failed dismally and when Customs saw what was on the tapes they contacted us at once. Dave Flanagan and Graham Passingham were assigned to the operation and brought the tapes back to the office. Most of the stuff was the sort of distressing material we saw all the time, but one film was of a kind we had not encountered before. It showed a young boy of about eight or nine being bound, gagged, beaten and buggered by an adult male. Quite apart from the appalling cruelty committed on the boy, there was an atmosphere of menace in the film that made us suspect the victim's life was in danger. In another segment of the same tape, there were scenes of a girl of about ten having needles thrust through her genitals.

It seemed to us that the sadistic scenarios common to many of the adult films we regularly seized were now being mirrored by child pornographers. We could not help speculating: did this film show an emerging trend already familiar in adult porn? Were the jaded child-porn customers demanding harder and more bizarre material?

Several things needed to be done. First, priority had to be given to finding the victims. Then we had to uncover the abusers, find out how they had distributed this stuff, and try to shut down the supply.

Customs searched a number of addresses in East London,

Essex and Cornwall. One of the two Underground drivers, Barry, owned a bus, which our officers searched. They found nothing in it, but nevertheless it was decided that the operation should be called 'Routemaster'.

Eventually, fifty pornographic videocassettes were found in a car parked at Wickford railway station in Essex. Both men were charged by UK Customs with importation of illegal material. They were subsequently dealt with at Croydon Crown Court and sentenced to terms of imprisonment.

In the meantime we contacted Interpol and the Dutch authorities and told them about the disturbing child pornography that had come into our possession. We then transferred the video film on to U-matic format and analysed the contents frame by frame. We saw that the boy being abused wore a sweat band on his wrist with the word *Liverpool* printed on it. This meant that he was most probably British, although football souvenirs are sold all over Europe. We also saw that he had three distinctive moles on his face. We consulted both an eminent dermatologist and Richard Neave, the cranial reconstruction specialist at Manchester University. Both men told us that moles actually move around through time, and while it would have been possible to pinpoint them accurately on the boy's face at or near the time the film was made, the moles could have grown or shrunk in size since then, and they could now be in different positions on his face. We also looked for evidence of the age of the film but there was none, and the boy's haircut was not typical of any particular fashion period.

If we could have done it, we would have taken a still photograph of the boy from the taped footage and published it in the national press, with a caption saying we needed to identify him because we were concerned for his safety. Try as we might, we could not find a frame in the whole of the film which we could freeze and use to make an acceptable still picture. In every one his face showed either agony or distress.

We wrestled with the problem and came up with a partial answer, which was to have an artist make a sketch of the boy's face, which was then shown to millions of viewers of BBC's *Crimewatch* programme, transmitted on 11 April 1991. This was a bit awkward for me because it was a week or so after Jacqui had left me, and the piece on the mystery boy would be presented either by her or by Superintendent Dave Hatcher. Rather than get involved, I left it to my deputy, Bob McLachlan, to negotiate the appeal.

There was one interesting response from Great Yarmouth, where the local police and social services were acquainted with a boy who was a known victim of abuse. In spite of a very striking similarity, however, he was not our victim. The drawing was also distributed throughout the country in police gazettes and transmitted to Interpol. We did all we could by conventional means, but in the end the boy was identified in a most amazing way.

Detective Inspector Paul Fahey from Huddersfield was a member of their Force Drugs Squad. He had been a detective sergeant dealing with child protection and retained an interest in the subject. He was visiting the National Criminal Intelligence Service in London and popped into the office to see our operation. As he walked into the viewing room, Dave Flanagan was showing the Routemaster tape to a number other officers. Paul Fahey glanced at the screen. Then he looked harder.

'I recognise that man,' he told Dave, pointing to the abuser on the film – whose face, incidentally, was not shown. Dave recognised the distinctive genitalia. As the tape went on he said, 'I know the boy, too.'

The following unfolded. In 1984 a Swiss lorry driver, a paedophile called Beat Meier, had befriended an English lorry driver and was invited to the Englishman's home. Meier offered – very kindly, it was thought – to take his host's two young sons, Peter and Andrew, on holiday to Switzerland. The offer was accepted.

Once they were in Switzerland Meier and another man violently abused Peter and taped the proceedings. Amazingly, when the boy was brought back home he said nothing about his ordeal. After that, Meier was a frequent visitor at Peter's home.

A year or two later, a teacher noticed that Peter had started to play truant. When he was questioned about this he mentioned Meier's name; the teacher became more and more suspicious and encouraged the boy to talk about what had been happening to him. Finally the teacher became alarmed enough to call in the police.

Meier was eventually found living in a flat and the police arrested him for indecent assault. Paul Fahey had been an officer in that case. Meier pleaded guilty at Leeds Crown Court, was sentenced to eighteen months' imprisonment and recommended for deportation.

However, the true extent of the offending had still not been discovered. Peter had told no one about what happened to him in Switzerland. But now *we* knew. The hunt was on for Meier. Since the crimes against Peter had been committed in Switzerland, Meier would have to be dealt with by the authorities there.

I contacted Interpol with this new information, and we discovered where Meier was. He had been arrested by the police in Paris in February 1993, on suspicion of abuse against German children in Switzerland and a French boy in France. The French police had incarcerated him in Paris and kept him in custody for several months. They finally dealt with him at the Paris Criminal Court, fined him for a relatively minor matter and deported him on 3 June 1996. In Switzerland he was charged with assault against the German boys; in November 1997 the charges were found proved and he was ordered to be detained for an unlimited time.

As for the abuse committed against the English boy, Peter, the authorities took the view that the offences were time-barred because, at the end of the film, Meier was seen handing the boy money. They asserted that because of that, the time limit was five years under Swiss law!

While Meier was still being held in Paris, I went to Norway to a meeting of the Interpol working party and we discussed Meier in some detail. It transpired that the film featuring Peter had been distributed in France, Germany and Holland. The police agencies in those countries had been as anxious as we were to identify the boy. There had been a fair amount of duplication of effort, and that highlighted the need for a worldwide index at Interpol – a need which still exists – so that finds and identifications can be available to investigators on an international basis, and quickly. There is already an international database for stolen art and antiques, a fact which pinpoints the low priority given to children who have no money and no votes.

In the meantime, it is certain that countless copies of that video are still circulating around the world, being passed from hand to hand, under the counter, over the Internet, perpetuating the victim's agony down all that time since he had the childhood driven out of him. Prolonged and exhaustive efforts failed to identify the other man in the film. We never found out who the little girl was, either.

The *Oxford English Dictionary* tells us that pornography, in its original meaning, was a 'Description of the life, manners, etc., of prostitutes and their patrons'. In the influential book *Sex Offenders: An Analysis of Types*, P. H. Gebhard and his co-authors give an updated definition that is now widely accepted. They say that the word 'pornography' commonly implies 'material, predominantly sexually explicit, which is intended to arouse the viewer, and usually has that effect'.

But there can be other effects. The market for filmed pornography has increasingly demanded the depiction of extreme acts of perversion, the so-called paraphilias. The depiction of cruelty, some of it unbelievably extreme, is also in big demand among the aficionados of filmed pornography – and then, of course, there are the videos produced specifically for paedophiles, featuring the abuse and degradation of children. The effects of all this material, viewed day in and day out by people whose work it is to evaluate the content, can be seriously damaging.

Even before I arrived at the Dirty Squad my boss, Dick Monk, had been concerned about the possible long-term harm being done to the civilian staff, who had the job of viewing the bulk of the seized videotapes. I was quick to share Dick's concern. In particular, I worried about the combined effects of having to view harrowing material, hour upon hour, while being obliged to work under pressure because of the time limit imposed on case preparation.

People had their strategies for coping, of course, and some were more effective than others. Detective Constable Phil

Hills, a very quiet and easygoing sort of man, was asked one day to listen to an audio tape to see if he could identify the voices. The tape featured a man who was either pretending to be a teacher, or really was one. He was taunting a very young boy, building up the fright as he threatened the child with a caning. Finally he administered the punishment. The boy was obviously in terrible distress. Phil was sitting at his desk with the headphones on, making notes on a pad in front of him. Suddenly he stood up, pulled off the headphones, strode across the room and threw a crashing punch at a grey metal filing cabinet. He stepped back, flexed his hand, then without a word he went back to his desk and put on the headphones again. It was a good example of an officer off-loading tension, and many of them could do just that, but I was still concerned that there was enough residue from the accumulated shocks and horrors to do my staff harm, whether they were aware of it or not. Worrying would get me nowhere, though; I had to find a practical way of relieving stress that would work without drawing too heavily on our precious time.

I raised the matter at a meeting with Dr Graham Lucas, a Consultant Psychiatrist to the Health and Safety Executive and to Guy's Hospital. He suggested that it might benefit our staff if they learned a régime of psychological techniques for handling pressure – techniques which, once they were learned, could be used without the involvement of anyone else.

I went away and thought about that. The idea of a self-administered formula for relieving stress was bound to have appeal; people were often shy about sharing their difficulties, so a system that meant they tackled the problems themselves was bound to have the edge on conventional counselling. I enquired into ways we could give our staff that kind of opportunity as part of a personal development programme.

Eventually I learned about a course in something called Autogenics. It was being offered by the Positive Health Centre at Harley Street. Through joint work we did on cases of child sex abuse I had already met the Principal of the Centre, Dr Malcolm Carruthers, a consultant pathologist at the Maudsley Hospital, and his wife Vera Diamond, a psychotherapist. I called to make an appointment and went along to see them.

'Tell me about Autogenics,' I said.

It was a series of easy mental exercises, they explained, designed to switch off the body's stress-related 'fight-or-flight' reaction and switch on its rest, relaxation and recreation system. An important point was that the course didn't need any special clothing and it involved no difficult body contortions. A person could do the exercises sitting in a chair or even lying in bed. The word 'autogenic' means 'generated from within'; it also indicates that people who learn the system can turn to Autogenics, independently and at any time, to break the vicious circle of stress.

I needed to know a little more and Dr Carruthers was happy to tell me. Autogenics was a well tried and tested technique which had been practised and perfected over a period of fifty years. Recently the staff of the Centre for Autogenic Training, which was part of the Positive Health Centre, had been instructed in the latest, most streamlined version of Autogenics by the world's leading authority on the subject, Dr Wolfgang Luthe in Montreal. Now they had brought the refined technique to Britain.

A lot of people were already using Autogenics. Specialists at the centre were teaching the technique to international competitors in rifle and pistol shooting, and in rowing and canoeing. Airlines were beginning to use Autogenics to combat jet-lag in their personnel and the insomnia that affected many of them when they stayed in strange surroundings. Industrial groups used the technique to reduce stress in employees at all levels from the shop floor to the boardroom. More and more people were realising that Autogenics could produce the benefits of tranquillisers and sleeping tablets without any of the hazards. The more I heard, the more the technique appealed to me. I wasn't just thinking of Autogenics as a life-enhancing tool for our civilian staff; if it was as good as Dr Carruthers and his satisfied trainees said, then I wanted it for everybody in our squad.

First, I had to be convinced. Dr Carruthers knew that, and he was so confident I would find Autogenics to be everything he claimed that he offered to give me a complete course of training – ninety-minute sessions, once a week, for eight weeks. I jumped at it.

After three sessions I knew this was going to work. My levels of stress became easier to regulate and I could sense a growing control of my moods and my capacity to relax. One of the claims made for Autogenics is that it can be used to mobilise a person's creative ability by balancing the activities of the left and right sides of the brain, which gave added benefits in concentration and co-ordination. Well, I could believe that, too. As the course progressed I still felt like the man I had always been, but now I was much more in control of myself, and my general sense of well-being had soared.

Others in my training group were just as enthusiastic about the improvements in themselves. There was a psychiatrist, a stockmarket whizz-kid, a harassed mother of young children, a lawyer and six or seven other people, all of them very pleased with the changes Autogenics made. At the end of the course we were better equipped to tackle our stressful environments than we had been before. For my part, I felt distinctly evangelical about the course, and I was determined that every member of the Dirty Squad should have Autogenics training.

When the first group from the squad trooped down to Harley Street for their initiation, they were largely sceptical. As time passed, they made a few guarded admissions about the useful elements of the programme. Then the blue spots started appearing in the office. This was an important part of the course; a blue spot was used in Autogenic training as an aid to concentration. Staring at the little disc of blue helped focus positive mental energy, in much the same way as a mantra is believed to exert a strengthening effect on the mind, the emotions and the body. One person in the squad room stuck his blue spot to the telephone, another put it on the side of a pencil tidy on his desk. Scepticism, essential to any male-dominated environment, was still very much in evidence, and a lot of jokes were made about the sinister mind-altering effects of Autogenics, but the fact was that the squad had benefited, and they knew it.

In August 1991, still concerned that only the right people should be taken on to do the work of viewing videotapes, I asked an occupational psychologist, Dr John Jones-Lloyd of the Directorate of Performance Review and Management Services, to produce a report on what he felt to be the best selection procedures to use with applicants for civilian vacancies in the future. Dr Jones-Lloyd agreed to carry out the work and he was assisted by Mrs Tracey Goreing, also an occupational psychologist.

As a first step, it was decided that existing members of the civilian staff would be interviewed to get their views on the work they did. The two psychologists planned at first to speak to only three of the staff, but then they began to worry that members of this small group might feel inhibited about exposing their true feelings, so they finally interviewed all eight civilian members of the staff. The psychologists designed a questionnaire to probe the civilians' motivation in applying for the job, as well as inquiring how they dealt with the effects of the material they had to look at and what they felt about the contribution they were making.

Some of the findings of the interview sessions were predictable, others were enlightening. In general, the reasons given for joining the branch were trite and uncontroversial; for example, 'I had passed an EO board', 'I knew somebody who had worked here already'. But a few admitted they were motivated by curiosity, interest in the work of the branch, and the desire to work in a high-prestige job.

A few interviewees said they had been briefly shocked at the first sight of some of the pornographic material, but after two or three weeks the unanimous view was that the material became very much 'part of the job'. One man gave the analogy of nurses dealing with serious injuries; he said he saw no real difference between supposed trauma in that kind of work and trauma in his kind of work. The only difference, in his view, was the sexual component, which by now had no special impact on him or his colleagues.

In the main, the staff reported that their work had broadened their outlook on life. They were now a lot more aware, for example, of the suspect nature of some people's behaviour in public places like swimming pools and beaches.

Everyone realised that management outside the branch expected, to some degree, that they would have emotional problems; but not management within the branch, so they reported. This certainty was based largely on the fact that they knew they could tell their own management if they were unhappy about carrying on in the squad – they also knew that counselling or a transfer could be arranged.

Everyone who was interviewed was able to identify good points about the job. They liked working with police officers; they liked seeing a piece of work through from start to finish; they all liked the family environment of the branch, where everyone was open with each other and the atmosphere was always sociable. They viewed themselves as a closely knit team carrying out a very worthwhile job. They liked going on raids.

There were only a couple of bad things. The biggest pain for everyone was the overcrowded office and, particularly, the lack of space in the viewing room. The actual viewing of the obscene tapes was held to be unpleasant at times, but the staff qualified that by pointing out that the impact of the material was minimised by the fact that while they watched it, they were kept busy completing a form which related numbers on the tape counter to specific acts of indecency that were being depicted on the screen. None of them felt that viewing the material was a necessarily 'bad' aspect of the job; it was more of a modest downside.

None of the people interviewed reported any detectable behaviour changes in themselves; nor could their families or friends, so far as they knew.

Among the ones who had already attended the Autogenics evenings in Harley Street, the psychologists detected a degree of scepticism, but nevertheless, the interviewees said they saw no harm in attending. They found the techniques useful in managing their lives, even if they didn't feel it was really necessary for them. However, when they were asked if they thought their successors should undergo Autogenics training, they said yes, they should.

The ideal person to work in the branch, according to those interviewed, had to be male, mature in outlook, sociable, outgoing, not a new recruit to the Metropolitan Police (that is, someone who has already worked in several branches); he should have conspicuous common sense, be easy-going, be able to enjoy a laugh, and be one of the lads. He should be confident, extrovert, and have a capacity for hard work.

All of the interviewees were against women joining the branch. They freely admitted their view was chauvinistic and perhaps irrational. Some of them even identified women's physical limitations as disqualifying them from working in the branch – things like the difficulty of carrying heavy bags full of videotapes.

Dr Jones-Lloyd and his associate believed our civilian staff were open and frank with them, and came to the conclusion that these eight civilian staff were not suffering from severe or even moderate levels of stress. The amount of stress that was evident seemed to come from the volume of work they had to deal with and the deadlines they had to work to in order to be effective – that is, in order to get convictions. A major part of their stress could be attributed to their working conditions – the cramped office, and the tiny, claustrophobic viewing room.

Dr Jones-Lloyd also concluded that the Autogenics training should continue. While there was some level of denial that it was necessary, there was an agreement that it helped staff to relax, to 'switch off' if they were tensed or stressed.

In their summing up, Dr Jones-Lloyd and Mrs Goreing emphasised that the Autogenics training was 'a most sensible prophylactic measure initiated by the head of the branch', and indeed that it could usefully be extended 'to constitute a highly professional external counselling forum. It is in our view, an initiative that the MPO [Metropolitan Police Office], under its declaration of being a caring employer, should be happy to see continue and we suggest that the Director of Occupational Health should be made aware of this initiative.'

The report put final emphasis on the need to tackle the accommodation problem. This clearly was an open sore, the psychologists said, in an otherwise happy and efficient working environment. 'Given a dramatic improvement in accommodation,' they concluded, 'we feel that some large part of the frustration experienced by the staff would be alleviated.'

So we still had problems, and I could detect more on the horizon. But on balance, I reckoned, we were tackling our difficulties and making improvements, inch by relentless inch.

14
Electronic Porn

Late in 1991 a curious case was brought to our attention by the *South London Press*. The editor rang us and said they had a videotape which had been posted through their letterbox with a note saying, '*You better have a look at this. The woman is a teacher at Tripton School.*'

Lennie Yeoell brought back the tape to the office where he and his sergeant, Phil Jordan, ran it in the viewing room. It featured a woman having sexual intercourse with a dog – a Great Dane. There was no indication of the woman's identity, simply the information that she taught at Tripton School.

The tape was shown to a few officers from other teams and suddenly one of them, a man from a Child Protection Team, said he recognised her. He had seen her at various PTA meetings. He studied her face again on one of the closer shots.

'Yes, that's her all right,' he said. 'Pam Predeth. She's the deputy headmistress.' He was even able to supply her home address.

Meanwhile we had been examining the tape closely, and we noticed someone else at the edge of the picture. We reduced the size of the frame on screen so that we had the full image from side to side. We could see a man, his face clear enough to be identified.

Lenny and Phil went to Kent House Road in south-east London to check out the address. As they sat in the car watching the house, Pam came out and crossed the road to the fish and chip shop. Phil got out of the car and followed her. He stood directly behind her in the queue. When he got back to the car he was nodding at Lenny.

'Yeah,' he said, 'that's *definitely* her.'

So we applied for a warrant. On the due date Phil and Lennie stood on the doorstep, waiting for somebody to answer the door. Lennie heard the sound of a dog barking. The door was opened by Pam Predeth's current boyfriend.

After the usual introductions, Lenny said to Pam, 'I think you know what this is about. It might be better if we spoke to you on your own.'

'No,' she said, and pointed to the boyfriend. 'He knows all about me.'

Lenny said, 'You're sure?'

'Yes.' She nodded firmly. 'Yes.'

So then Lennie told her he was arresting her for bestiality, and he cautioned her. The boyfriend looked astounded. This was something he *hadn't* known about her. Pam denied nothing, and she did not appear to be distressed in any way.

She proved to be a model of co-operation. The other person in the video, she told us, was her previous boyfriend, James McFarland-James, who owned and operated a commercial garage. I went there myself, armed with a search warrant, and I searched all the cars until I came to a big

American vehicle which was locked. McFarland-James had a rummage through a desk, but he said he could not find the keys. We sent out a message to Traffic Patrol and a few minutes later a locks specialist arrived on his motorbike and tried to open the boot. He could not do it.

'All right,' I said, 'we'll just jemmy it.'

At which point McFarland-James miraculously located the missing keys. We opened the car boot and found several videotapes. In the screening room they turned out to be more prints of the original incriminating video, and others depicting Pam having sex with an Alsatian and a collie. We later learned she had dropped McFarland-James and he wanted her back. When she rebuffed him he made copies of the tapes and planned to sell them as an act of revenge. Sending a tape to the *South London Press* had been a spur-of-the-moment act committed through anger and spite.

Pam Predeth and James McFarland-James appeared before Judge Verney, the Recorder of London, and they were both sentenced to three months in prison, which in Pam's case was suspended after she had spent a short time inside. Following the court hearing and the sentencing, a national newspaper offered Pam £10,000 to pose in her underwear, complete with stockings and suspenders as she had appeared in the videos, and be photographed outside Battersea Dogs' Home. Pam found the suggestion amusing, but she declined.

In December that year, and the following year, Pam sent Lenny Yeoell a Christmas card, which confirmed our impression that she bore the police no grudge and not the slightest animosity. For our own part we found Pam to be a pleasant and wholesome-seeming middle-class woman. She freely admitted that she enjoyed having sex with dogs; she had even had a special protection harness made so that their claws would not hurt her. Her wish to have the sexual acts with the animals captured on videotape was a perverse vanity which I am not sure she entirely regretted.

It was always possible for me to argue and fight my department's case against perceived irregularities in the law, or in the way the law was selectively observed in certain quarters. It was quite another thing to be presented with a wrong – but legal – move that was virtually impossible to reverse.

James Ferman, the Director of the British Board of Film Classification (BBFC), used to meet regularly with myself and Jeremy Naunton, an official from the Crown Prosecution Service. We would discuss what was current in commercial film productions, and examine the developing trends; we would look at troublesome film clips and scrutinise the variety of difficulties raised by the need for a system of film classification. My relations with the BBFC and its director were always cordial and civilised, and I never had any reason to feel I was being kept in the dark over matters that might concern me.

Then in September 1992 the BBFC passed a number of sex education videos as suitable for home viewing, giving each of them an 18 certificate. These films were already on the market and I didn't know about it until somebody told me. Up to that point I didn't even know that the films existed. They had never been mentioned to me. I was surprised.

Shortly afterwards the newspapers were in touch, asking me what I thought. I said I would have a look at the films and give them my response. I viewed all of the tapes in question and I was surprised by the familiarity of the content – they incorporated many of the elements I was used to seeing in hardcore pornography. My surprise edged into annoyance as I detected a *fait accompli*. Had I wanted to take action against the BBFC, it would have been futile, because when they issue a certificate, action cannot be taken against them without the consent of the Attorney General.

On the front page of the *Sun* for 2 September 1992, under the heading 'FURY OVER SEX TAPES', there appeared a colour photograph of a naked man embracing an equally naked woman as they stood in front of a blazing fireplace. Another heading alongside asked 'IS THIS REALLY EDUCATION?'. The accompanying article declared that a top policeman had branded sex education videos openly on sale in High Street shops as 'nothing more than thinly disguised pornography'.

The article went on: 'Detective Superintendent Michael Hames of Scotland Yard claims the law allows "instructional" videos to feature sex acts that would get porn merchants arrested and their films burned. He says, "Turn the volume off and just watch the action – as I am sure most people who buy these tapes do – and what have you got? Porn. It's the sort of stuff we seize every day, yet this is legal."'

Further on, in a two-page spread featuring stills and cover shots of the videos, I was quoted again: 'Most people think they know what is classified as porn – the material we would seize and which most magistrates would order us to destroy. Fully aroused male sex organs? Penetrative sex? Oral sex? Actual acts rather than simulated sex? Gay scenes? . . . All this goes on in these "education" videos.'

This was interpreted in some quarters as a value judgement, but as far as I was concerned, I wasn't doing that. I was saying that what people see in those tapes is pornography liable to seizure. That's it; I have no other axe to grind. The Board passed the films because the perceived educational element justified an exemption under the Obscene Publications Act. I was saying the videos make the law look like an ass. The Obscene Publications Act at that time was – and to a huge extent still is – really rather silly.

At the time I learned the 'educational' tapes were being sold openly, I recalled a lunchtime meeting I once had with James Ferman and Jeremy Naunton. The talk got around to the nature of our jobs and we agreed, in the spirit of specula-tion, that if we three decided to move the goalposts and make the sale of pornographic films legal, we could do it quite easily, without consultation with anyone else. Now I realised that what we talked about that day had virtually come to pass. It had been accomplished by stealth rather than by mutual consent, but the outcome was the same.

I don't think it is within the power of governments to control the spread of adult pornography, and there is no longer much evidence of a will to do that anyway. But the determination of governments all over the world to stop paedophiles trans-mitting child pornography is as strong as ever. For our part, we at the Dirty Squad went from dealing with adult pornog-raphy and a *little* of the child pornography which was circulating, to changing the agenda so that 90 per cent of our concern was with child abuse.

To effect the change, we took a decision to let the policing of adult pornography slide away to other quarters, and we did that for two major reasons. One, we had to make the best use of available resources – I had only sixteen officers, a number wholly inadequate to cope with the volume and spread of pornography throughout London. Two, the more important job for us was, as it should always have been, the protection of children. As our knowledge improved and as our seizures of paedophile-related material increased, I deployed more and more resources to deal with child abuse.

From 1990 onwards there was talk about the use of computers for transmitting pornography. We were being told by the media, increasingly, that computer disks with pornography on them – at this stage it was ordinary adult hardcore porn – were being swapped in playgrounds by children who downloaded the stuff from the Internet. Manchester Police had an officer in their vice squad, Sergeant John Ashley, who already had this new offshoot of the trade under active investigation. When I was asked what we in the Met were doing about the problem I said we were looking into it, which in truth we were *trying* to do. But we could not do it very adequately because we didn't have a computer. I applied through the usual channels for a machine we could use to begin our online investigations. I also singled out one of our officers, DC Kevin Ives, who had an interest in computers, and I urged him to get himself thoroughly computer literate as fast as he could.

Time passed and we still didn't have a machine. A number of suspect floppy disks were passed to us and Kevin had to take them home with him and use his son's computer to view the material. He made a video of the contents and brought that back to the Yard for us to see. It is amazing to think now that, at that time, we had nothing at all at the Yard that could tackle the simple job of reading the data on a few floppies.

I tried to put on the pressure, but I was told that all these applications had to go through committees, and mine was pretty far down the list. I could not imagine any way that we were going to get a computer in the foreseeable future. Then a couple of charities actually offered to pool resources and donate a machine. I thought about it and decided it wouldn't look very good – in fact it would look pathetic – if we were forced to go to one of the children's charities to get equipment necessary to do our job.

Meanwhile I was being pressured to show my worth. What was I doing about this trading of pornographic material among school kids? As much as I could, I would reply – as much as I could considering I didn't even have a single computer at my disposal.

I simply had to get one. The facts were stark and unequivocal: villains used computers to transmit child pornography, *ergo* I needed a computer of my own to catch them. I put a report out to the Director of Administration, through channels, saying in effect that it would be catastrophic for the image of the Met and the British Police Service in general if the media found out that Scotland Yard didn't have a computer on which this new threat – which was becoming more and more a focus of attention from the press – could be tackled. Within three days I had a phone call: the cash was now available. Kevin Ives went out and bought a 286 computer through our Provisioning Branch.

Now, at last, we were making progress, and soon we were prosecuting individuals engaged in one- and two-way transmission of child pornography. Early in 1992 I was at a meeting of our Interpol committee where Don Huyck, my friend from the US Customs Service in Washington, told me that he and his team were investigating the use of computerised bulletin board systems for the transmission and collection of child pornography. This, he believed, was a problem increasing at an exponential rate.

A bulletin board system (BBS) is a service run on a computer dedicated to the purpose. The board is for the use of subscribers who can connect their own computers to the BBS by using an ordinary telephone line and a modem. The subscriber simply dials the number of the BBS, the modem connects his computer to the bulletin board, and once he has provided his password he has full access to whatever is on the board.

Bulletin boards permit users to read messages and view pictures left by other users; callers can make contributions to the board, or download material for their own use. Huyck and his team had found child pornography was being produced by the use of scanners – devices that capture an image and convert it into a set of electrical signals – to turn pornographic magazine pictures or photographs of children into computerised pictures which were stored on a computer's hard drive or on floppy disks. This transformation allowed the electronic transfer of the pictures to computers serving as BBS centres, and from there the material could be downloaded to anywhere in the world.

Huyck and his team were looking at a particular bulletin board in Denmark which operated under the name of BAMSE; the investigation of this BBS was part of an operation called Longarm. It had been found that people were uploading and downloading child pornography to and from the board, which contained over 400 different pornographic pictures of children, which is very few compared to current capacities, and 700 other types of obscene photographs.

Don Huyck and another US Customs investigator, Gary Narz, who worked out of Miami, went to Denmark and together with the Danish police they seized the offending computer system and took it away for expert inspection and scrutiny. By examining the database files on the machine's hard drive they obtained the names of 1,100 people who had been in contact with the bulletin board. Of this number, approximately 300 were US citizens; most of the remaining 800 were from Europe. As a result of the investigation Huyck and Narz arrested and questioned the majority of people whose contact details had led them to addresses in the United States.

Later in the year the two Americans were due to come to Britain to share their information with us. The conference at which they were to speak would be held in Manchester, where Huyck and Narz had been in touch with the police, comparing notes on the extensive work already carried out there by John Ashley. Also at that time the producers of *The Cook Report*, the investigative television programme headed by the journalist Roger Cook, were keen to do a follow-up programme to one they had screened seven years earlier on the subject of child pornography. This time their topic was computer pornography in general.

In due course Manchester police called together a conference of officers involved in possible action against people in the UK who had downloaded material from BAMSE, the Danish bulletin board. Bob McLachlan, myself and Kevin Ives went up to Manchester to attend the conference. Don Huyck gave his presentation and we were surprised to see that reporters from *The Cook Report* were present. In fact we were more than surprised, we were concerned: Huyck was, after all, disclosing sensitive police information. But that was how things had been arranged, and we were in no position to argue about it.

There was another surprise when we learned there was a feeling among British Customs representatives at the conference that they would not be having much, if anything, to do with the policing of computer pornography. They took the view that their main concern was the smuggling of illegal items through ports, not via the airwaves or telephone lines. US Customs took a different view and they still do. They see it as their duty to monitor and to act, where necessary, against material illegally imported by whatever means, and that includes child pornography brought in over the telephone lines.

After his presentation to the conference, Don Huyck gave us the addresses of British citizens who had used the Danish bulletin board to download or upload material. We then talked to *The Cook Report* people and basically took over the initiative from Manchester.

The television team was allowed to come with us on some of the raids. When we arrived, complete with camera, light and sound, and crept up the stairs outside the riverside apartment of one suspect, we were using an early-morning stealth-and–surprise tactic, so he would have no warning we were there, and therefore no time to switch on his computer and destroy his files. Alex Coe, twenty, a former public-school boy with a private income, was in bed when we took off his front door with a hydraulic ram and went into the apartment. His wife took immediate and noisy exception to us being there. While officers placated her, we explained to Coe that we had a warrant to search the apartment on the suspicion that he was operating a bulletin board which supplied subscribers with child pornography.

We began the search for the disk that carried the electronic information to reproduce the images. Coe offered to help. As he showed us how the computer set-up worked he told us that running the bulletin board was his major preoccupation. For a while he appeared to be perfectly co-operative, but as we worked through the files on his floppy disks, he suddenly grabbed the external hard drive and threw it on the floor. As

Roger Cook remarked in the eventual broadcast, it was hard-core evidence, but the means of storing it was extremely fragile. Fortunately, the rash attempt to destroy the evidence failed. Pornographic files in abundance were found on the hard drive and formed the nucleus of the case that was eventually made against Coe.

The TV crew were also with us when we visited William Crookes, a former BT engineer who ran a bulletin board called Merlin's Cellar, and they secretly filmed computer consultant Jason Manger before we took him in for questioning.

In the case of Crookes, we found pornography on his database files, but although much of it was sickening, none of it featured children.

Jason Manger was another matter. We had evidence that he had downloaded material from BAMSE, the Danish bulletin board, and we knew he placed cryptically brief advertisements in *Private Eye* and other publications, offering adult electronic images. The producers of *The Cook Report* paid him a £350 consultancy fee and filmed him secretly as he laid on his service for an actor he took to be just another client.

Manger had three degrees in computer science and an abiding fondness for money. He claimed to have unrestricted access to hard-to-get material, and said he had supplied a number of new bulletin boards with a wide range of pornographic pictures. For the £350 fee he provided the bogus client with several thousand images, and he offered him access to tens of thousands more.

When Roger Cook finally confronted Manger and told him he had been filmed on a number of occasions, the young man appeared unconcerned. He insisted he had done nothing illegal. He argued with Cook, claiming that all he did was supply clients with the means of obtaining what they wanted; he did nothing improper, because he merely gave access, and whatever use people might make of that access was no concern of his. This would not stand up in court and, besides, it was a lie. Manger nevertheless maintained his slightly aloof stance and when he was asked if he would accompany Detective Inspector Bob McLachlan back to the Yard for questioning, he readily agreed, and was seen doing so on camera.

From a policy point of view we were very pleased that this was all aired on television, but we wanted enough influence on the outcome to have the cases and the other content highlighted as we wished, and that was not possible. We had no editorial control, although we did work as closely as we could with *The Cook Report*, and we used the opportunity to make sure we – that is, the Dirty Squad – got the best slant we could from the finished film.

When the programme was transmitted it contained one or two images of children being abused; the scenes did not go into sexual detail, but the apprehension of the young victims, bordering on distress, was patent and the scenes were prolonged for rather too many seconds. We were unhappy about that, but the images had been sanctioned for use seven years earlier in the previous *Cook Report* programme on child pornography. Beyond that quibble, I would say that we were happy with the outcome. The programme was mentioned in Parliament by Ann Winterton MP on the day of transmission, and it has been mentioned since then in several parliamentary briefings related to legislation.

A couple of days after *The Cook Report* was shown, we heard that a very senior officer at the Yard was criticising the episode and was saying that we had conspired with the production team to make a titillating programme. Apparently he

had not actually *seen* the transmission, but his driver had, and
he had told his boss that he thought the programme was
dreadful, because there was this little kid in it who was being
abused, and so on. The atmosphere of disapproval was unmis-
takable, yet nobody had the guts to say anything. I wasn't
called on to any carpet to be given a roasting, and nothing
was said by way of official displeasure to any other members
of the squad. All that reached us was stiff-lipped rumour.

Some intriguing problems can arise when items of evidence
defy the specifications of the law, or when the letter of the law
accidentally creates anomalies. Television companies have to
adhere to the Obscene Publications Act, but in 1993 an
attempt was being made by certain satellite broadcasters to
get round the Act and transmit electronically scrambled
pornographic films via set-top decoders into the homes of
British subscribers.

It was my job to object and I objected. The situation, I
pointed out, was becoming ludicrous. I was asked to explain
myself, and I did. It was all right, I pointed out, for people to
sit at home and watch this stuff on television. But if any of
those people were to record the material on to videotape and
try to sell it or swap it, that would constitute publication of an
obscene article, and they would be liable for prosecution
under the terms of the Obscene Publications Act. The situation, I pointed out again, was anomalous and silly.

As a result of lobbying by myself and others, the government finally proscribed the satellite channels in question,
which meant that none of them could sell their decoding
cards in the United Kingdom.

A tougher legal point was raised by the case that became
known as Operation Shakespeare. It began when we received

a call from an irate woman in Watford who told us that her husband had child pornography on his computer.

Kevin Ives and his sergeant, Steve Quick, went to Watford to investigate. They seized the accused man's computer and found the offending image on the hard drive. He had created what is now known legally as a pseudo-photograph. First he had obtained a nude picture of a woman, a pornographic shot which placed emphasis on the crotch. Then he used a photograph of a young girl's head to replace the adult head in the picture; next he employed photo-manipulation software to remove the hair and breasts from the adult torso, thereby creating the semblance of an immature female body, lewdly posed, complete with a child's smiling face. While evidence of the manipulation was visible on close inspection, to all intents and purposes this was nevertheless a pornographic photograph of a child.

So what did the image amount to in law? It was not a photograph of a child, because it could be demonstrated that a photograph of an adult woman's body had been electronically airbrushed and retextured, with the photograph of an actual child's head superimposed – the head of a relative, as it happened, which contributed a lot to the wife's outrage when she found the picture.

The Protection of Children Act is clear on the subject of photographs, but we could not be sure this would fall within the definition of a photograph, therefore it posed difficulties over what we were going to do. Would it pass the test of obscenity? We believed that it could be classified as an *article* within the meaning of the Act, but would it be classified as obscene? The Crown Prosecution Service were as concerned and uncertain as we were, and in the end no prosecution was mounted.

We were determined to have clarification of the law in this case, and in order to press our cause we included the picture in an exhibition we held in the Jubilee Room of the House of Commons on 24 and 25 February 1993. The exhibition was organized by Ann Winterton MP and fifteen of her cross-party colleagues. Over 300 other MPs had accepted an invitation to attend the exhibition at which, in the words of the press release, 'The Obscene Publications Branch of New Scotland Yard will provide briefing on the obscene and porno-graphic material which is now increasingly available in the United Kingdom and to explain the weaknesses of the Obscene Publications Act. Items on display will include tapes, books, magazines, and satellite and computer-generated pornography. The material includes child abuse, bestiality, oral sex, both homosexual and heterosexual group and anal intercourse and other violent and abnormal sexual behaviour which it would be inappropriate to list.'

'I am certainly no prude,' Mrs Winterton was quoted as saying, 'but I was deeply shocked that such material is now increasingly available, largely because of the lack of political will to tackle the weakness of the Obscene Publications Act. The Act is a threadbare garment, woven in a different age, which can no longer provide the cloak of protection which women, men and children need against the most horrific, exploitative, and damaging pornography.

'I am not talking about soft porn, or about material which is titillating. I am talking about an exhibition of material which is so horrific that not one Member of Parliament at the private viewing held a short time ago was able physically to endure viewing all the exhibits in question.

'We have met with the minister to discuss the issue. We have explained our concerns in detail and it is now clear that the only way to get across our message that the Obscene Publications Act is no longer relevant to today's technology and the free market in filth, is to mount this gruesome and nauseating exhibition.'

The exhibition produced the desired effect by triggering a move by the Home Affairs Select Committee to urge the government to make amendments to the Criminal Justice and Public Order Bill. When the Select Committee came to Scotland Yard in June to consult us on the growing problem of child pornography, we took the opportunity to go into detail with them over the dilemma raised by Operation Shakespeare. In addition Kevin Ives prepared an excellent paper on the technical details of the case.

As a result of our lobbying and the Select Committee's determination to implement reforms, the law was changed, within months, to make it more adequate in the area of child protection.

The use of computers to transmit and produce pornographic images has always been difficult to police, but nowadays it is virtually impossible. Sophisticated developments in image compression and electronic storage make it hard even to detect that anything illegal is taking place. Invisible files stored on hard drives, on CD-Roms, and on floppy disks are hard to detect, and the more sophisticated peddlers of illegal material split the invisible files over several disks, rendering each piece useless as evidence – even if it can be made visible. Fragmented invisible images can only be restored as whole, visible files via complicated software that is often tailored to a particular disk or set of disks.

Anyone surfing the murkier corners of the Internet can now download, for a fee, a program that will alter the way he switches on his computer. The program works by pausing the start-up for ten seconds after switching on, during which time the computer owner must add a five-digit code number from the keyboard. When that is done the machine starts successfully. If the five-digit number is not added at switch-on, the machine will still start after the ten-second delay, but in the process of starting up it will erase everything on its hard drive.

Another wipe-clean program, originated in Germany, has the ability to destroy every file on a hard drive in a maximum of four seconds, and it can do the job remotely, from a hand-set, on any computer with an infra-red sensor. On conventional machines, the program is triggered by a two-button combination entered on the keyboard.

For those collectors of pornography who wish to hang on to their files and at the same time escape prosecution, a Dutch vendor on the Internet offers a randomising program at a cost of fifty US dollars. When a preset combination of keys is held down, every file stored on the hard drive is scrambled into a senseless jumble of letters, numbers, and symbols. Order can only be restored by restarting the computer, then entering a pre-set key combination which is different from the combination that scrambled the files in the first place.

A new and daunting arrival on the scene is a cheap, high-capacity storage system that can store over seventy-six times more than a conventional floppy on a disk measuring only 10cm by 10cm. Photographic images – including movies – can be stored on these disks in significant numbers, and security for the user is higher than ever before.

Using these new disks, paedophiles and others can safely send their wares through the mail, or even pass them over a counter, because the disks cannot be viewed on a computer

without a password first being entered. Even the manufac-
turers of the disks cannot reveal the contents without the
password. If the password is lost or forgotten, there are two
options: erase the disk and at least salvage it as a ready-to-use
blank, or destroy it.

Pornographers selling their wares on this new medium do
not, of course, supply a password with the individual disk; it
is either telephoned or e-mailed to the recipient, in the same
way that a credit-card PIN is sent separately from a new card.
Knowing the password, the owner now has the further option
of changing it, in case the original is discovered. If he wishes,
he can change the password every day. No matter how
viciously hardcore and copious the pornography on a disk, as
long as it is password-protected, and as long as the owner of
the disk is the only person who knows that password, he is
immune from prosecution.

All of this sophistication comes about at a time when the
paedophile threat to children seems to be at its most ominous.
In the end, vigilance and solid legislation offer our only hope,
since we can never effectively combat the best technology
when it has fallen into the worst possible hands.

15
Broken Childhoods

In carrying out investigations I have always stuck to the serious strategy underlying a comic line of Inspector Clouseau's: '*I suspect no one, I suspect everyone.*' To reach a reliable conclusion a detective has to keep a completely open mind. It is just as important, as the investigation moves along, to connect all the items of evidence with great care, then view them in a context that will properly explain them.

An example. A roll of film is handed in for processing at the local chemist's. The staff discover that most of the roll consists of photographs of a twelve-year-old girl at bathtime. She is naked in every shot but she has not been provocatively posed. There is no obvious attempt at obscenity. In most of the photos the child's genital area or her buttocks are visible. No one else appears in the bathtime pictures and the remainder of the roll is taken up with shots of an evidently happy family – mother, father and other children.

The staff at the chemist's are uncomfortable. They know

the pictures are not obscene and to all appearances they are innocent. But they are pictures of a naked little girl, presumably taken by an adult.

The manager at the chemist's decides to call in the law. The police, for their part, feel that at the very least a few questions should be asked. They go to the house and discover that the person who took the photographs is not the girl's natural father, he is her stepfather. It also turns out that the mother was not present at the time the pictures were taken, and furthermore she did not know they had been taken.

The stepfather says the pictures are entirely innocent. The mother says they *have* to be innocent. The girl, questioned carefully by Child Protection Officers, convinces them that nothing improper has ever happened between herself and her stepfather.

The police decide to take no further action. Some people would say that in the situation as I have described it here, the police should never have intervened in the first place. From my experience, I would say that not only was the chemist's manager right to report his misgivings, but that the police would have been doing less than their duty if they hadn't made further inquiries.

Only by taking that course could they learn the facts, amalgamate them, then examine them within a context (in this case the family unit and its state of balance) which clarified their meaning. That procedure cleared the stepfather of any wrongdoing. It also determined that the child was at no risk, and that the bathroom photo-session was not the first step in an extended process of barrier-removal that might have led to serious abuse.

A case where questionable snapshots proved not to be

innocent was triggered when a branch of Boots in Penge, south-east London, got in touch with the police about a batch of photographs that had been sent in for processing. Most of the shots were ordinary, but three or four were pornographic pictures of a little blonde girl about six years old. The name and address of the man who sent in the film for processing was on a receipt slip. We got a warrant the same day and officers paid him a visit at his flat first thing next morning.

The man was called Derek James. He was in his mid-fifties. As an officer spoke to him at the door, quite unexpectedly the girl in the photographs came out behind him, from his bedroom. We later learned that she lived a couple of doors along from James, who was regularly paid to be a babysitter for the girl and her four-year-old brother. When we went into the flat we found the boy playing in the bedroom.

A search of the place uncovered a number of undeveloped films, plus several packets of pictures similar to those handed over to the police by the technician at Boots. This time there were obscene pictures of both the boy and the girl. When the officers asked James about these pictures, he said the kids had done it themselves – the boy had photographed the girl and she had photographed him.

Derek James was arrested on suspicion of having sexually abused both children. He was taken to Penge Police Station, where officers did what they could to interview him. He would not say much, beyond trying again to blame the children themselves for taking the pornographic pictures.

We spoke to the children's mother, who was convinced that Derek James was a thoroughly good person. When she learned about the photographs she became distraught. Shock and disbelief were evident as she tried to talk the facts down into something harmless and insignificant.

We charged Derek James later that day with taking indecent photographs of minors and he was bailed, pending an examination of the undeveloped films we had found, and pending an interview with the girl by members of a Child Protection Team. During this meeting the girl said that James had interfered with her; at his own interview the boy said the same: James had interfered with him on several occasions.

Even at that point the children's mother could not bring herself to believe that Derek James had sexually abused her children. By all accounts James had lived at that address for a long time, and he had done what many paedophiles do once they have targeted a child or children of a particular household: he had built up a strong bond of trust with the mother. By the time we intervened, the bond was strong enough to make her disbelieve the truth even in the face of overwhelming evidence.

Shortly after being charged, Derek James killed himself. He left a note saying he had not been guilty of sexually interfering with the two children, even though his suicide was a clear enough indication of his guilt. The note also left pressure on the children, because no matter how convincingly they detailed the assaults, the dead man's note would always leave a cloud of doubt over their testimony.

Inevitably, the unanswered questions in a case of this kind outweigh the certainties. We have no way of knowing how many children Derek James abused over the years. We do not know, either, why he was so naïve as to send his incriminating photographs to Boots for processing. It is possible he was simply stupid enough to think that the laboratories never look at the pictures they process, and there was certainly evidence at his flat that many of his obscene pictures had been commercially processed in the past, without any kind of repercussion.

Intriguingly, it has been suggested that a part of Derek James, consciously or unconsciously, wanted him to be caught. We will never know about that. We do know, however, that the principal warning at the heart of this case is repeated, over and over, year after year: parents must be rigorous in the way they scrutinise people who are to be entrusted with the care of their children.

Operation Cathedral began as a result of a raid by Devon and Cornwall police at the home of a man called Williams. The police found letters during the raid which prompted them to circulate names and addresses from the letters to a number of police forces; it was strongly suspected that the people named had obscene pictures of children in their possession.

Canterbury police raided the home of a schoolteacher and eventually called us at Obscene Publications. They said, bluntly, that they had found some nasty child pornography. I assigned DS Graham Passingham and DC Dave Flanagan to the case. A short time later they viewed the tape that became pivotal to the case known as Operation Cathedral.

'It consisted of various home-made clips of a boy of about thirteen or fourteen being abused – masturbated,' Flanagan reported. 'He had a noose round his neck at one stage as he fellated the man in the tape.'

A shorter clip showed another boy, a child of about seven, lying on a bed, being wakened by a man. He knelt over the boy, holding the video camera in one hand as he masturbated. Although both policemen were experienced in this area of investigation, they were seriously disturbed by the tape.

'The boy's distress is obvious,' said Flanagan. 'He's whimpering and saying, "Please, no more." But in a way, *The Snowman* music in the background . . .'

The animated film *The Snowman* was on television in the background, Flanagan explained.

'I found the two in conjunction very distressing. My kids like *The Snowman* music, and *The Snowman* is a story that entrances children. To have that in the background while this child was whimpering, "Please, not again . . ." or "You're squashing me." Well, I don't like that music now.'

It was certainly as ghastly as anything I had ever seen, and DS Passingham said the same.

On one of the video clips there was a shot of the older boy sitting in a Jaguar car outside a block of flats. The car's registration number was perfectly visible. There were two things going on in this video, Passingham reported. 'You had the very young boy who was being sexually abused on a bed, and that kept being intercut with scenes of an older boy being sexually abused in the car, but they weren't filmed at the same time, as you were meant to think. They were separate incidents.'

On the video clips both boys were spoken to by a man with a strong Geordie accent. This, in addition to the number from the car's registration plate, was all the working evidence we had at the start of the case.

One of the first things we did was get a voice analysis of the two clips. That came back saying that the Geordie in Clip A, with the car, and the Geordie in Clip B, kneeling astride the boy, were almost certainly the same man. So that was a step forward. We took a step backward when the voice analyst seemed to think one of the boys might be a Geordie as well.

Up to that point, a DVLC history of the Jaguar from the date of manufacture, December 1987, until the day the inquiry began, had pointed the investigators in the direction of Nottingham. But now they were not so sure. A painstaking strategy was set up. A team of police officers and civilians would research the car's ownership from the time it left the factory until the most recent registration.

The car was bought in the first instance by a company in Wellingborough, who leased it straight away to a pharmaceutical company in Cambridge. When the lease had run its course two years later, the car was returned to Wellingborough.

Then we had to decide if we should go to the pharmaceutical company. The danger was, if we went to the main man there, the one who was using the car, he might very well be the man we were after, and the last thing we wanted was to alert him. In the meantime, Jaguar had supplied us with information about places all over the UK where the car had been serviced. At that stage it was a dishearteningly widespread inquiry.

Standard procedure after the Jaguar lease had expired was for the leasing company to sell the car at auction. It was duly auctioned and sold to a dealer from Mapperley, who sold it on to the most recent owner, a man in Nottingham.

The current registered owner was no longer a likely suspect. We still needed to eliminate everyone from the inquiry leading up to him. So we went to the car dealer's in Mapperley and spoke to the owner. He looked through his papers and discovered he had actually sold the car once and bought it back a few months later, before selling it to the most recent owner.

The man who had owned the Jaguar for those few months had been shrewd enough not to register it for the short time it was in his possession, but he hadn't been clever enough to give the dealer a false name. He was stupid enough, in fact, to let the number plate be seen on the video.

Flanagan went back to the Anti-Vice Squad Office in Nottingham. They checked their records and found that a man with the same name as the man who briefly owned the Jaguar was known to them. He had a record of indecent assault against minors. The photographs of the man on the file showed strong similarities to partial images of the man in the video clips.

'He was just the right kind of suspect with the right background of offences,' said Passingham. 'The details of an earlier offence were typical. He enticed two youths into his home and forced them to strip at knife point, then he fondled their genitals and forced them to engage in mutual oral sex. In 1981 he had been sentenced to two years' imprisonment at Newcastle Crown Court. Since that time, I don't think he had come to the notice of the police.'

Passingham and Flanagan were convinced they were on to the right man. To tighten the certainty they made efforts to identify the locations visible on the video; a number were checked and were found to be near where the suspected man now lived. One particular location actually turned out to be one of his previous addresses.

'We still didn't know where the offences took place,' said Passingham. 'We knew one of the addresses appeared in the film, and that seemed to indicate where they had been committed, but it still wasn't definite. I remember we had a lot of discussions about this, because where the case is eventually dealt with is quite important – you know, where the children are now. After various meetings it was decided, on the balance of probabilities, that the children lived in the Nottingham area and that the case should fall within the jurisdiction of the Child Protection Team there.'

The Nottingham Child Protection Team set up the operation for the arrest of the suspect. He lived in a house on the outskirts of town. On the morning that the police turned up to arrest him, DC Flanagan was with them.

'I was in the rear garden when he came out through the back door,' Flanagan said. 'He tried to run off down the garden. I just grabbed hold of him and took him back into the house. It was like watching a pin jab a balloon. He deflated. He didn't break down in tears or anything like that, but he looked incredibly shocked.'

The accused made no attempt to deny the charges that were put to him. His daughter was too young to understand what was happening, but his wife was distraught.

'That's another part of this job that I don't like,' Flanagan said. 'It's all very well arresting the offenders, but then you've got their families there, and they're just fall-out victims. They're not guilty of anything, are they?'

At Nottingham Crown Court in October 1992, the accused pleaded guilty to a number of indictments of indecency against children. He was sentenced to six years' imprisonment. Passingham and Flanagan were as surprised as I was at the severity of the sentence. In our view, sentences for offences against minors are generally too light. Both officers believed that in this case, the visible evidence of the younger boy's pain and fright, in bizarre contrast with the lyrical music in the background, must have demonstrated to the judge, better than any spoken description, the hideous nature of the crime.

The children in the video clips were identified. The older boy, who had been fourteen at the time the tape was made, was able to identify the younger boy for us. By the time the suspect was arrested, the older boy was twenty-one and already had a child of his own.

*

One morning in September 1992, I had a telephone call from a detective at Evesham, in the West Mercia Constabulary. He told me that he had been on a raid with Customs Officers early that day and that they had found something which disturbed him. He said that the owner of the house was a man called Peter Righton, that he appeared to be a paedophile, and that from correspondence found there, it looked as if Righton was a very influential figure in child care. The name wasn't familiar, but I told the officer I would make inquiries and call him back.

I rang Valerie Howarth, the Director of ChildLine, a person of great integrity who sat on various committees with me. I asked her if she had ever heard of Peter Righton.

'Oh yes,' she said. 'He's an adviser to all sorts of organisations. He was the Director of Education at the National Institute of Social Work, and he's pretty much a national figure in child care.'

I told her briefly what had happened and she agreed not to say anything.

I went along to the Dirty Squad main office and asked Terry Bailey and Dave Flanagan what plans they had for the day. They said they were tied up in paperwork on various jobs. I told them to be on standby to go somewhere fast. I phoned the West Mercia officer who had called me, told him that he had netted a big fish, and that I proposed to send a couple of officers to help him, if he didn't mind. He told me he would be grateful. I passed the phone to Terry and a few minutes later he and Dave set off for Evesham.

When they arrived they asked for the low-down on what had happened during the search at Righton's house. The officer told them and it was immediately apparent to Terry and Dave that a lot of potential evidence had been overlooked. In fairness to the officers at West Mercia, this was and is a specialist area. Policemen are used to looking for stolen property, not for the sort of material that will substantiate a child-abuse inquiry. In this case they had not seized videos and correspondence which are essential to investigations involving the possibility of child abuse.

Dave and Terry suggested a search warrant be obtained on the basis of the new information and that they all go to Righton's house. They duly did, and they took possession of a large amount of material which they took to Evesham for examination.

Before very long it was obvious to Dave and Terry that the local police had stumbled on an important case. They immediately suggested that the inquiry be continued at a school in Gloucestershire, where Righton's partner, Richard Alston, was the headmaster and Righton was a governor. This suggestion was not received with much enthusiasm. Dave and Terry returned to London.

In the meantime I had spoken to Herbert Laming, now Lord Laming, the Chief Inspector of the Social Services Inspectorate. He came to my office and told me that government ministers were anxious, as he was, that the police get to the truth and that a comprehensive inquiry be established. In short order a full investigation into Righton's activities was begun by a joint police and Social Services team in Hereford and Worcester.

We discovered that Righton had been a founder member of the Paedophile Information Exchange and had made little secret of his sympathy for those who had a sexual preference for children. He had contributed a chapter in a book entitled *Perspectives on Paedophilia*, published in 1981.

In due course Righton was charged with possession of

indecent photographs and pleaded guilty. He was fined. That was the limit of the action that could be taken against him under the criminal law. Had this incident occurred prior to 1988, when the possession of indecent photographs became an offence, he would not have been convicted of any offence, and he would have the value of the 'possession' legislation had been proved.

As we delved further into Peter Righton's past, we established that although he had not hidden his sexual preferences from many of his colleagues, he had used the pretence that he was homosexual, a cover which effectively diverted most of them because of their reluctance to be thought homophobic. Eminent practitioners like Barbara Kahan, who had carried out the Pin-Down inquiry and who was the Chair of the National Children's Bureau, and Daphne Statham, Director of the National Institute of Social Work, both knew Righton and had been blind to his paedophilia. It was to these women's credit that they subsequently acknowledged publicly the way they had been fooled by him. Others were not so forthcoming.

An example of the extent of Righton's influence, and the support that he and other offenders were able to give each other, is clear from correspondence between Righton and the Department of Education in 1981, when he urged them to remove another PIE member, Charles Napier, from List 99, which is the list of banned teachers.

In April 1972 Napier, from Thames Ditton, had been convicted of indecency with schoolboys in his charge. He was sentenced to three years' probation with the condition that he submitted to psychiatric therapy for one year. In January 1981, Peter Righton sent a letter to the Department of Education, on the headed notepaper of the National Institute for Social Work. In his opinion, he wrote, Napier no longer constituted a sexual risk to children. He wrote:

> In my view, Mr Napier is a gifted teacher of both adults and children. I believe that, during the years since his conviction, he has acquired a knowledge and disciplined mastery of himself which would justify the conclusion that he no longer constitutes a sexual risk to children in his charge. It would give me great pleasure – and cause me no anxiety – to hear that the Secretary of State had reviewed his decision of 24 October, 1972, in Mr Napier's favour.

In July 1981, Napier's ban was revoked where establishments of further education were concerned. He was told that he could make another application for full reinstatement in 1984.

In 1990 he applied once more, and at his own request he was referred to Dr Morris Fraser, a consultant psychiatrist at University College Hospital, who would prepare a report on Napier's condition. In 1981 Dr Fraser, like Peter Righton, had contributed a chapter to *Perspectives on Paedophilia*. By 1992, Dave Flanagan had already prosecuted the good doctor for possession of indecent photographs of children. After a third conviction Dr Fraser was finally struck off.

Napier remained on the banned list.

While an investigation into Righton's activities was being carried out in the West Country, we had established a wide-ranging intelligence-led investigation codenamed Operation Clarence. The two officers responsible for the operation were Graham Passingham and his partner, Dave Flanagan. The operation targeted schoolmasters and people involved in education in particular. We soon traced links between Righton and other offenders.

David Blomfield, the chief executive of a charity called the Standing Conference on Schools Science and Technology, was another principal target. A team of us raided his flat in South London one morning. We found child pornography, as we had suspected we would, and in the kitchen was a letter from Charles Napier who, by now, was employed by the British Council as a teacher in Cairo. The letter boasted of Napier's abusive behaviour towards boys in his new posting, and how much he enjoyed the freedom from the restrictions of the British legal system.

We alerted the British Council and they immediately suspended Napier. By the time he returned to the UK we had gathered enough evidence to arrest him and charge him with indecent assault. He was eventually sentenced to eighteen months' imprisonment at Kingston Crown Court. David Blomfield was fined for possession of child pornography and sacked from his job. He left England to live in Portugal.

As the list of contacts continued to grow we managed to build up a huge database, and to learn about the remarkable ways paedophiles organise themselves, and the support they give each other. Until we started to examine the networks in this proactive way, these offenders had been able to associate and develop their networks with relative freedom. Now we felt that even though we were a very small band, we could destabilise them with the glare of publicity and keep them on edge, wondering where we were going to pounce next. That was as much as we could do.

The inquiry in Hereford and Worcester finished in 1994. The results were disappointing. Righton was cautioned for an offence of indecent assault committed on a boy some thirty years before. Apart from that, all they achieved was a mountain of intelligence. The leaders of the inquiry recommended that a national unit be set up to investigate allegations against care staff. The Home Office left the recommendation on file.

My goal was, and is, the creation of proactive teams, backed up by the resources of a properly tasked paedophile intelligence team at the National Criminal Intelligence Service. I had hoped that by showing how effective we could be with just fourteen officers plus myself and the Detective Inspector, aided by a few civilian support staff, chief officers would be encouraged to pump more resources into an area of police activity which should be at the head of their priorities. I still have my hopes.

I remain convinced that we have only touched the tip of a huge national and international problem. The fact is evident from the never-ending allegations of sexual abuse in the child-care system, and the hundreds upon hundreds of social workers who have been convicted of the systematic, planned abuse of children in their care.

We have to ask how it is possible that crimes on such an enormous and often organised scale can go unnoticed. One reason is that the child-care system has been thoroughly infiltrated at all levels by abusers. They have protected each other by subtle processes of misinformation, by the creation of doubt about the credibility of their victims, and by steady reassurances that all is well. Blatant and arrogant denial, even in the face of incriminating evidence, is a reaction native to the mentality of the paedophile, and it gets more of them off the hook than might be imagined. The paedophile's progress is also helped, in many cases, by misguided notions of 'equal opportunities'.

In 1992 I called for the creation of a National Paedophile Register and in 1997 it finally came about. I never believed, however, that this alone would solve many problems, but it is important nevertheless that the authorities know where paedophiles live and where they work.

In calling for the register I realised that if the police know where paedophiles are, they will also have to assess their level of threat, which is a complex job. They will then be obliged to monitor the paedophiles' movements and to become seriously proactive. After all, if the police know where the paedophiles are, and the paedophiles attack children, then the public will want to know what the police did to prevent these men offending.

In my experience the Police Service is largely driven by fear of criticism, so it will not be too long before self-preservation will force them to establish the proactive units. Better late than never. It is a pity the motive by that time will be the wrong one, but the ends, where the maintenance of child protection is the issue, will always justify the means.

PART THREE

16
Going Undercover

For a number of years undercover operations have been carried out in all areas of major crime. The commonest way to infiltrate a criminal organisation is through an informant, who will ease the undercover officer into the environment he wants to investigate at close quarters. There are of course other methods of getting a man into enemy territory, and in 1990 we began examining them all with a view to putting an undercover officer into a paedophile network.

The places a covert operator finds himself are often dangerous, but the criminals he mingles with are essentially people he can identify with and impersonate; the motive for the criminal activity is simple greed, and we all have enough of that in our make-up to make it relatively easy to understand and imitate, even in its grosser forms. In the case of paedophiles, the overriding motive is lust for children, which is something that non-paedophiles, undercover officers included, find hard to accept, let alone imitate. So in dealings with paedophiles, an undercover officer's composure and his ability to act must both be of an unusually high order.

Another complicating factor is that paedophiles' behaviour is so far beyond the bounds of decency that no police infiltrator would ever join in. A paedophile is bound to be suspicious of any wavering or hesitancy on the part a man who claims that he, too, is a child molester.

Unless, of course, the other man is a consummate deceiver. And that was our specification: we needed an undercover officer who could pass himself off as a paedophile to real paedophiles without ever *doing* anything to prove it.

We began laying down scenarios, setting out ways we could use covert operations for maximum advantage. It was obvious from the start that because paedophiles operate like terrorists, infiltration would be incredibly difficult, and once an officer was in, the risks would be serious. Even so, we knew that if we could deploy an undercover man with an appropriate level of skill, he could increase our effectiveness tenfold. Not only would we bring more targets to justice, we would gain crucial knowledge of the ways paedophiles organise networks, how they contact each other, and how they set up their crimes.

I have to say that at that point we already had some methods of learning about paedophiles. One way was to talk to offenders in treatment. That was valuable, especially in terms of developing our interrogation strategies. But the clinical setting is not home ground, and clinical staff are not a patient's kindred spirits, so offenders were telling the therapists what they decided to tell them, and little nuggets of truth had to be extracted from an amalgam of fact and fiction. If we could put someone in 'on the ground', however, someone the paedophiles would trust, then we could gain first-hand information that was far more likely to be accurate than the material we were getting from the cells and clinics.

With a number of strategies already agreed upon, we addressed ourselves to finding an experienced undercover officer who could act the part of a paedophile well enough to convince the genuine article. It was a tall order, but by a stroke of astonishing luck we were introduced to the man I shall call Todd, who has been a full-time undercover policeman since 1971. Although he found the work he did for us traumatic and occasionally sickening, his contribution to our war on paedophiles lived up to every expectation.

Todd's association with the Dirty Squad began on a case which centred on a teacher who had erected a barricade of respectability around his sexual obsession with young children.

David Black (not his real name) was head of music at an exclusive public school in the Midlands, where in the early 1990s the cost of a pupil's education was £3,000 a term. Black was married with two teenage daughters and a son; they lived in a comfortable semi-detached house provided by the school. He was a respected senior master who, to all appearances, conducted his life with a decorum that was appropriate to his position.

He came to our attention when he put an advertisement in a contact magazine. The ad used coded language to tell readers that he was looking for pornographic pictures and videos of little girls. Todd, our undercover officer, replied to Black's box number, employing the kind of language paedophiles use in correspondence with each other. Inevitably there was some postal reconnaissance by Black – careful questioning to check the authenticity of his correspondent – before he revealed his identity.

'I started phoning him up after that,' Todd said. 'That's how we got into him. I said, "We've probably got the same sort of interests." He immediately said to me, "Where do you come from?" I told him London and he said, "I'll come and see you."'

A time was arranged and eventually they met on a platform at King's Cross station. They had no trouble recognising each other. Todd simply said where he would be standing and Black walked up to him and introduced himself.

'We shook hands and walked off together,' Todd said. 'I had a room on the fourth floor of the hotel next to the station. In the hotel room I showed Black a compilation tape. This was the first time that anyone in the service had been given authority by the Crown Prosecution Service to show a tape to a suspect. I guessed from the correspondence and the phone calls that Black was into girls, so I fast-forwarded the tape and showed him the segment with girls, then he told me he wanted to see the bit at the beginning, which featured boys. So he was into boys as well.

'He was sitting on the bed while he watched the tape. Without any warning at all he unzipped his fly, took out his penis and began masturbating. He asked me to join him. I said, "I would do, but I had one before you got here."'

This was Todd's first undercover job in the paedophile field and he was unprepared for what had happened.

'Of all the things I'd had to do since 1971,' he said, 'that experience with Black I found incredibly distasteful. It had nothing to do with fear, it was just that I found *myself* affected more than I would have thought. In the other jobs we do, it's fear that can upset you. But this was emotional in another kind of way, and it was much worse than being scared. I saw him getting turned on like that, with children . . . I thought of my own kids, and it was a nasty collision of emotions. He wasn't just a bad man, he was something foul, that was the reaction I got. When he left, I was physically sick in the bathroom. In fact it was touch and go whether he was going to leave before I was sick. I was actually thinking at the time that I would have to tell him I had a stomach infection.'

Todd arranged to meet Black a second time. When the arrangements were made I went up to the Midlands to liaise with the local detective superintendent, an old friend who had been to police college with me. We had dinner the night before Black's next trip to meet Todd in London. Later, before I turned in, I read over the notes on the case in my hotel room.

In the morning I woke with uncomfortably mixed feelings. There was the usual frisson at the approaching conclusion of a job, knowing a target was about to be hit. There was the other certainty, too: by evening, David Black's carefully structured life would be in ruins.

The operation was planned so tightly that I could almost time the stages in advance. I knew what train Black would take to London, I knew where and when he would have the meeting with Todd, and I knew where he would be arrested. So I could tell the approximate moment when his world would fall apart.

As I shaved I pictured Black with his wife and children. It was the perfect domestic tableau, a smiling middle-class family in their cosy home, secure and respectable, cocooned. I thought what a weak, wretched man he was to put his sexual fixations before his reputation and his livelihood, and to put a stain on the lives of everyone close to him.

I wasn't part of the surveillance team, but that morning I travelled to London on the same train as Black. Until then I had only seen photographs of him. I got to the station early and watched from behind my newspaper as he walked past me on the platform. He was in his forties, smartly dressed, carrying a Gladstone bag. He looked like any level-headed, unexceptional businessman.

The train pulled into King's Cross station just before one o'clock. A number of officers watched Black as he walked to the rendezvous hotel.

'At that second meeting,' Todd said, 'he brought his stuff down, a caseful of it. I had my stuff, which he liked, but I wouldn't let him have it. I said, "Well, this is for someone else actually, but I'll get you some." He seemed okay with that, and told me I could take his stuff anyway. "No," I said, "I don't want to take yours. Not today. I'm going on somewhere else after this, it wouldn't be safe."'

Forty-five minutes after Black had arrived at King's Cross, Todd met me in a pub across the road. He confirmed that Black had a bagful of pornographic tapes, and he was taking the bag back with him to the station. The arrest could go ahead.

Black was under surveillance again from the time he left the hotel. He did a little shopping then went back to King's Cross station. When he walked on to the platform I stepped forward with Detective Inspector Stuart Baker, who formally arrested him. Black looked stunned. He said nothing.

We went directly to Albany Street Police Station. Black was outwardly calm as he stood before the custody sergeant. He tipped out the contents of his bag when he was asked. A number of videotapes slid on to the desk. They were taken away for viewing and it was quickly confirmed that they were obscene films featuring children. Stuart Baker told Black he would be charged with possession of child pornography. Black looked down and murmured something.

At that point I left to take the train back to the Midlands. The arresting officers would take Black back by car when the paperwork was ready.

I arrived at six o'clock and went straight to see the bursar at the school where Black worked. He invited me into his drawing room. I told him why I was there, and what had happened that afternoon in London.

'Oh, my God,' he groaned. 'I'd better tell the headmaster.'

When the situation had been explained to the head he took the news stoically and assured us we would have his full co-operation. A few minutes later word reached me that Black had arrived.

We waited for him in the school music room. When he came in he looked calm and unruffled. He was asked to unlock and open a large cupboard in the corner of the room, which he did. Among the piles of stationery and sheet music we found his personal collection of child pornography: videos, magazines, photographs. Later we determined that he had originated none of the material. Every item in his possession had been bought.

Next came the search of Black's home. Officers from the local Child Protection Team came with us to the house, and although the children were not at home, the officers were later able to determine that Black had never abused them.

The visit to the house was a distressing episode. I went up the front steps with Black at my side. I knocked and Mrs Black opened the door. I identified myself, then told her that her husband had been arrested for possessing child pornography, and that I had a warrant to search the house.

'Good God.' Mrs Black looked astonished. She stared at her husband. 'David! Is it true?'

He didn't say a word. We went inside and into the sitting room. Suddenly, with no warning and to everyone's embarrassment, Black threw himself on the floor. He lay there sobbing and clawing at the carpet.

'Forgive me, darling,' he wailed. 'Please forgive me. I'm so sorry, so terribly sorry . . .'

He crawled towards his wife on all fours, convulsed with sobs. His wife stared at him, showing her contempt. It was a terrible scene. I asked Mrs Black quietly if we could search the house and she nodded. We set about the job discreetly and as inoffensively as we could. We found no pornography. Black had obviously kept his perversion separate from his domestic life.

In due course Mrs Black left her husband. David Black was dismissed from his post, and because the family home was owned by the school, Mrs Black and the children had to be moved to a council house. Black went to live with his mother. He was later fined for possessing child pornography.

'I hadn't had to give evidence, so he didn't suspect me at all,' Todd said. 'He had my covert mobile phone number, and maybe a couple of weeks later, after he had been fined and had apologised and told the court it was a moment's madness and all the rest of it, he rang me up. "Oh, Todd," he said. "I wonder if you could help me out? Can you get me some stuff, some videos?" He sounded a bit distressed, so I asked him what was up. "Well, a terrible thing's happened," he said. "I was arrested and they've taken away all my stuff . . ."'

'I thought for a minute, then I said, "You've been arrested, and you're phoning me up?" I made myself sound really indignant. "Listen, don't you ever phone me again."'

That same day, Todd had the number on his covert telephone changed.

We heard some time afterwards that David Black was teaching music privately somewhere on the south coast. Following the court verdict we put his name on List 99, which means he is prohibited from working in a school. There is, however, nothing to prevent him, or any other teacher on the list, from working as a private tutor.

Throughout my time at the Yard there was steady speculation, mainly in the media, about the existence of snuff movies. My own definition of a snuff movie is a film in which the maker has set out to record a killing, but it could include filming in circumstances where death occurs accidentally during bizarre and dangerous activity. News footage, such as the widely screened execution of a suspect Viet Cong guerrilla in the street by a South Vietnamese soldier, would never be included in the category of snuff movies.

It was widely rumoured that the murder of Jason Swift, a young boy killed by a network of predatory paedophiles, had been filmed. The police have never believed that is true, and in spite of vigorous efforts to find even a trace of evidence, nothing has ever been found to suggest that this terrible episode was recorded. I don't doubt, however, that if the technology had been available in 1962 when Myra Hindley and Ian Brady set out on their orgy of child-killing, they would have recorded their activities on video.

We often seized tapes, and occasionally some were sent to the office, in which people were depicted being killed, usually as part of an extreme sado-masochistic scenario. Some of the tapes were quite plainly faked; others were more difficult to interpret and in these cases we would call on Iain West, one

of the finest pathologists in the country, to give an opinion.
The British Board of Film Classification occasionally found
themselves with similar films on their hands. None of them
ever turned out to be genuine.

It is possible, though, even likely, that real snuff movies
exist. There is certainly a market for them. They would command a high price and would certainly be kept in a very
secure place, since the film would be first-hand evidence of
murder and would expose the participants to detection.

In 1993 we had direct experience of a man who wanted to
murder two prostitutes and make a film of the event, so we
know there are people out there with the desire. The man's
name was Alec Doughty. He wrote to a pornographer – we
will call him George – and told him without preamble that he
wanted to make a sado-masochistic video featuring himself
and prostitutes. As his letter got into its descriptive stride, he
went further than that: he said he wanted to kill two prostitutes on video. It was his misfortune that the pornographer he
wrote to was a police informant, who contacted our office
immediately. We told him to call Alec Doughty and suggest a
get-together at which George would introduce him to a man
who could make the video for him.

A meeting was arranged in the upstairs bar on the con-
course at Euston station, and at the appropriate time George
arrived in the company of Todd, our undercover officer.
Doughty arrived shortly afterwards and they all shook hands.
Todd was introduced as an expert producer of pornographic
videos.

'I was using a tape recorder,' Todd recalled, 'so when we
went to the bar I tried to get as far away from the actual bar as
possible, so I wouldn't pick up the sound of all the people
talking and ordering drinks and the tills banging and so forth.

So I got myself up into this corner, then somebody put money in the juke box and I realised I was standing in front of one of the biggest speakers you've ever seen. The music was so loud it vibrated in my chest. So I said we'd have to go outside when we were ready to talk business, because I was a bit deaf and I couldn't hear a word they were saying.'

They had a drink at the bar, then George said he had to get back to business. When he had left Todd went outside with Doughty and sat beside him on a low wall in front of the station.

'Right from the start he got on well with me,' Todd said. 'He didn't hesitate about going through what he wanted to do with these two girls – it had to be two girls, one to watch what was happening to the other one. He had made expert drawings of what he was going to do.'

'If it's an ordinary girl I'm not interested,' Doughty said. 'If it's a working girl who opens her legs for money and sells sex then what little conscience I've got left would be quite unaffected, I could really go to town.'

Todd asked him if there was any reason for that.

'A personal hang-up of mine, I suppose,' Doughty said. 'I've seen tarts opening their legs and hawking themselves and I think they deserve all they get, and it's much nicer if they can do some suffering first.'

Doughty had prepared a list of items that would be needed for the various tortures he planned to inflict on the women.

'Most of it is going to be household stuff,' he told Todd, running his finger down the list. 'You get a long cane from the garden centre, a dildo – well, I think I can make one of them. Then there's some tree wood, pliers, wire-cutters, a blowtorch, Stanley knife, car battery acid, salt.'

Doughty emphasised that every item was important to his

plans. Nothing should be left out, because everything had a specific place and purpose in the ritual. Doughty's enthusiasm grew as he talked. He made tight, swooping hand gestures as he described the scenario to Todd.

'What I want to do is grab them one at a time. We mustn't lose control of them. Not at any time. We'll use chloroform.'

He was anxious, he said, that the women's suffering should be drawn out as much as possible before they died. He also wanted to arrange the tortures so that he could investigate some things he had been curious about; he wanted to know, for instance, what the inside of a breast looked like.

'And I want a second camera. There, right on the spot where I stick the poker, focused right on her, and a monitor mounted along the table where she can see it.'

From time to time Doughty would stop talking and hark back to something they had discussed minutes earlier, as if it was the first time the topic had been raised. He kept emphasising how important it was to keep control of the women until they were tied down and helpless.

Doughty had worked out that he would dispose of the corpses in a fire. He explained that they could not simply put the bodies on the ground and build a fire around them. They had to be raised, so there was fire underneath and around them. That way a draught was created and the resulting intense heat was powerful enough to ignite the body fat. When that was ablaze, even the bone would burn to ash, he said.

'That's all we want left. Ash. The cleverest scientists in the world can't tell much from ash, and it certainly doesn't prove anything. Ash isn't any kind of proof. That's worth remembering.'

As they parted company Doughty gave Todd a list of telephone numbers where he could be reached.

'He never gave me a private telephone number to get in touch with him,' Todd said. 'It was always a phone box in Hertfordshire, a different phone box for different times of day.'

They met several times, and each time the plan became a shade firmer than before, a shade more real. Doughty was going to supply the victims, Todd had to lay on the photographic expertise, the cameras, the lighting and the sound equipment. He had to provide the building they would use, too. It had to be well away from other buildings or places where people might be walking, so the screaming would not be heard, and there had to be a walled yard where the women's remains could be cremated.

The last time they met, Doughty gave Todd a bottle containing a liquid he called chloroform. We later learned it was not chloroform. It was trichlorethylene, a strong industrial grease-cutting agent which in its pure form – the form in which Todd received it – was the key component in several powerful anaesthetics. A pharmacologist confirmed that the liquid had the same effect as chloroform.

'Try it out on yourself,' Doughty told Todd. 'Just a little bit. Inhale it and you'll feel yourself going.'

By now it was obvious that Doughty was doing more than fantasising. The fact that he had gone to the trouble to obtain a dangerous chemical was a clear enough sign that he was serious.

Then he seemed to drop out of sight. Todd had no contact with him for months.

'Then, right out of the blue, one day he phoned me,' Todd said, 'and he told me, "I've got the victim."'

She was a prostitute living in Surrey. Doughty gave Todd
her telephone number. An officer checked it out and he confirmed he had spoken to a prostitute on the other end of the
line. The case having reached that stage, with a woman's life
potentially at stake, we decided we could not let matters get
out of our control. The police arrested Alec Doughty.

In the end the case never reached court. Doughty was considered unfit to plead and was committed to an institution for
the criminally insane. He is likely to remain there.

17
Operation Framework

While any undercover policeman will agree that his work brings a huge variety of experience into his life, the officer who infiltrates paedophile networks is bound to comment on the curious monotony he finds in the company of child molesters. There is a dominant *sameness* in the outlook and day-to-day behaviour of men who are sexually obsessed with children.

'Rich or poor, educated or illiterate, they all come across as being much alike,' Todd said. 'Nothing in their lives is so big that it distracts them from that one central preoccupation.'

Frederick Chambers was essentially no different from the rest. He was a very, very rich man who owned a number of companies dealing in electronics and advanced video equipment. He was contracted to Sky Television, where one of his teams was regularly engaged to film major sporting events. Chambers had also been responsible for installing the video cameras in the Houses of Parliament.

One day he went into a sex shop and asked for sex videos featuring very young girls and boys. The manager of the shop said he did not sell that kind of stuff, but he knew a man who did. He gave him the telephone number of our undercover officer. Chambers called Todd the same day and they arranged to meet in the Tower Hotel.

'That first time I met him,' Todd recalls, 'he said he was acting on behalf of two other people. He said he wanted one lot of tapes with girls, one lot with boys.'

Todd had to explain that there was no question of working with a go-between. 'I'll certainly speak to your two clients, though. Whatever they want, I'll get it for them.'

Chambers looked disappointed. 'You can't do the business directly through me, then?'

'No,' Todd said firmly. 'I would never do it through someone.'

Chambers said that was awkward, because he was the one who laid out the money.

'Money doesn't come into it,' Todd said. 'There is no money involved, they pick out what they want and it is normally operated on an exchange system.'

'Oh, I see.' Chambers looked very glum. 'It's going to be difficult.'

'If it was one of your two clients I was talking to here, we would be well into it by now,' Todd said. 'Probably I'd be showing them my stuff by this time.'

After more hesitation, Chambers said he didn't think he could deal with Todd in the way he insisted. Todd asked him what was so difficult.

'It's the position these people are in,' Chambers said. 'They are very wealthy people and one of them is the son of a lord.'

'All the more reason I should deal with him directly,' Todd said. 'I get to know exactly what the client's into, I supply him with whatever he wants, and that's it. Clean cut and straight-forward, no messing with middle-men.'

Chambers then appeared to get playful and friendly, per-haps hoping to soften Todd up and get him to drop the rule about middle-men on this occasion.

'Listen, Todd,' he said, 'I've got five hundred pounds in my back pocket now that says you can't shock me.'

Todd looked at him and thought, *I've got a warrant card in the office that says I can.*

'Sorry,' Todd said, 'I can't do business with you. You've got my number. If your interested parties want to contact me, then fair enough.'

A week later, Chambers phoned Todd. 'I've got some tapes,' he said. 'They're my own tapes.'

'What about these other two people?' Todd asked.

'They don't exist.'

'Pardon?'

'It's me, just me. But I have to be cautious.'

Chambers said he was going on holiday for three weeks, but when he came back he would meet Todd.

'So we arranged a meet. He would bring his tapes and I would bring mine, and maybe we could do business between us. So I met him again at the Tower. We had a drink in the bar, talked about this and that. He told me he had been on holiday and had gone into the public toilets where all the young kids were. He had spent a lot of time hanging around near them. Then he said he had videos of some girls cavorting and had angled the camera up their skirts.'

When they had finished their drinks Chambers said, 'Right. Shall we go for a walk? I've got the car on the third floor of the multi-storey at the top of the road.'

They left the hotel and started walking towards the Tower of London. As they went, Chambers told Todd about some of the campsites he visited on holiday on the continent. He made a practice of going into the latrines early in the morning and usually he would find little girls on their own there.

'You can cop a grope,' Chambers said. 'I've had some wonderful times.'

They took the lift to the third floor of the multi-storey, then Chambers realised he had parked on the floor below. They went down the fire escape to the second floor and Chambers pointed to a large Range Rover. It had been backed into an alcove.

'Nothing overlooking us, Todd. Nice and private.'

Chambers told Todd to get into the back. As Todd sat down he saw a portable TV set with a built-in video recorder mounted between the front seats facing the rear seats. Chambers started the car's engine, then he came and sat in the back beside Todd. He took a videotape from a compartment behind the driver's seat and put it in the machine.

'I don't know whether you've got this one or not,' Chambers said.

Todd watched as the picture came up on the screen. A little girl was lying on a bed and a man was removing her underwear.

'How old is she?' Todd asked.

'Six or seven.'

When they had watched some more footage it was time for Todd to show the material he had brought. He pointed out that it was a relatively short tape.

'I don't mind,' Chambers said, loading the cassette. 'I like everything.'

Chambers switched on the machine. On the screen a girl of

about twelve was seen in what looked like a doctor's surgery, being sexually abused by a man in a white coat.

Todd asked Chambers if he had seen the tape before.

'No,' Chambers murmured, his eyes glued to the screen. 'Bloody good quality, by the look of it. I love it, it's very sweet, that . . .'

'If you fast-forward it,' Todd said, 'you'll see it's got a bit of a story to it.'

Chambers became visibly excited by the tape. 'I tell you, I'm a bugger, Todd. I really do like that, that's brilliant, that really turns me on . . . Wonderful, absolutely wonderful!'

The arrangement was that now each knew what the other liked, they would meet again and do a proper swap.

They got out and walked round to the front of the car. Chambers took a bundle of money from his pocket and offered some to Todd. He refused it.

'I don't want your money. It's just nice to see one of my own.'

They shook hands, which was the signal for police officers waiting nearby. Chambers was arrested and Todd melted away towards the fire escape.

'I remember, as I was shaking his hand,' Todd recalls, 'he said to me, "I don't want to be too late tonight, I'm filming the Coca-Cola Cup Final," and I thought, I don't think you are, actually.'

Chambers was sentenced to six months' imprisonment for taking indecent photographs.

Operation Framework arose from our serious concern that a number of British men were taking children abroad, principally to Amsterdam, where they were selling them into prostitution and pornography. On the day the final swoop was made we obtained thirty-one search warrants, one of them against a man called Warwick Spinks. Our intelligence was that although Spinks had no convictions, he was a paedophile and had associations close to the heart of the trade in children. It was felt that he was probably so dangerous that he would warrant the kind of scrutiny that only an undercover operation could accomplish.

So once again we called on the expert talents of Todd, our undercover officer. In the story of how he gained the confidence of Warwick Spinks, I asked Todd to tell the tale himself, exactly as he recalls it.

In November 1992 I was tasked to gain the confidence of a man called Warwick Spinks, who lived in Norwood. After gaining his trust I was to monitor his movements and activities with a view to bringing a prosecution. I had to pass myself off as a homosexual paedophile, but this time I had to do it without letting the target know that I knew *he* was a paedophile. To make matters even more difficult, this man had never been convicted of anything, so I had to work on a person who had no form for me to study, and who also possessed an apparent ability to run rings around the law. It was not going to be an easy job, and we knew this would be a long-term operation.

Spinks had placed advertisements in *Boyz*, a free homosexual magazine, offering flats to rent in Poland and Amsterdam. I called the number in the advertisement and Spinks answered the telephone. I introduced myself as an executive in an insurance and finance business, and I said I would like to use his flat in Amsterdam. We arranged the dates and agreed the terms, and I gave him a special office number so he could contact me if there was any need. He told me I could pick up the keys from him at the flat in Amsterdam, as he would be there on 17 December, the date I was due to arrive.

Spinks had been under fairly regular surveillance, and a couple of days before I was due to meet him he was seen in Victoria station, talking to a teenaged boy he was definitely aiming to pick up. I was shown a photograph of the two of them in the station as part of my briefing before I left for Holland.

On my arrival in Amsterdam I met up with a young Dutch police officer who was to work with me. He was using the name of Mark. In the early afternoon he drove me to the Amstel district and parked outside a large block of flats with the name 'Amstel 294' on the front. Mark waited in the car and I went into the foyer of the building. I pressed the intercom for one of the flats. A man answered and told me to take the lift to the fifth floor. When I got there I knocked on the door of the flat.

Warwick Spinks opened the door. I recognised him at once from the various photographs I had seen. He looked younger than his years; he could easily have been taken for a man of twenty-five, rather fat but quite flashily good-looking, the type anybody would assume to be a ladies' man. He took me inside and introduced me to the same youth he was photographed with in Victoria station.

'This is my friend Ken,' he said.

Spinks then gave me a cursory tour of the flat, which was one big room with kitchen facilities and a fold-down bed, plus a separate shower room and toilet.

I said to Spinks, 'I've met a friend of a friend of mine over here. He's downstairs. He doesn't know Amsterdam, perhaps we could all go out this evening?'

'Sure,' Spinks said. 'In fact we can go for a drink right now, just so you get the feel of the place, then tonight we'll all go out for a proper pub crawl.'

'That's marvellous,' I said. 'I'm here for three days, and I don't want to miss out on anything. If you really don't mind showing me round . . .'

'It'll be a pleasure, Todd.'

'Great. I'll pay for everything. I want to see the right places. You know ...' I winked, 'where they've got the younger element.'

Downstairs I introduced Mark, then the four of us walked through the cold sunlit streets to the Marcella Bar in Princengracht. We sat at a table and Spinks ordered our drinks in Dutch. He was extremely friendly and I appeared to hit it off with him without any difficulty. He commented on my Cockney accent, and I told him that I came from the East End. He told me he was from South London.

I tried to ask Ken about himself, but Spinks did all the talking.

'Ken lives in Kent. He's fifteen,' he added, with the shadow of a wink.

Later, when Ken went to the toilet, Spinks told me that he had had sexual intercourse with the lad the night before. He said it was Ken's first sexual experience and that he had pretended to be drunk and asleep throughout the whole scene.

When we were on our second drink Spinks asked me what I was going to do during my stay in Amsterdam. I told him I would like to look at some videos and visit a few gay bars. He told me that there were plenty of chickens – young boys – in the gay bars around the city. I did my best to look pleased about that, then I moved the subject on to videos.

'I'll tell you what, Warwick,' I said, 'I bought a few videos back in England but they were very poor quality.'

'Yeah, well, they would be.'

He told me he had run a porno video business in Kent at one time, using the name of J. Heath. He said all of his stock of videos had been confiscated by the police, but he hadn't been caught.

'Do you still have any contacts in the business?' I asked him.

He nodded slowly and smiled. He said that he could get any kind of videos I wanted right there in Amsterdam.

'I don't think I'd like to run the risk of taking them through Customs,' I said. 'Have you got any back in England I might have a look at?'

'Sure, I'll fix you up, Todd. Don't worry about it.'

Later, while Ken and Mark sat saying nothing, looking around them, Spinks told me he had other flats for rent in Warmoestraat, which was in another part of Amsterdam.

'But they're for straight punters. I've got flats to rent in Prague and the Canary Islands, too, if you're ever interested.'

'I quite fancy Prague,' I said. 'Never been there, mind you.'

Spinks told me drink and cigarettes were cheap in Prague. He had plenty of supplies in England and he would be happy to sell some to me cheap.

I noticed that Spinks was getting more talkative the more he drank. He told me he had been coming to Amsterdam since he was fifteen years old. He also said that he had been married and had two children, but he had left his wife and was living with a nineteen-year-old Polish boy in Thornton Heath. He referred to this boy as 'the wife'.

When he showed some interest in my own background I told him I was the executive manager of an insurance and finance company. I was single, I said, and usually inclined to keep myself to myself.

Spinks told me that tonight, just for a change, I could come out of my shell. He said he would show us round the best gay bars in Amsterdam. Then he looked at his watch.

'I have to go. I've an appointment to keep.'

We arranged that we would meet again in the evening at seven o'clock, at Amstel 294. Before he and Ken left the bar Spinks gave me a set of keys for the flat. I waited five minutes, then left the bar with Mark. We met up with other Dutch officers and went to a hotel where a room had been booked for me. We spent the rest of the afternoon making notes.

Later I went to the flat with Mark, where we sat and waited for the other two to show up. At about half-past seven Spinks buzzed the intercom and told me he was in the foyer with Ken. Mark and I went down and all four of us went to the Amstelhoek, a gay bar. While we were there Spinks told me he wanted to show me as many bars as possible that evening because he was going back to England with Ken the following day.

We stayed in Amstelhoek for about three minutes and then went to Chez Manfred on Halvemassteeg. It was full to the door with gay men of all ages. There were also two middle-aged women, who were walking along the bar, putting lipstick on the men as they passed. We declined their offer and went to another bar opposite. This place was decorated entirely in white, with white cloth on the walls and ceiling.

'It's like walking into a giant condom,' Spinks said.

Like the other places this was a gay bar, as busy as the one across the road. Two black men behind me were dancing, and after a minute I felt two hands closing around my genitals. I looked over my shoulder, trying not to panic, and I saw that one of the black men had turned towards me and was dancing with his front to my back. He grinned at me and so did Spinks. I pulled away from him perhaps a little too sharply, then I quickly explained to Spinks that he had been making me spill my drink.

We left this bar after ten minutes and went to a quieter one on Amstel. There were only four other customers and the bar had no disco, so it was possible to have a conversation. Spinks drew me to one side.

'Todd, I want your stay in Amsterdam to be a memorable one. There's lots of other gay bars I want to show you, but I've got a problem. I didn't get a chance to go to the bank, so I'm running low on money. Could you lend me three hundred guilders?'

'No problem.'

I handed him the cash, and I had the immediate sense that I had passed some kind of test. He put his mouth close to my ear.

'The next bar we go to,' he whispered, 'I'm going to fix you up with a chicken.'

So events were fitting the required scenario. Spinks had taken to me. I had won his confidence, and he accepted me as a paedophile, all on my first day in the job. The only snag so far was that I had to make sure I had no part in the soliciting of a minor, and I had to do it without making Spinks suspicious.

'Listen,' I said, tapping my chest, 'I've got to be careful. With this heart condition I've got, a frisky chicken would probably kill me.'

'Nah.' Spinks shook his head. 'You won't have to do anything. You can just cuddle, or the boy can give you a blow-job. It won't cost you a thing, either. It'll be my treat.'

He said I could take the boy back to Amstel 294N, and at some point during the evening we could swap partners. He would let me sleep with Ken while he had sex with the boy he had supplied for me.

Now I felt a little flutter of panic. I told Spinks it seemed like a good idea, but the fact was, I fancied Mark.

He frowned at me. 'Isn't he a bit old for your taste?'

'He is, yes, but he's the boyfriend of a friend, you see? It would give me a bit of a kick if I could make it with him. I won't get a chance after tonight, so I'd like to take a shot at it, if you won't feel offended.'

'Do you think Mark will go for it?' Spinks muttered. 'He doesn't look all that interested to me.'

I said I would speak to Mark, and if he wasn't interested, I would take Spinks up on his kind offer.

'Fair enough,' Spinks said.

I asked Mark to come outside for a minute. He followed me out on to the cold street.

'Look,' I said, 'me and you have got to fall in love very, very quickly, otherwise we're both in the shit, big time.'

Mark understood. We walked back into the bar hand in hand. 'I'm in with Mark,' I whispered to Spinks. 'But thanks for your offer, anyway.'

Keeping my voice low, I told Spinks that not only had Mark agreed to sleep with me, but he was going to drive me back to his house where I could stay the night, so Spinks could have the use of Amstel 294, which would save him driving across the city to the place where he was staying.

'Suits me fine,' Spinks said, and I could see he had swallowed the story. He looked at his watch. 'I'll have to phone the wife soon. He's a jealous lad and gets stroppy if I don't keep in touch.'

At about 9:30 I told Spinks I was keen to leave with Mark, now we had an understanding. We said our goodbyes and I thanked Spinks for making my first visit to Amsterdam so enjoyable.

I left the bar with Mark and we then drove to my hotel, where we made our notes. I was confident, by that time, that I had made a sound contact with Spinks, and that he not only trusted me and accepted me as a paedophile, but appeared to want to stay friendly.

When I returned to England I allowed time for Spinks to get back, then I telephoned him, because I had to give him back the keys to the flat in Amsterdam. I said I would bring them round. He told me not to bother, I could just post them. I said I didn't like the idea of putting keys in the post, I'd much sooner give them to him.

So I met him down in Norwood, and he introduced me to the man he had referred to as his wife. We had a drink and as I left he said he wanted to have a natter with me again really soon. We kept in touch fairly regularly after that. I used to meet him at Compton's and similar places in the West End. It was an easy-going arrangement, smoother than I had imagined at the outset.

Then without any warning Spinks moved to Hastings to live. I made excuses to keep in contact with him there, too. Operation Framework at that point had been running for about two years; they now had a list of numerous names and addresses where they would soon make simultaneous swoops nationwide. The big day was about to dawn. I went down to Hastings to find out if Spinks would be there the following Tuesday, when the raids were due to take place.

When I was alone with him in his house he said, 'I had two lovely boys here. Fourteen, they were, both of them.' He winked. 'I took photographs.'

'Local lads, are they?' I asked him.

'No fear. They're from a children's home in Doncaster.'

I told him I would love to see the photographs. He said he hadn't had them developed yet.

'I'm going over to Amsterdam next week, I'll get them developed then.'

I asked him what the boys looked like. One was fair, he said, and was called Tom; the other one, Ricky, was dark-haired.

'Lovely,' I said. 'I'd definitely like to see them.'

Because of that conversation, the Framework invasion plan was put on hold until we had a date when Warwick Spinks would be back home at Hastings.

Meanwhile, going on the descriptions of the boys I had been given, plus their names and the location, the police were able to go to the only children's home in Doncaster where they found, sure enough, that two boys with those names and fitting those descriptions had run away several days earlier.

Later, when the boys had been found again and brought back to the home, one of them described how they had been picked up in Hastings by Spinks and taken to his home. He had sodomised them at knife-point, then made them sodomise each other. One of them was taken to Amsterdam and sold to the owner of a club called the Blue Boy. He eventually escaped through a window and went to the British consul, who brought him back to England.

Meanwhile, Framework had to be re-scheduled, so I called Spinks in Amsterdam and said I was thinking of coming over to Hastings the following Wednesday, which was when the officers running Framework wanted to make all the raids.

'I'll be home that day, sure,' he told me. 'Earlier than that, most likely. Come down when you like.'

'I wondered if you'd have the photos of the two lads you told me about,' I said.

'I should have them by then, yeah,' he said. 'You won't be disappointed, I can promise you.'

'Great. I'll see you next Wednesday, then.'

Spinks was duly raided the following Wednesday. Among other material, the police found the negatives of the photographs of Tom and Ricky from the children's home.

At Lewes Crown Court Spinks pleaded not guilty to a number of charges. After I and everyone else involved in the case had given evidence, Spinks was found guilty. He was sentenced to seven years' imprisonment.

The value of photographs in the above case would be hard to overestimate, especially where their existence could be directly incriminating. The shift in the law which made it an offence for a person to possess indecent photographs of children meant we no longer had to prove direct wrongdoing against a child or children before we could prosecute.

Around that time the emphasis of the work of the Obscene Publications Branch altered in much the same way. We shifted our focus from the prosecution of obscene publications, where the corrupting effect of pornography had to be proved, to the prosecution of specific, illegal acts depicted in films, videos or still photographs. It was a shift from subjective policing – that is, the attempt to prosecute material which a jury might not judge was obscene – to the *objective* pursuit of individuals who took part in acts which the law had already decided were punishable. In the case of child pornography, we prosecuted the people who distributed the material; the definition of 'child', incidentally, was someone who *appeared* to be under sixteen years of age.

Paedophiles must have heaved a collective sigh of relief when attempts to include mere *possession* of child pornography in the 1978 Act met with failure. We found a letter in one raid in which the writer praised Parliament for failing to pass 'that ridiculous possession law'. For a further ten years, unless it could be proved that any child pornography we seized was destined to be distributed in some way, it had to be given back. It was incredibly frustrating to have to do that, knowing that these men were in possession of pictures of children being abused and exploited, and were using them for their pleasure. We all found it almost too much to bear. It was not until 1988, when the law changed and possession of indecent photographs of children became an offence, that the police could really get to grips with the problem. Apart from closing a gap in the law and strengthening the hand of those engaged in the protection of children, the possession law made it easier to identify paedophiles. Someone who possessed indecent photographs of minors, and who was convicted of possession, could then have his name entered on a paedophile register and be identified as a danger to young people.

Critics of our work occasionally called us the Thought Police. The implication was that we found means to censor what people could see and hear, and that in the process we restricted their imaginations and their freedom to express themselves. When the people allegedly being treated in that way are paedophiles, I don't deny that we have always been interested in curtailing their access to anything that stimulates or sustains their deviant behaviour towards children.

Photographs can be an eloquent gauge of a paedophile's fixations, and a guide to the severity of his obsession. That was certainly the case with the serial killer Robert Black. He was arrested in Scotland after grabbing a young girl on the street and dragging her into his van. A neighbour saw what had happened and telephoned the police. Black was arrested shortly afterwards.

The murder squad in Edinburgh were convinced that Black was the man responsible for a number of unsolved cases of abduction and murder of young girls which had been carried out in various parts of the country over a number of years. They invited me to Edinburgh to examine material they had found in Black's flat in Edmonton in London. They wanted to know my opinion of his level of threat, based on my experience in dealing with paedophiles. I took Sergeant Bernie Meaden with me and we were well received by the team. They had put their case together painstakingly, using a system that became known as Catchem, which pinpointed Black's movements and eventually led to him being convicted for several more offences.

The material taken from his flat was truly astonishing. He had a vast collection of child pornography videos and photographs, but there were also a number of Polaroid pictures he had taken of himself which vividly illustrated his obsession with bodily orifices. He freely admitted this fixation after he was convicted. In the Polaroids he used a mirror to photograph himself pushing objects – one of them a telephone receiver – into his anus. He was compelled to penetrate bodies, even his own, and his compulsion strongly echoed the sadistic treatment inflicted on the girls who figured in the unsolved murder cases. He also made a chilling comment during an interview with an expert on paedophilia: he admitted he had a compulsion to push objects into little girls, but he felt that since he had no wish to hurt them, they would have to be dead first. In other words, the abuse he was driven to commit was so extreme that the victims would have to die in order to be spared the pain.

Black's video and picture collection was undoubtedly the hoard of an extremely violent and dangerous child molester. We could confirm, straight away, that the murder squad detectives were correct in believing they had arrested one of worst deviants in British criminal history. Black was not tried for the murders, since the cost of mounting a case, not only in money, but in hours and manpower, would have been horrendous, and little would be achieved in law, since Black was already behind bars for life. He never confessed to the murders, but his movements throughout the eight-year period when the girls went missing, and important clues he let slip in his conversations with the expert on paedophilia, leave little doubt that Black was the killer of at least six little girls.

There is special pleading, from time to time, on behalf of paedophiles at the other end of the scale from Robert Black, the men who never make sexual contact with children. They are the ones who use pornography alone to satisfy their needs, and it is argued that they channel their urges safely and are therefore guilty of no offence. But that argument is badly flawed. If a man uses child pornography he takes pleasure from the brutal abuse of young lives; if he seeks out this material, he contributes to a demand that can only be satisfied at the price of violated children. The collector of child pornography may prove that he has never laid abusing hands on any young person, but that atones for nothing. His actions have made him as culpable as any predatory paedophile.

18
Brushes With Media and Death

Press and television exposure formed a crucial part of our working policy. With our limited staff we needed media interest – and, therefore, media coverage – to maximise our impact. Information about paedophiles and their methods had to be communicated to the public. It was a crime-prevention strategy. It is also a fact that the public will take far more notice of the police as an authoritative source than, say, Social Services or any of the charities. This is undoubtedly because the police complement their information with real-life cases, which end up in the criminal courts and can be reported. So often, cases dealt with by Social Services are resolved in the Family Division and cannot be publicised. The police have credibility and are used to dealing with crime and social-affairs correspondents practically every day.

In such a contentious area there are bound to be pitfalls when it comes to running a high-profile media strategy. We know that sex sells newspapers, so it is important that child abuse is not reported in a way which can be viewed as exploitative. We tried to maintain the initiative; it did not always work and sometimes we were driven by the demands of the news medium. In these cases, we endeavoured to make the best of the situation, and by and large it worked.

All areas of the broadcast media bombarded us daily for opinions, statements, and expert information. We always did our best to help. I got an average of twenty telephone calls from them a day, and we had excellent staff from the Department of Public Affairs who dealt with requests for facilities, and would put our responses on topical matters into the Press Bureau to reduce the burden on us. I tried always to be as open as possible with the media. It is a policy that works, even if it does expose one to easy scrutiny.

The biggest problems always came from the Sunday tabloids. If they gave us information, they would want us to carry out any raid on a Friday night, so they could print the results on Sunday.

One occasion when the whole exercise ended in failure, from our standpoint, was in the execution of Operation Butterfly. We were contacted by a reporter at the *News of the World* on a Thursday; he told us that a pornographic film was to be made the following Saturday night. The location for the filming was to be the King's Hall Leisure Centre in Hackney, where arrangements had been made for the crew to be let in after the public had left and the centre was closed.

The movie, we learned, would be directed by a man who was already known to the police as a pornographer. The storyline would depict extreme sado-masochism, and would feature an eighteen-year-old girl who would be portrayed as a twelve-year-old schoolgirl. The girl in question, the daughter of a known brothel madam who operated in Paddington, was already working on the streets as a prostitute. During the shooting of the film, the mother was to be part of the back-up team providing tea and coffee for the crew. We listened to tape recordings of telephone conversations that confirmed the plans, and we learned that the film was intended for the paedophile market and would be sent to Holland for distribution.

We gathered what intelligence we could on the suspects and assembled a team of twenty officers from our office and from Hackney Division. We briefed at Scotland Yard on the Saturday afternoon and set up the observation in Hackney at 6:30 P.M. Time wore on, but no film team appeared. We were covering their various home addresses around London but there was no activity to report. By ten o'clock we realised the film was not going to be made that night. Bob McLachlan and I approached the newspaper photographer, who had been lurking nearby waiting for the story to break. We told him he could go home. He looked startled at that, and then hurried away.

Keith Driver was sent out for an early edition of the *News of the World*. On page 7, under the banner headline, 'TV NAZI TORTURES GIRL AGED 17 IN SEX VIDEO', was an account of the plans to make the film. Newspapers are forbidden, under the *sub judice* rule, from publishing details of a crime and the people involved in it between the time they are charged and the end of any subsequent trial. So by publishing that account before we had charged anyone, they had got themselves a story and at the same time avoided the legal stricture. They had also made certain that the suspects would never turn up – not after their plans had been set out in the *News of the World*.

My own view was that in the medium term, there would have been a far better story if the paper had held back from publication and let us finish the inquiry. They could have claimed, correctly, that they had helped the police to set up the job, they could have printed their account from the 'inside track', and it would probably have made two or three pages of splash copy instead of a piece on page 7.

The reality is that newspapers have short-term preoccupations and feel obliged to print as early as they can. I accept that there is a lot of competition in the industry. There is always the danger of a story being bagged by a rival, and certainly the Sunday papers are more vulnerable to that than the dailies. But forethought and a bit of reflection should also play a part in these deals. In this case the information was good, we had identified the people who were part of the set-up, and from our perspective the whole conspiracy hung together. We did not know why it didn't go ahead. There was no reason to think the suspects had been alerted to our involvement, or to that of the paper. There was every reason to suppose that the filming would have taken place on another day, and we would have been waiting for them. We had committed a lot of time, energy and public money to the enquiry and all for no result. It was a frustrating night.

Overwork and other stresses, among them my recent divorce from Jacqui, combined to undermine my health and bring about a crisis. It happened on 2 September 1993, a Thursday. It was a day no more or less stressful than any other at that time. I got into work at 8:30, as I usually did, and settled down straight away to deal with the routine correspondence. After two hours of that I chaired a meeting to review and discuss the caseload being handled in the office. The meeting lasted until 12:30, and then I went to lunch with Peter Burdon, the chief crime correspondent of the *Daily Mail*.

At that time Peter was working on a story about the

Children of God sect. A woman whose daughter was a member of the sect was trying to sue the leaders for custody of her grandchild. Peter, who had interviewed the woman at length, was passing me new information to supplement a three-year study we had done on the Children of God. After lunch I had more correspondence to deal with, another meeting, then an informal end-of-day confab with my team to discuss worries, dilemmas, breakthroughs and progress in general.

I left the office at 6:30 and drove home to my partner at the time, Elizabeth. There was some confusion that night about where we should eat. After a while we decided that the four of us – myself, Elizabeth and her children Elizabeth-Anne and Daniel – would go to a Mexican restaurant a short drive away. When we got there it was fully booked for the night, so we had to think of something else. Young Daniel decided he wanted take-away fish and chips; nobody else wanted that, so we took him to the chip shop, picked up some fish and chips and dropped him off at home. By now the rest of us were getting grumpy with hunger. We finally plumped for the Rose & Olive Branch, a favourite pub near the Royal Holloway College at Virginia Water.

The food was superb and the choice was always difficult to make, but finally we ordered: fillets of salmon for the girls and Beef Wellington for me. We sat down in a corner with drinks.

I was starting on my second pint of Speckled Hen when I began to feel very strange. Within seconds it went from strange to terrible. I felt profoundly ill. I didn't remember feeling ill ever before, apart from when I had 'flu. There was a fierce crushing pain across my chest and it was spreading down my arms.

The Beef Wellington arrived. I started to eat it but it was a struggle. Each mouthful made me sweat. I told Elizabeth I felt dreadful.

'Stop eating, then,' she said.

I shook my head. 'Rod'll get upset. He's very sensitive about his cooking. He'll give me a terrible bollocking if I leave this.'

Elizabeth told me not to be so stupid. 'Just stop.'

By this time people were beginning to notice something was wrong. One of the joint licensees, John, came over and asked what was the matter.

'I feel dreadful,' I said. 'Never felt so bad in all my life.'

He said he would drive me home.

'No,' I told him, not sure why I was saying it. 'I'll drive.' I pushed aside my plate. 'I will drive . . .'

I got up. The pains were worse now and I was starting to feel dizzy. I went outside and pulled open the car door. Elizabeth argued. She said I was in no state to drive. But I was adamant, I was going to drive us home and there was no point trying to stop me. I felt as if the pain had shoved me halfway into another dimension. I think I knew, in a remote way, that I was being amazingly irrational, but knowing it wouldn't stop me being that way.

So I drove back home with Elizabeth beside me and Elizabeth-Anne in the back. I must have looked like a crab, gripping the wheel with my arms all angular, hunched up with the clamping pain in my chest. As I remember it, I was reacting to an orderly imperative, a plain insistence somewhere in my head that the car must be driven home and neatly parked. That made perfect sense, and it was just as obvious to me that I was the only one who could do the job.

Somehow I got us back safely. Once I was inside the house I decided I wanted to go upstairs and lie down, rather than slump on the settee in the hall and wait for the doctor to show up.

Elizabeth-Anne sat beside me as I lay on the bed. The pain by now was overwhelming and I was ready to admit what was happening. I looked up at Elizabeth-Anne's worried face.

'Tell Mummy not to bother with the doctor,' I said. 'Get her to phone the ambulance. I'm having a heart attack.'

She rushed downstairs. I remember thinking the pain couldn't get any worse. Then it got much worse. It swelled until it was bigger than me. I had never suspected my body could hurt me like that.

After an age, which was probably only a few minutes, two paramedics strode into the room. They moved confidently, studying me with competent eyes, reading my signs. They sprayed GTN (glyceryl trinitrate, a blood vessel dilator) under my tongue and put an oxygen mask on me. They strapped me into a chair, then the poor devils had to carry me all the way down the stairs which I should never have climbed in the first place.

As soon as I was anchored in the back of the ambulance we took off for St Peter's Hospital at Chertsey. The oxygen had rallied me, although I was still in tremendous pain. I was alert and worried enough to try and make a joke of the situation.

'Blues and twos,' I called to the driver. 'Quick as you can. It's not my bloody turn to die. I'm too young.'

At the hospital they put me on a trolley and hurried me to Accident & Emergency. A long minute passed then a nurse appeared at the side of the trolley. She was holding a clipboard and a pen. She asked me for my name and my date of birth.

I couldn't believe it. I had to be catalogued and pigeon-holed before they could get down to saving my life. It was like something out of Orwell. Later, in a calmer frame of mind, I would see the point of it all, but at that moment I wanted to start yelling.

'I don't remember my date of birth,' I told the nurse. 'I'm in agony, for Christ's sake . . .'

A doctor came hurrying out. I stared up at him and thought *Oh my God*. He looked about sixteen. He had blond hair with one of those ratty little ponytails. *That's it,* I thought. *I'm dead.*

He asked me something and I babbled something back. The pain had hit a pitch where I felt it might kill me. Another doctor appeared. I learned later he was a registrar. He had glasses and reminded me of the Milky Bar Kid. I guessed he was maybe eighteen. I know my perception was skewed, but right then it seemed terribly sharp. My life, I thought, was in the hands of a pair of children.

'Give me something to take the pain away,' I begged.

The registrar said they couldn't give me morphine yet. 'It would reduce your blood pressure, and that isn't a wise thing to do until we know what we're dealing with.'

I had an ECG and a blood test in short order, then I was taken for a chest X-ray. When they brought me out of Radiography the registrar had the X-ray plate in his hand. He looked at me, half smiling.

'Here's a surprise, then,' he said, 'there's a shadow on your lung. You've obviously had TB somewhere in the distant past.'

I glared at him. 'I'm not interested in bloody TB! I'm having a heart attack! Do something!'

They wheeled me into Intensive Care and hooked me up to the support machinery. They injected me with 1.5 million units of streptokinase, an anti-clotting drug, and then, at long last, they gave me something for the pain.

Approximately three hours after I had arrived at the hospital, one of the doctors told me I had suffered the kind of heart attack known as a myocardial infarction. Part of the heart muscle had been damaged when the blood supply from one of the coronary arteries was severely reduced.

'If we hadn't seen you having a heart attack,' he said, 'we would have assumed you'd never had one. The tests show that the amount of damage is minimal. You ought to be fine.'

I was relieved to hear it. What I should have done right then was sink into a dreamless sleep. But the machinery of life support makes an incredible amount of noise. With that racket going on, and with bored night-nurses keen to talk to the only conscious patient in the unit, sleep was practically out of the question.

The following day the Deputy Commissioner, John Smith, paid a visit. He told me that when I was on my feet again I should go and see John Coltart, who was the Force Physician and a consultant cardiologist at St Thomas's Hospital. I promised I would do that.

Time passed. I learned that when I had first become ill, Detective Chief Inspector Jim Reynolds was moved across from the Stolen Motor Vehicle Squad to take charge in my absence. Jim was a career detective who had worked in the Detective Training School and the Fraud Squad as well as at Division. (When I eventually got back to work Jim stayed with me and I was glad of that, for the work load had increased. When I finally retired, Jim took over the squad.)

Another of my visitors was Dick Monk, my former commander and mentor, who was by then with the Devon and Cornwall Constabulary. The visit was memorable, among other things, for the presents he brought me: a toy police helicopter with a siren, and a box of paints and a painting book.

After three days I was moved from Intensive Care to Cardiac Care, and that was a marvellous contrast. It was a place where people spoke in whispers and the machinery hummed and sighed instead of buzzing and beeping. I spent several peaceful days there until I was considered fit enough to be discharged from hospital. When I was ready to leave, Bob McLachlan came to pick me up. I gave the paints and painting book to the registrar, and to the impossibly young doctor with the ponytail, whom I called Jesus because he brought me back from the dead, I presented the little police helicopter.

At home I called Dr John Coltart and he arranged a consultation in his rooms at Wimpole Street. 'I'll tell you right now,' I said, 'I haven't any private health insurance. I did have BUPA but it got very expensive, and what with the financial demands on me this past year I let the insurance go. Foolishly, as it's turned out.'

'That's all right,' Coltart said. 'I'll deal with you through the hospital and it'll all be done on the NHS.'

He said the first thing to do was establish what kind of shape my heart was in. To do that he would have to take an angiogram. By injecting a radiopaque substance into the heart and taking a series of X-rays while the substance worked its way through the vessels, he could get a clear picture of the functioning heart and any defects that might be there.

'Call my secretary at the hospital and set up an appointment,' he told me.

I did that. The secretary told me I could have the procedure done in nine months' time. *Nine months.*

I couldn't believe it. For all I knew, and for all anybody could tell me, I might be dead in nine months. I didn't know if I was fit enough to go back to work. I couldn't be sure there wasn't a time-bomb in my chest. The doctor certainly wasn't sure either, or he wouldn't have decided on an angiogram.

I rang up Coltart. 'I suppose if I put my hand in my pocket,' I said, 'I could have the angiogram next week.'

'You want it done privately?' he said.

'That's right.'

'What are you doing tomorrow?'

So next day I went down to his clinic in Harley Street, shelled out £1,200, and had the angiogram.

He showed me the results, fully animated on a videotape. There was a clearly visible blockage in the left anterior descending coronary artery.

'That's all there is,' Coltart said.

'So what'll it take to fix it?'

'You need an angioplasty.'

The operation, he explained, involved passing a catheter into the blocked artery, then inflating a tiny balloon at the tip of the catheter. The balloon would dilate the artery, and at the same time it would flatten the deposits of plaque which were causing the obstruction.

'Call my secretary at the hospital and she'll set up an appointment,' Coltart said.

I called, and sure enough, she told me I'd have to wait another nine bloody months.

This time there was no question of me having it done privately. An angioplasty has to be performed in a fully equipped operating theatre with a cardiac team as back-up, so that if an emergency develops during the operation, they can go ahead and perform a full bypass. The cost of the straight angioplasty was prohibitive; a bypass would have broken the bank.

I thought it over and finally I rang up an old pal, a general practitioner. I put him in the picture. With a minimum of delay he made arrangements for me to go to the Hammersmith Hospital instead of St Thomas's. He fixed an appointment with the cardiologist there, Professor Oakley, for one week later.

When I went to see her I took the tape of the angiogram and she looked at it. She confirmed there was a clearly visible blockage.

'You don't have to have the angioplasty,' she said. 'But if we don't do it there's always the chance you'll have another myocardial incident. It probably wouldn't kill you, but a heart attack's the kind of thing a sensible person avoids.'

I said I wanted to go ahead with the operation, and three weeks later it was done at the Hammersmith. It went smoothly and the blockage in my coronary artery was effectively removed.

There were exchanges of correspondence on the matter of the strange differences in waiting lists for emergency surgery at two central London teaching hospitals, i.e., nine months for an angioplasty at St Thomas's, three weeks for the same operation at the Hammersmith. No satisfactory explanation was offered by politicians or hospital administrators.

My annoyance lingered for a long time. I appreciated it wasn't Coltart's fault, but if I hadn't been lucky enough to have a friend who knew the ropes, I would have been at the mercy of the boneheaded system and would have had to wait for the best part of a year, like hundreds of other poor souls, to find out if I was sick or fit or what. The maze of inequities in the NHS can be a frightening place to get lost.

I went back to work three months after the heart attack.

I wasn't back inside the Yard ten minutes before people were saying things like, 'You can retire now, can't you?

You'll get an ill-health pension, and it's index-linked immediately.'

There was no way I was going to do that. I had unfinished
business. The branch was under attack from the inside, the
whole matter of paedophilia needed to be addressed in the
country at large, and I felt we were at the forefront of making
that happen. I needed to carry on where I left off; I had to
make sure the branch was safe; I had plans to push through a
clutch of proposals for changes in the law, and I had to get
down to a hundred other important, unfinished projects.

In short, I wanted to walk out of the Metropolitan Police
having done my full duty. And in the end that's what I did.

19
The Battle to Survive

The 1992–93 Commissioner's Report, which was the first to be issued by Sir Paul Condon, mentioned the need for organisational change, with the creation of a corporate structure to bolster our capability and help us perform at peak efficiency. The view was that more responsibility should be given to divisions, the operational command units which Condon saw as the hub of police activity. In short, optimum policing could be best delivered locally. I had absolutely no argument with that.

As for how this affected us, the report said: *'Headquarters would be streamlined and reduced to a level necessary for carrying out functions that cannot be done effectively at a local level.'*

I saw no problem with that either; we were in a position to support, advise and give operational help to local police, not only in London, but anywhere else. We had been checked out by the Force Inspectorate twice since my appointment and they praised us fulsomely, along with the usual small

administrative observations that one expected and indeed
hoped for. I viewed inspections as an opportunity for someone on the outside to look at the branch objectively and help
us to streamline our performance.

The Service Restructuring Team (SRT) began its work and
asked us for the usual information about branch duties, functions, and our regular operations. While I knew perfectly well
that we were laying on a service second to none, and knew
moreover that we tried very hard to be a centre of excellence,
I had an uneasy feeling that we were being lined up for sacrifice. Put it down to something in the tone of their approach.

So I examined our weaknesses. We could be shot down on
statistics, if anyone cared to try: by concentrating our ener-
gies – about 90 per cent by then – on countering paedophilia,
I was exposing the branch to the charge that we were
neglecting the problem of adult pornography. While we did
carry out a number of operations against the major suppliers
of pornographic videos, these were significantly fewer than
before. The officers of the West End Clubs Office, with
whom we had no quarrel, were waiting quietly in the wings
and I knew that they would make a play to take over responsibility for policing adult pornography the instant an excuse
presented itself.

Another part of the Commissioner's plan was to give functional as well as regional responsibilities to the new Assistant
Commissioners (ACs) who were to be appointed to the new
areas. The AC appointed to central London would have a
functional responsibility for vice and licensing. It could be
argued, therefore, that the best place for the operations
against pornographers would be at the heart of his area.

Powerful arguments were being made for wholesale
change. I found it hard to come to terms with what I saw as

the destruction of Scotland Yard. Until then it had been a monolithic model of law enforcement, renowned as the best police organisation in the world. Moving the functions away from the centre, and pushing out policy along with them, struck me as a flawed strategy.

Our cause was not helped by the fact that, at that time, we were having a struggle to educate the senior management about the proportions of the paedophile problem. The reluctance of the public to discuss it was mirrored inside our organisation. Senior officers' eyes would glaze over at the very mention of the topic; far better to concentrate on robberies, burglaries and public order. I had no wish to argue with the need to deal with everyday crime, but I was determined to make the point that we needed to commit more resources to targeting men who were curtailing and killing off so many childhoods.

Getting any argument through to the top men was hard, especially when they had dismissed it before it was actually put to them. It was Dick Monk who warned me about a demoralising tactic they used: you would be encouraged to press your point as hard as you could, then they would say, smiling slightly, 'In the blood, is it?', dismissing your earnestness as cranky obsession.

We also faced a proposal that Child Protection teams, with whom we always got on well, might take over our role. It was a profoundly daft proposition. Our staff had all been on the same training courses as the Child Protection Officers, and we regularly lectured to them. We liaised on a daily basis, too. I asked many members of the teams what they thought of the proposition that they take over proactive targeting from us, and I got the same answer every time: they were already snowed under and they had no spare capacity. On top of that, they had no guarantees that they would be authorised to make investigations outside their allotted areas. Most of our operations had country-wide ramifications, in fact a lot of them had international connections, and we were free to pursue all of them.

In spite of what we considered to be overwhelming arguments to retain our central role, I still had an uneasy feeling about the future. Then in April 1994 the Met's own newspaper, *The Job*, carried a supplementary newsletter from the SRT and the Personnel Department. The newsletter was called 'The Future', and on its middle-page spread, under the sub-heading 'HQ responsibilities', a spokesman for the SRT wrote, 'Research has revealed that the time is now right to review and re-organise Specialist Operations. The impetus for this is the need to prioritise resources by matching them to demand over the Service as a whole.'

There had been growing rumours and gut feelings that moves were afoot to have us summarily liquidated, and it struck me that those two sentences in the newsletter might be the prelude to a bombshell. I read on. Sure enough, nine paragraphs later, in the middle of a clutch of the SRT's observations taken from a study of the central squads, the following little knell rang out:

> Obscene Publications: It is suggested that their
> dealings with paedophile offenders could be
> undertaken by Area Child Protection Teams while their
> dealings with obscene publications could be devolved
> to the Clubs Office. Intelligence functions could be
> transferred to the Central Intelligence Unit.

We were up for the chop, nothing was surer. There was a

note later in the newsletter emphasising that none of the proposals contained in the summaries had yet been decided. The note did add, however, that the summary proposals were intended *as an introduction to the subject and a vehicle to identify broad areas of agreement*.

That said it all. Broad areas of agreements brought sweeping change in their wake. So we were on the way out and no amount of nifty pussyfooting would soften the fact. Unless we fought back. But at that time a fair fight was hard to organise and, as far as I could see, my hands were tied. The senior officers in line of command above me were in the same position as myself. They had fought for us without success. We were also told not to speak to the press.

I thought about our position, and I thought about it again. I got angry. Our work, our dedication, our concern and heartfelt commitment were to be denied any further existence, allegedly in the interests of improved efficiency. It was a grotesque obliteration of something vital that could not be replaced. A unit with the success of ours, with that quality of accumulated knowledge and expertise, could not simply have its function extracted and put to work elsewhere; professional excellence did not work that way, and plenty of people who knew it were simply turning their backs, dismissing us without even the need to argue.

I decided to lobby. I went to the House of Commons and to the House of Lords. Over several days I put our case to people in power who believed that power carried responsibility. I put forward our record of success and dedication, and all our arguments for continuing to exist and provide an unequalled service. I asked that the Obscene Publications Branch have the support of caring individuals whose opinions could make a difference.

We also fired back a multi-point criticism of the SRT consultation document, which had managed, among other blunders, to comment that 'some' special skills had been developed within the Obscene Publications Department, ignoring the fact that as a part of the International and Organised Crime Branch, we were in fact a *totally* specialised unit. We also pointed out that another remark in the SRT document, referring to a 'drift' towards concentration on paedophile offences, was entirely misleading, and that, far from having drifted, we had undertaken a strategic tasking of our small staff and limited resources and had focused them, quite properly, on the investigation of child pornography and paedophile offences. So successful had this strategy been, we added, that both inside and outside the service we were acknowledged to be the most informed and effective police unit in the UK.

On 21 April, shortly after we set our defence in motion, the following appeared in *Hansard*, which is the official report of the proceedings and debates of the Houses of Parliament:

Mrs Ann Winterton (Congleton): Will my Right Honourable Friend [the Home Secretary] take note of early-day motion 1057? The motion, which is tabled in my name, concerns the proposal to disband the obscene publications squad at New Scotland Yard.

Is my Right Honourable Friend aware of the success of that unit, and its commitment to bringing child pornographers and paedophiles to book? Is he aware of the strength of our belief that the squad should be given more resources and more power within the restructuring process? The proposal to disband it will be applauded by peddlers of pornography throughout

the United Kingdom. Can my Right Honourable
Friend find time for a debate on the subject very
soon?

The motion referred to by Ann Winterton read as follows:

That this House commends the commitment and
dedication of the personnel in the Obscene
Publications Branch at New Scotland Yard; recognises
their unique national role and expertise in
investigating child pornography and paedophile rings;
notes the ever-growing complexity and the volume of
computer pornography with which the branch deals;
and calls upon the Home Secretary to ensure that the
Commissioner abandons any plan to close the Obscene
Publications Branch and that this specialist squad is
assured a continuing and strengthened place in the
Metropolitan Police on the conclusion of the current
restructuring review.

Eight days later Ann Winterton sent the following letter to
the Home Secretary, Michael Howard:

Dear Michael
            Future of the Obscene Publications Squad
We have met and corresponded a number of times over
the last year about Obscenity Law reform. You know
my view that while the provisions in the Criminal
Justice and Public Order Bill are welcome, especially
those on child pornography, a more fundamental
review is necessary. Although we disagree on this issue,
I had accepted at face value the assurance that a central

plank in the government's strategy is effective enforcement of existing law.

You will understand my dismay, and that of the 100 Members from six different parties who have already signed my Motion on this subject, when I learned that the future of the Obscene Publications Squad is in jeopardy as part of the current review of the specialist functions of the Metropolitan Police.

It would appear that under the totally unacceptable proposals currently being considered the squad would be disbanded, the seizure of 'adult' material would be dealt with by the Clubs Office in Soho, the vast amount of successful work currently being done on child pornography and the investigation of paedophile rings would be undertaken by the already overworked Area Child Protection Teams, and the computer pornography work would be absorbed elsewhere at New Scotland Yard.

I am deeply concerned that the Commissioner could even be contemplating a move of such breathtaking foolishness, and that he could envisage the loss of the Obscene Publications Squad with its unique national role and expertise in investigating child pornography and paedophile rings.

The squad is also increasingly involved in the ever-growing complexity and volume of computer pornography, which spans nations rather than just counties, and it is imperative that we have an organisation that can take an overview of the international supply of pornographic material that is developing with new technology.

The review of the future of the squad is entirely

misconceived, it is at odds with the spirit of the
provisions of the Criminal Justice and Public Order
Bill, it will be a major boost to those involved in the
vile trade of child abuse and pornography, and it will
be a move for which we will pay a heavy electoral price
in surrendering all claim to hold a mandate as the
party of law and order.

Far from being disbanded, the squad should be
strengthened, and supported, as a major plank of law
enforcement in the battle against paedophiles and all
forms of explicit, thoroughly degrading and violent
pornography.

Yours sincerely

Ann

On 5 May, in the House of Commons, Nicholas Winterton,
MP for Macclesfield, asked the Home Secretary when he last
met the Metropolitan Police Commissioner to discuss the
future of the Obscene Publications Branch, and what was the
view which he expressed at that meeting. The reply was to the
effect that no decision had yet been reached on the future of
the squad.

Minutes later Richard Ottaway, MP for Croydon South, got
up to ask the Home Secretary how he intended to combat the
trade in computer-generated pornography, and wondered if
the Home Secretary would be making a statement to the
House. The reply was as vague and inconclusive as the
response to Nicholas Winterton's question; in rough terms,
things were moving, but nothing much had happened yet.
The important thing, from our point of view, was that pressure was being piled on.

The House of Lords spoke up in *The Times* of 10 May:

Sir, We note that a House of Commons early-day motion, calling on the Home Secretary to guarantee the future of the Obscene Publications Branch at Scotland Yard, has been supported by more than 140 MPs. We wish to express our profound concern that the branch may be under threat of closure and its work distributed to other branches.

An exhibition of the work done by the branch was held in the Palace of Westminster last year. Many colleagues were shocked by what they saw and were deeply impressed by the work of the branch.

The Obscene Publications Branch has a unique national role and expertise in investigating child pornography and paedophile rings. The House of Lords will consider the Criminal Justice and Public Order Bill in detail over the next few weeks. We welcome the new provisions that strengthen the fight against child pornography and computer pornography.

However, we urge the government to ensure that the effect of the provisions is not undermined by disbanding the specialised and dedicated team in the Obscene Publications Branch. Rather, we believe the branch needs strengthening to increase its efforts to protect the children in our society.

Yours faithfully

ROBERTSON of OAKRIDGE, ASHBOURNE, BROUGHAM and VAUX, GARDNER of PARKES, BUTTERFIELD, LUCY FAITHFULL, DAVID RENTON, STRANGE, SWINFEN

House of Lords

In the Commons on 13 May, Ann Winterton tabled two questions for the Home Secretary:

1. What recent discussions had he had with the Commissioner of the Metropolitan Police about the future of the Obscene Publications Branch?
2. What recent representations had he received from Right Honourable and Honourable Members concerning the future of the Obscene Publications Branch, and how many of those representations had opposed, and how many had supported the disbanding of that branch?

The Home Secretary was now being leaned on rather heavily. On 16 May he wrote to Ann Winterton, saying nothing to indicate whether the moves to eliminate our department were to go ahead or not. In closing he wrote, 'I shall certainly have in mind the points made in your letter when the time comes for me to consider the Commissioner's proposals.'

In the end we were left alone. The axe did not fall. I take the view that we were under powerful and unfair attack, and because we took the trouble to fight back, we won. It was reassuring to know how many prominent people were prepared to stand up on our behalf, and all of us in the Obscene Publications Branch were heartened to know that they considered us worthy of their support.

Afterword

Nowadays, having left the hubbub of a policeman's existence behind me, I find life has a gentler and more agreeable pace. I am kept in touch with trends and events in the Met by friends still serving, and through contact with my daughter Kirstie, who is a police officer at Notting Hill. I am happily married to Caroline, a beautiful actress and interpreter, who is half Polish, a quarter Greek, and the rest Russian. We live with our Persian cats Oliver and Maxwell, who have stayed with me through all my ups and downs over the past ten years.

Shortly after I left the service the Obscene Publications Branch was split. Responsibility for policing pornography went to the West End Clubs and Vice Squad, as predicted, but the core of our work in paedophilia stayed with the team of officers best qualified for the job. The squad was renamed the Paedophilia Unit of the Organised Crime Unit, which operates under the leadership of Bob MacLachlan, who has been promoted to detective chief inspector. We have survived and the vital work goes on.

Then there's the bad news. The number of officers in the Paedophilia Unit has been cut to thirteen. It is nothing short of scandalous that this is the total proactive effort made against paedophiles by the Metropolitan Police. I know the answer to that criticism would be that Operational Command Units (they used to be called Divisions) or the overworked Child Protection Units will deal with cases as they arise. That is nonsense. We need more than token resources to deal with crimes against children. A simple, blinding statistic makes the scale of the problem clear: we now know that approximately one adult in sixty is a paedophile, which means that in the United Kingdom there are one million people, mainly men, who want to have sex with children.

If the Commissioner or any other chief officer were to announce that they intended to mount a sustained, large-scale operation to track down and deal with paedophiles, their standing with the public would soar. So why don't they do it? Is it because they don't comprehend the seriousness of the crimes? I don't think so. Is it because they can foresee a realistic operation running away with the budgets? That is more likely.

Police priorities need to be revised. For example, although I would never play down the harm done by drugs, I am sure there is a case for putting child protection higher on the action agenda than drug addiction. We now have a Drugs Co-ordinator at national level, devising strategies to prevent drug abuse, the victims of which are mainly volunteers. Children *never* volunteer to be sexually abused.

And what of obscene publications? As expected, the Internet has thwarted and undermined most attempts to control the distribution of hardcore pornography. Nowadays, few juries would find anything but the grossest images obscene within the definition of the Obscene Publications Act. The law has been neutered by its insistence on proving the damaging effect material has on an individual, rather than calling for an objective assessment of words or images. The policing of obscenity is a nonsense and I will predict, in passing, that the written word will never again be prosecuted for obscenity in the United Kingdom.

When I retired in September 1993 I had no regrets. I felt a lasting gratitude to the service which let me earn a living doing something I regarded as an adventure. At the end of thirty years' service I had faced a familiar dilemma: should I stay on to the maximum age of fifty-five, or would it be better to go while there was still a chance to make a new career for myself? If I stayed my pension would get no bigger, although I would have to go on paying contributions. There was also pressure at that time for middle managers to leave, because after the Sheehy report into manpower we were told that the ranks of chief inspector and chief superintendent would disappear. I made my decision and became one of several hundred senior officers who opted to retire from the Met after being told they had no future there. I believe that exodus of experienced people has had a serious and damaging effect on the running of London's police force over the past five years. But I digress.

For two years before I left the service, I had been thinking about what I would do with the remainder of my working life. This was at a time when scandals in children's homes had begun to erupt throughout Britain. No one knew better than we did that many of the paedophiles targeted by our operations had infiltrated the child-care professions, or did voluntary work in areas that brought them into contact with children. After Frank Beck was convicted at Leicester Crown Court on charges of sexual and other offences against children, Norman Warner was appointed to evaluate the recruitment and selection methods being used to hire staff in children's homes. That struck me as a worthwhile thing to do, and when I retired I decided to put my accumulated knowledge to work. In consultation with all the people I knew in the child-care network, I assembled and eventually operated a system of vetting and evaluation that helps ensure that anyone planning to work with children is suitable for the job. I continue to do that work.

Appendix:
Legal Definitions

Prostitution occurs when a woman offers her body for sexual intercourse or other sexual activity in return for money. Prostitution is not a crime in itself, but a number of related pursuits do breach the law. Advertising details of prostitutes may amount to a conspiracy at common law or an obscene publication. Certain offences concerned with brothels and living on immoral earnings also apply to male prostitution.

Brothel: a place used for female or male prostitution. A contract for the hire or renting of a brothel is without value in law, because such a contract is held to be contrary to public policy. It is an offence, therefore, for a landlord to rent out premises in the knowledge that they will be used as a brothel. It is also an offence to help or manage a brothel or for a tenant or occupier of any premises to permit the premises to be used as a brothel.

Kerb-crawling is the offence of soliciting a woman for prostitution in a public place from a motor vehicle, or having just stepped out of one, when the soliciting is so persistent as to amount to importuning, or is likely to annoy the woman or cause a nuisance to other people in the vicinity.

Living on immoral earnings means knowingly using the proceeds of another's prostitution for one's upkeep or subsistence. It is an offence which is punishable by up to seven years' imprisonment for a man, but *not* for a woman. The crime is usually committed by a man who cohabits with a prostitute and is entirely or mainly supported by her, or by a man who operates a brothel or in any way compels or helps a woman to commit prostitution. In all these instances a man is presumed to be knowingly living on a woman's immoral earnings unless he is able to prove that he is not. It is also an offence for either a man or a woman to live knowingly on the proceeds of male prostitution, and it is punishable for one woman to force another into prostitution, or to help her indulge in prostitution for gain.

Procurement is persuading or asking a woman to have sexual intercourse. The following instances are offences of procurement: a) getting a woman to have sexual intercourse with oneself or anyone else, at any place in the world, by means of threats or false pretences; b) persuading a girl under the age of twenty-one to have sexual intercourse with a third person, at any place in the world; c) persuading a severely subnormal woman – that is, one who had no ability to guard herself against exploitation – to have sexual intercourse anywhere in the world. (These three instances constitute offences only if sexual intercourse occurs.) d) persuading a woman to take up prostitution, or to leave Britain with the intention of frequenting or taking up employment in a brothel. All of the above offences can be punished by up to two years' imprisonment.

Soliciting is when a prostitute plies for clients in a street or other public place. It is an offence punishable by a fine of up to £100 on first conviction and up to £400 on subsequent conviction. Any act committed by the prostitute may amount to soliciting – even smiling in a way that could be construed as provocative; on the other hand an advertisement inviting men to call on her does not constitute soliciting. If a prostitute in a private house makes efforts to attract the attention of men in the street, for example by tapping on the window, or simply sitting at the window lit by a red lamp, this could be considered soliciting 'in a street'. The offence of soliciting by a man is when he persistently accosts a woman in a public place with a view to having sexual intercourse, or importunes an individual in a public place for immoral purposes. 'Persistently' means one invitation each to a number of different people, or two or more invitations to the same person.

Conspiracy at common law: the law still recognises some forms of criminal conspiracy, which are limited to a) conspiracy to defraud, which means committing fraud or theft, obtaining property by deception, infringing a copyright, or causing an official to act in a way that runs contrary to his public duty; b) c

onspiracy to corrupt public morals; and c) conspiracy to outrage public decency, which might, for example, include an
agreement to put on an indecent exhibition.

Obscene publications are articles or materials that tend to
deprave or corrupt. Under the Obscene Publications Acts
1959 and 1964 it is an offence to publish an obscene article or
to have an obscene article for publication for gain. The question of whether or not material is obscene must be decided by
a jury; expert evidence is rarely permitted. Material that has a
tendency to shock or disgust is not obscene. The author's
motive in writing or depicting is irrelevant.

'Publishing' an obscene article includes distributing, circulating, giving, hiring or lending the article or offering it for
sale or hire; the latter does not include displaying such material in a shop. An 'article' may be something that is meant to
be looked at rather than read, and can include a film negative
or any such item used to reproduce material to be read or
looked at. This offence entails strict liability, but there is a
defence of lack of knowledge, if the defendant can prove he
did not look at the article he published and he had no reason
to believe that publication would be an offence. There exists
a special defence of public good, which applies when the
accused shows that publication was justified because it was in
the interests of science, literature, art or learning. Expert evidence as to the merits of the material *is* admitted when this
defence is put forward. If a person possesses an obscene article in the expectation of publication for financial gain, this
situation is also subject to the defences of lack of knowledge
and public good. If a magistrate suspects that obscene articles
are being kept at a specific location to be published for gain,
he may issue the police with a warrant of authority to search

for and seize the articles. If the articles are judged to be obscene, the magistrate may order their forfeiture.

The Acts do not apply to material published on television or radio, but they do apply to cinema performance and staging in a theatre, with the proviso that prosecutions in such cases must have the consent of the Director of Public Prosecutions or the Attorney General, respectively. In these offences, too, the *public good* defence may be used, in this case defined as serving the interests of drama, opera, ballet, or other art.

There are a number of special offences relating to obscenity, for example publishing obscene advertisements, sending unsolicited material describing sexual activities, or sending through the mail any 'indecent or obscene article'. The latter offence is limited to sexual obscenity, but also incorporates matter which is merely indecent.